# BLACK
# WATER
### AND
# TULIPS

# BLACK WATER AND TULIPS

*My mother, the Spy's Wife*

SARA
MANSFIELD
TABER

a mother-daughter
memoir

*atmosphere press*

Published by Atmosphere Press

Cover design by Josep Lledo

atmospherepress.com

*to our mothers,*
*who love as best they can*

*One wanted fifty pairs of eyes to see with, she reflected. Fifty pairs of eyes were not enough to get round that one woman with, she thought.*

— Virginia Woolf
*To the Lighthouse*

*We are not wholly bad or good*
*Who live our lives under Milk Wood,*
*And thou, I know, wilt be the first*
*To see our best side not our worst.*

— Dylan Thomas
*Under Milk Wood*

*Sadness, in order to sing*
*will have to drink black water.*

— Jose Luis Hidalgo
"Sadness"

*The only legend I have ever loved is*
*The story of a daughter lost in hell.*

— Eavan Boland
"The Pomegranate"

# BOOK ONE

**1**

I

# TWO MOTHERS
*Kamakura, Japan*

*Life began with waking up and loving my mother's face.*
– George Eliot

"I was so blue when you were born, I was ready to jump out a window." This was the first of two stories my mother told about the early days following my emergence into the world.

The home into which I was born was set high on a mountainside overlooking Japan's vast Sagami Bay. The house was an ancient structure of dark wood slats and sliding rice paper doors. An airy abode whispering with salt sea breezes and fragrant of oranges and pines commanding a vista of islands set in endless blue, it was a dwelling lovely but also deeply lonely.

That house was lonely, for my mother was far, far from home. An Indiana country girl until only a few years before my birth, my mother had now been transformed into the wife of a clandestine intelligence operative and dropped onto this remote corner of Asia a full quarter-world away from everything she had ever known—a land of once and future beauty crawling out of the ravages of war...

In addition to being dipped in feminine hormones and loneliness on a mountain slope near the Great Buddha of Kamakura, my mother was, it seems likely, experiencing a flood of black, roiling fret and fear—an inner tumult that swapped intermittently with rainbow splashes of gay ebullience—to which she was prone. She had learned young that life was full of perils. What would become of her new daughter, and, indeed, of herself? Perhaps a daughter possesses a kind of deep knowledge or perhaps this is an act of imagination. Whichever it may be or a blend, I can hear the urgent rhythms of her mind thrumming within my own body decades on. They ran something like this:

*I cannot. I cannot. I can't go on... What on earth have I done? I*

3

*thought this was going to be so thrilling. And, well, it was, in Hong Kong—living in the apartment with the view over the harbor, eating that delicious Chinese food in those little dirty places, being announced at official British parties as Mrs. Charles Taber. But now this...It's all just plain too much. I'm just a good-for-nothing and always have been. I'm a burden on Charlie and an abject failure as a mother. Here I thought I wanted eight children and now I'm a wreck. I can't even cope with one hungry baby. I should just disappear. It would be better for everyone...*

At this time, summer of 1954, my 29-year-old father was working miles away on a hidden base in the scruffy Japanese countryside, training young Chinese to take over Red China. Meanwhile, my mother, cached alone in her own perhaps even more hidden redoubt, had marshaled all her resources to support her country's and her husband's noble effort. Her part, she'd determined, was to give birth to her first child in an utterly alien terrain without a single wince, *come hell or high water*, for she was a person harsh on herself, with exacting standards, and exhilarated by service and sacrifice. Without suffering, after all, how could a woman, denied conscription because of her sex, show that she was brave? Beyond the effort to demonstrate stoic courage, my mother had, in addition, exerted strict self-discipline to gain only five pounds during her pregnancy, following her U.S. Navy doctor's order to the letter.

My mother was a 27-year-old energized by self-discard, but by the moment of my birth she was emaciated and almost strained to breaking. Hell *had* come in an unexpected way, and her spirits had plunged into darkness. She, who had always been the epitome of competence, who, as a physical therapist, had cared for victims of polio and of war, was certain now that there was no way she, Lois Taber, could keep a baby alive. The

4

responsibility was too enormous—far beyond her.

Adding to my mother's present dislocation to a strange land was the fact that, as a spy's wife, she could not even use her real name. All she had ever known, including herself, seemed to have slipped away. And the prospects for self-recovery must have seemed dim as there was only more displacement ahead. After Japan, for the next 25 years, she would be whisked to the Philippines, to Taiwan, onward to Europe, and then back again to several Asian posts. Her life was to assume a strenuous pattern of moving every couple of years, as my father, a covert officer for his country, tried to discover and sabotage the actions of Communist China.

Why not slip away altogether now? Why not step out a window from this strange overlook to become a disappearing female form hurtling toward the glimmering sea?

For a time after my appearance, as this first story of my mother's told, she lived in a dark and desperate and hollow orb. While she gripped baby me in her arms, it was as if she were experiencing, pulsing within her, as but a brand-new mother, the ancient losses and brave sorrows of Demeter, the Greek goddess of maternity.

The ancient Greeks passed on to us a beautiful tale about a mother and a daughter, here adapted from *The Homeric Hymn to Demeter*:

One joyful day, Demeter, the golden-haired guardian of the harvest, gave birth to a daughter named Persephone, a little being she adored. Demeter's life thereafter was one of casting light and seeding bounty over the earth, and blissful days passed with her delightful flower-faced girl—until, one day, Hades, the lord of the underworld, snatched the lovely Persephone and transported her into the earth's deep, misty realms of darkness.

Stricken by the loss of Persephone, the frantic mother

goddess searched and raged, destroying the plants and threatening to starve the whole human race if her daughter with the delicate ankles was not restored to her.

Witnessing from on high the destruction that furious, grief-wild Demeter was willing to wreak, the king of the gods at last intervened with the god of the underworld.

Bowing to Zeus' command, Hades finally relented and permitted Persephone to return to her mother and the realm of forests and meadows above.

Upon their reunification, the mother and daughter basked in each other's presence, embracing with love and forgetful of sorrow, and each received joy from the other and gave joy in return, but there was more in store...

Before allowing Persephone to depart his kingdom, Hades had ensnared the reluctant Persephone and compelled her to eat a honey-sweet pomegranate seed. This partaking obliged the young woman to spend one-third of each year in the earth's dank depths with him, and only the remaining two-thirds with her beloved mother, sowing the cornfields and rose-flowered pastures above. Mother and daughter were overjoyed to be reunited but their lives were forever after dimmed as they were now left, like the earth, to live part in light and part in shadow...As have been left, perhaps, all mothers and daughters.

For my mother, perched on a Japanese mountain, a heavy, archaic, premonitory grief had pervaded her body. It was as though she'd lost her daughter before she even had her.

Beholding, through time's spyglass, this vision of my too-thin and desolate mother on her isle, I wonder about her, and about me, that clutched babe in arms: Can the interplay at the very constellation of a mother and daughter, such as this at the very first joining of my mother and me, be the point when a seed of trouble is planted? Might a half-starved pregnancy and postpartum depression stamp the relationship between a mother and daughter, predisposing it to contest, to animosity, to eternal rubbing? And: If the eyes looking back at a baby are hollow ones, if the first world-outlook taken in is bleak, might this set the child up for melancholia? "The precursor of the mirror is the mother's face," wrote the psychologist D.W. Winnicott.

There was this dark story my mother told about my beginning, and then there was another from a couple of months after my birth.

My mother's other story of my babyhood was celebratory: "When you were new, my milk just came and came. *Bloop! Bloop!* There it was: spurting, overflowing all the time. Everything I wore was drenched. I was a fountain of milk and my milk was whipped cream!" Telling the story about her fountain of milk, my mother always chortled and shook her head, half repelled, half wondrous, as the words laughed from her lips. With her colorful earthiness, she joyfully exclaimed, "You were a butterball!" a fact verified by photographs which show a baby wriggling and thriving in a wicker basket, with plump legs and a round bowl for a tummy.

This second account sprang from the days after my father, comprehending his wife's peril, had hired a baby amah to help my mother and also arranged a part-time job for her as an assistant at his own hidden base, where, though the boss would pinch her bottom, she would feel of use. She had lucked upon a perceptive husband who understood her clamor and need to contribute to the work of the world. And so, by the time of her second story my mother had emerged from her dark orb and felt rise in her again the bubble of happiness.

In this second story, my gleeful mother, shooting sweet cream, was Demeter in her joy and glory. Brimming with delight at the luck of holding a daughter in her arms, at last sensing her existence to be snug and secure, she felt as bountiful and overflowing as that mother goddess who fed her small one upon earth's finest ambrosias and nectars. What finer way for a mortal parent to impart love than through a pair of generous breasts? What greater and happier endowment could a small daughter desire from a mother?

The two stories my mother told about my infancy—the tales of a desolate and of a jubilant mother—bequeathed to me twin, rivalrous visions: one of my infant self as a source of anguish for my mother, the other as a fount of joy.

Chilling moments of darkness and delicious moments of light were to compete for ascendance in our relationship. Their flipping back and forth would haunt me and yank at my spirits from my birth onward. In my first three decades, the light moments counterbalanced and outweighed the darker ones. Then, around my thirtieth year, there was a sharp, inexplicable tilt toward the dark and our relationship was rendered torturous. To identify its cause has been a primary preoccupation of my adult life, my desire to sort it out once and for all the spur behind these pages. There is something ancient in a human being that desperately needs an intelligible life story, but a coherent story of my relationship with my mother has long remained elusive.

Ever since I was a small girl, I have been curious about people and what makes each of them who they are. As a young person growing up in many countries, I watched and watched. Once grown, I first approached this puzzle of human natures via the study of psychology. After my undergraduate training, I acquired a social work degree and worked with multiply troubled adults and children in low-income families. Then, wanting to explore the impact of culture on human development, I added a doctoral degree that combined further studies of psychology with anthropology.

As I read in psychological anthropology, I became enthralled with ethnography, oral history, and literary journalism as further channels for exploring and writing about human beings. It was as though I couldn't gather enough perspectives to satisfy myself or answer my questions about people and their ways. No one field seemed adequate, so I kept adding more. Perhaps somewhere in me I sensed that I faced a formidable opponent ahead and needed to marshal all the equipment I possibly could in order to have the possibility of triumph.

Finally in my searches, I turned to literature and the classics. I had, of course, read novels and one or two memoirs before, but now it was as though a new, vast store of enlightenment poured out before me like jewels. Literature was a fresh lamp both in terms of comprehension of human beings and for translation of human experience to the page. Seized, I tutored myself in literary techniques, wrote books and articles about the lives of people in America and abroad.

After years of dedicating my pen to portraits of others, I turned toward my own life. For a decade, while tutoring others in creative nonfiction, I worked away on a memoir about my father and my relationship with him. Even though a spy trained to be hidden, he was the easier parent to encompass. When I would tell my friends stories about my mother, they would inevitably say, "Your mother takes the cake."

After delivering a moving eulogy at her memorial service, my mother's Unitarian minister commented to me privately, "Your mother wasn't always an easy person. She was a force of nature." Finally, after years of keeping at bay the writing task for me most daunting of all, it came time to take the dare and chase the slippery tail of my mother.

# THE PURSUIT

To lay hands on my quicksilver mother and bring her into the light was easier embarked upon than achieved.

For months that turn into years I sit alone at my desk. Now and then I glance out the window as the garden's hues shift from summer's green, to russet and brown, and back again to green, but mainly, I think. I sit tracing through the vapors of the past a certain pert five-foot-five woman with a determined set to her lips and a pair of shining, hazel eyes that, like those of a fox, miss not one thing that flits in her surrounds. She possesses a straight back, a full, womanly bosom, and a pair of arms strong from childhood cow-milking and expert for her adult work of helping disabled people around the world regain the power of their bodies...

To many, my mother was straightforward and plain. They could easily identify and peg her. But to me, her daughter, she was a tricky, confounding being, constantly escaping capture.

As might have been predicted, the task of writing, itself, was as baffling and complex as the mother and the mother-daughter relationship it concerned. Ceaseless alteration characterized the relationship between my mother and me. Our relationship morphed and morphed. Constantly, it spun. Ceaseless alteration, thus, was also a feature of—and continuously foiled—my attempts to fashion a sturdy, enduring story. As a writer endeavoring to capture the relationship on the page, I was forever trying to chase after it, catch it by the hem as it flung off its clothes. My mother was an expert operative, unexpectedly shifting her guise, routes, and times. At moments I felt like yet another spy in our household, spying on my own mother, trying to trail a quarry that spurned both entrapment and written record.

The inherent fickleness of the story was further heightened, as I wrote, due to the shifting nature of my medium: memory. The bond between us, as viewed in the slideshow of the mind, shifted from dark to light scenes, and to shades between, many times in a week as I tried to write about it.

Because of life's ever-unfolding and changing nature, some propose that only a chaotic collage can accurately represent life as it's lived. To fashion a narrative may violate the seeming randomness of life as experienced moment to moment, but to create narrative is basic to the way life and minds and literature work. Something in a human being craves intelligibility and so we write ourselves along. All we writers can do, and the best we can hope to achieve, in terms of an embracing, comprehensive account of ourselves and our relationships with loved ones, is an attempt, an *essai*.

A relationship between a mother and daughter is composed of moments beyond counting. My simple hope was that, if the truth in all its baffling complexity were pursued with rigor, the sum of those infinitely compiling moments might add up to something grander and more embracing than their mere assembly. It has been my ardent wish that, by the end of this exploration, the placement of the last shimmering transparency on the mounting pile would lend a sense of a whole and yield, once and for all, a sigh.

So many factors make a woman who she is: genes, family, culture, and on and on. Among the many influences on my mother's life, a primary and particular one was its context—that of international espionage. Hers was a womanhood spent in a kingdom of shadows. Just how the stresses inherent to being a covert operative's wife played in my mother and rippled out to her daughter is an integral part of this hunt—this, and the intense emotions that erupted from them. It is astonishing how, as life unfolds, deep love and ferocious anger can intermingle in human beings devoted to each other. In a sense, this book is a study of that potent tangle.

To begin my fathoming, I return to the start—if ever there is a start to a mother and daughter emerging out of the universe. I gather here a variety of moments to try to meet three inter-lapping inner calls. First, my aspiration is to reckon up the blithe spirit and disconsolate soul that was my mother. Second, my desire is to lay out the dimensions of the relationship between us. Third, I am giving rein to an urge to uncover something more of that elusive, multiple, flitting thing, the affiliation between females, one emerged from the womb of the other… What is the nature of the interplay between a mother and daughter as they pass, hand-in-hand, into time? Where does a mother end and a daughter begin?

**2**

# ARMY ANTS

*Fair seedtime had my soul, and I grew up*
*Fostered alike by beauty and by fear*
— William Wordsworth
  "The Prelude"

"Charlie, Charlie," my mother says, "the ants are coming!"

The "butterball" baby that was once me wriggling in Japan has grown into a butterball toddler and our three-person family is now in the Philippines where we have been assigned to a small house identical to dozens of others, set down in the flat grid of an American army base. I don't know what my father's intelligence task in the Philippines was, but happily for my mother, in this temporary posting, there are other American mothers nearby with whom to swap baby tips so she is less alone than on her Kamakura mountain. The house has behind it a small square of lawn backed by a steamy, thick, deep green jungle in which my mother can, if she wishes, watch and hear monkeys hanging and chattering in the trees.

This particular day, my mother, pregnant again, has heard a droning-clattering-clicking sound rising from out of the forest. When she looks out the window, she sees a vast force coming toward the house in which she is standing. Immediately, her stomach jolting, she hoists me onto her hip.

The ants are a horde, billions of evil-looking, yellowy creatures scurrying, dashing and toppling over one another across the lawn in a wide, martial swath, bent on eating their way through our little army house. My mother is able to identify them because her neighbor was just forced out of her identical billet by this battalion's cousins.

Clutching my legs as best she can around her belly and holding my head as tight to her bosom as possible, my mother's heart ratchets in her chest as she watches the insects marauding from outside and marching up the walls toward her at the

15

window. Her breath is frantic. Quickly, she shouts to the amah to take me, and grabs the telephone.

"Charlie, Charlie, what do I do?"

My father tells her to hold tight while he calls the base extermination squad. He assures her they'll be there lickety-split. They're on alert.

My parents met one another in 1950 at Washington University in St. Louis. My father, a slender birch of a man, was a keen student of political science and my math-smart mother, in physical therapy school, nourished within her ambitious heart a yearning to advance even further in the field of care for human bodies.

A year or so after they met, on their honeymoon trip to Washington, D.C., my father was offered first one job with the government and then another—with the new Central Intelligence Agency. Clandestine operatives' wives in this era were, according to the government's definition, part and parcel of a man's employment package and expected to play a demanding and exacting supportive role. This being clear, the very first action my mother took, to prove she was a good wife and a dedicated government servant, upon my father's receipt of the CIA's offer, was to give up her spot in the next entering class of Georgetown University Dental School. As the first woman ever admitted to the program, the coming of an impossible dream, it was a sacrifice that broke her ambitious heart. But a woman's job in the 1950s was to support her man; a man's career always came first. So, this plucky young woman with a ponytail put her chin up, gritted her teeth, smothered her heart, and thrust herself body and soul—even more passionately than did my father, it could be said—into the job set before her. And so, at the age of 25, my mother was blown, like a seed of Midwestern prairie grass across the sea from America to Asia—

and into a dazzling life of glamour and exotic locales spiced with secrecy and ever-incipient catastrophe. How she coped with it all is a puzzle left for her daughter to piece together.

*What on earth am I doing here?* my mother must have thought to herself as she beheld the marauding ants, her heart thumping, clutching me to her bosom, and waiting...

Another day, as all days in the Philippines, it is as hot as an oven and my mother has only a small fan with which to ward off the bugs and the swelter. She is frazzled and overheated, is covered in bites, and feels like she has a piglet rolling around inside her. She is sweating through her madras shift, I am pulling at her arm, and she is ready to screech.

Finally, she bursts. "Okay, just go on, Sara, out the door!"

We don't wear shoes in the house—a custom we've transported with us along with our few household effects, from Japan. At one and a half, I throw a fit every time my mother tries to shove my chubby feet into a tiny pair of zoris.

I've been insisting all morning on going out to the front sidewalk, where I like to take walks. I've refused to put on my sandals, and my mother has had it. She decides to let me learn for myself, *goddamnit*.

She opens the door and lets me stagger confidently out.

Within seconds I am shrieking as my feet hit the burning pavement.

My mother feels a stab of guilt and perhaps also a secret spurt of satisfaction while the amah rushes out to rescue me.

# NUNS

I am now almost two and chattering to myself as I squat on the floor of a Catholic nursery school run by Chinese nuns.

My father has been transferred to Taipei, a city bedraggled by poverty and clamorous with jigsaw vitality. For most of the next five years—save for a dividing year when my father is sent to Yale to study Chinese—I see out of the window of our Rambler sedan, and experience up close when we walk through the crammed and noisy city: ramshackle huts huddled cheek by jowl with new multi-story office buildings, housing developments, and gaudy temples topped with dragons.

For this next half-decade, my father, with his colleagues, will be working to identify and cultivate relationships with those having contacts in Red China who might pass on information about Chinese military developments and schemes—so that the U.S. might overturn and sabotage them. My father will continue to be engaged in this grand anti-Communist effort throughout his career in each subsequent post. Virtually all of his activities toward this goal will be unknown to me. I will be told at age 15 that my father is a spy, and be instructed to keep his cover, but that will lead me into no further knowledge as to the content of his days. On rare occasions, I will pick up intimations of his activities and glimpse my father's uneasiness, frustrations, and concerns in scraps of terse sentences uttered to my mother— via references to "messes" or "eejits" at "the office"—but I will have no sense at all as to what they pertain.

I do know that ethical concerns about Agency actions haunted my father almost from the inception of his association with the CIA. For instance, while he was working on the covert base in Japan when I was a baby, there was much debate among my father and his colleagues about the merit of their mission.

18

Wasn't it a bit audacious to think that, by parachuting saboteurs onto the Mainland, we could really build a viable democratic force? And wasn't it morally questionable to plant this notion into the minds of the young Chinese they were training—and then proceed to drop them into China, quite likely, to a fate of imprisonment or worse? I know, from one of the extremely rare tales my mother told me about my father's work, that one of these Chinese trainees with whom my father had developed a close relationship was descended into the Mainland never to be heard from again—and presumed dead. His contribution to this tortured my father and made him, from the age of 29, question the absolute wisdom of his country.

Another part of my father's portfolio in Taipei pertains to an even more perilous clandestine U.S. objective: to build a "third force," that is to support and nurture an underground democratic groundswell with the aim of routing dictator Chiang Kai-shek, our ostensible ally.

I am attending a small Taipei school, in the basement of a church we do not attend, for just a couple of mornings a week while my mother goes to help little children who don't have mothers and fathers. My mother has explained that I am very lucky because I have my mother and father, and Mary our amah who love me, while those other children have no one special at all. Some of those children are sick and hungry and they need my mother, who knows about bodies. My father and my mother are both working hard in "Free China" to help the Chinese people, who wear ragged clothes and have only rice to eat, to get back on their feet after their country's war.

To me, prattling plopped on the floor in my little Taipei school, the nuns are like giant white storks. They flap and flap around all of us children playing on the mat, and now and then one of them swoops down like a tall bird to pick me up. She holds me against her starchy habit, and as she carries me around, she shows me to the other nuns, and comments on my big eyes and the fair color of my hair, and she strokes my head and nuzzles my cheek. She does this for as long as she can since I am special, until one of the other children—they are all Chinese except for me—starts to whimper, at which point she reluctantly and gently sets me back down.

When a nun sets me down, I play with little plastic dolls with little Chinese faces and black Chinese hair alongside real little Chinese girls with little Chinese faces and black Chinese hair, and I snack on rice crackers and lychee juice and chat to my neighbors until my mother appears in the doorway.

Most of the time when my mother arrives, I am being held in the wings of one of the large white bird nuns, and the nun hands me to my mother, making appreciative, high-pitched sounds as she says good-bye.

As we walk away, with my mother holding my hand, my mother says to me, "Is that all the sisters do all day? Carry you around and snuggle you?"

My mother's own mother probably never snuggled her; she was her mother's ninth and last child. She always said of my grandmother, "Mom didn't want all those children."

Life at my mother's childhood home, the log house of "the forestry" at Clark State Forest in Henryville, Indiana, was a life of work, work, and more work. Clark State Forest was the first of Indiana's state forests, established in the early twentieth century to preserve the state's dwindling but economically essential woodlands. It became an experimental laboratory for forest care, and was designated a training center for the Civilian Conservation Corps during the Great Depression. My grandfather was an arborist who knew in his own limbs the needs of the species, and, during the 1910s through the 1940s, with the help of the CCC, led the cultivation of great stands of trees to replenish the Indiana woodlands. As an employee of the state, his job offered a steady but limited income for the support of his family, which bloomed like the saplings in his woodlots.

My mother's mother, Daisy Bell, a scrawny woman with ram-rod posture, made the best of her own lot as a wife and mother responsible for the feeding and clothing of her large household. She sewed, for instance, all her eight still-living children's clothes—identical baggy dresses for the five girls and simple trousers with suspenders for the three boys. She grew all the family's vegetables in the truck garden: green beans, tomatoes, carrots, potatoes, cucumbers, corn, and sweet peas. She scrubbed the long underwear everyone in the family wore, looking weary and shaking her head, and washed and wrung out all the other clothes too, and then hung them, cold and clammy, on the lines. She repaired the children's broken noses with Scotch tape and treated their infections with bread and milk or cold meat poultices. She cooked all day long, and forever. Breakfast was a huge laying-out of eggs and oatmeal and pancakes, and while supper was leftovers, lunch was "dinner," the big meal of the day. This meant the preparation of roast chickens or roast beef, potatoes, greens, carrots, home-baked bread, and pies. She cooked not only for her brood, but for the ravenous CCC boys who came and went like the corn and beans of the season. Then there was the hulking log house with the big sleeping porch to keep clean. As if this wasn't enough, rake-skinny Daisy Bell with a white bun by age 30 raised chickens and milk cows.

Daisy Bell's face almost always wore a severe look. My mother seldom saw her smile—at least not in response to her. Her scampy sister Marge could make her mother smile, and the boys could, but never Lois herself. The somber look was because of all the work, but on a deeper level, it was due to Fay. Even before the Second World War in Europe to which her boys innocently trundled off, disaster had hit. Fay, who was the little girl between Thelma and Marge (the girls went: Bernice, Thelma, Margerie, Norma, and my mother, Lois), fell into the well one day when she was four. She was discovered after five hours, and retrieved, but she soon died of pneumonia.

So, my mother spent her childhood in the company of a mother grieving. Daisy Bell kept her sorrows hidden behind a furious scrubbing. Bernice and Thelma, the oldest girls, served as Daisy Bell's hard-toiling surrogates, and the three youngest girls each had their distinct roles in Daisy Bell's crew. Margerie—the plucky, funny, quick one full of mischief—reminded Daisy Bell of her younger self, and could trick a grin out of her. Norma was sickly, so she demanded Daisy Bell's attention. Lois, meanwhile, was, to Daisy Bell, the annoying little scamp, the tail end, the last straw in this large and lumpy and lumbering family of never-ending work.

What all this work meant was the Guernsey kids were expected to help their mother, no questions asked. Lois' jobs included mopping the floors and cleaning the outhouse and sewing up tears in her brothers' britches, but it seemed to little Lois, and to bigger and then grown-up Lois, that she could never help or please her mother enough. No matter how many potatoes she peeled, or how many rooms she swept, or how many old socks she mended, her mother always ended up grabbing the broom and swatting her with it, saying, "Why can't you ever be quicker?" until she escaped out the kitchen door to the words, "You get back in here, young'un." Lois felt herself a rat to be swatted, constantly in the way despite her efforts.

When I nod to my mother here in Taipei that, yes, the sisters do carry me around and snuggle me all day, my mother squats down and her face goes all squiggles of mixed fondness and scolding. "Oh, you little rat," she says, and then she picks me up to carry me and snuggle me.

# LA PIETA

The week in 1956 my brother is born, my father grabs me up in his strong arms and we drive to the Seventh-Day Adventist missionary hospital, which resembles a blocky, white refrigerator, bordered by rice padis on a wide, empty Taipei road.

When we enter the disinfectant-reeking ward to greet little Andrew, prepared to be happy, my mother's eyes are too sunken and large, though, and the baby is covered in sores. He has contracted a form of impetigo that has spawned fluid-filled blisters all over his infant skin. This has meant—the doctor has delivered these instructions—my mother must immediately scrape the oozing scabs off his tender skin and apply ointments, or he will scar.

For the first week of my brother's life, the aching post-partum hormones sluicing through her like cataracts, my mother will weep and weep as she scrapes away at the cheeks and belly and legs of her wailing son.

On this day of our visit, Andy, as we will call him, is so sick with the impetigo as well as a displaced hip, and my mother so desperate and so in need of my father, that my parents send me home to the amah, with a driver, alone. Instead of playing with my new brother and climbing into my mother's lap in her hospital room, the U.S. Embassy car is whisking me away down a broad, fast road and I am staring at my own two small feet.

Back during her childhood on the forestry, my mother had learned, from her mother, that boys were more vulnerable and fragile, and more valuable than girls. All of my mother's three brothers returned from the European front damaged. Carl, the brilliant scientist, was so shell-shocked when he arrived back at the forestry that he barely spoke. Daisy Bell concluded that boys were in need of special treatment and protection, and my mother took in this wisdom through her pores. Thus equipped, she was determined. She *would* save my brother. Perhaps it is inevitable that boys have a leg up—an easy hoist into their mother's laps—because they have always been the ones to do a country's fighting. There is no *La Pieta* of a mother holding a dead daughter.

My mother's mother believed that, in contrast to boys, girls were tough as nails, like their mothers had to be. Daughters, rather than needing protection, were put on earth to help their mothers and were expected to absorb a little rough treatment from them, as had their mothers from their mothers before them. What was done to them as daughters, mothers would pass on.

By her ministrations throughout her life, my mother, following her own mother, tried to ensure for her son—that representative of the more vulnerable and therefore more valuable human kind—all the protections she could. As for her daughter, I think she, instead, held me up before a special pool and saw, in its reflection, her own twin. In that reflection, she beheld three flickering images: *her childhood self*—and all that child's hungers; *her best self*—the self she wanted to be, and to *be* through me; and *her worst self*—the side of herself she hated bearing all the flaws she would like to rub out. Only once in a while, when she held me up to the pool, did she see the real girl shining back from the water.

As for that delicate and treasured male offspring, no matter what she did, my mother would not be able ultimately to protect my brother…from his own human vulnerability. It seemed he could not resist danger. Variously, as a zoologist drawn to the most hazardous regions of the world, he would almost die in a shipwreck in the Falkland Islands, he would be thrown from a snowmobile in the Artic, and he would contract dire diseases in the Amazon.

A quarter of a century earlier, before all those perils hit, on this day of my brother's birth, I am sixteen days away from turning two, and being shuttled down a Formosan road in a long, embassy car. My shoes are sticking up straight out in front of me; they do not even reach to the car seat's rim. My father has hugged me close and said, "You'll be okay, Sara. Amah will be waiting," and has aimed his directions in Chinese at the Embassy driver in no uncertain terms—but, looking at my feet, alone in the whirring car without my father or my mother or my barely-seen brother, I feel sinking into my belly for the first time what it means to be forlorn. My father has until this moment always been my pal, my mother attending to my every wish as best she can, and what I note most there on the seat of that car is a vast and baffling incipient loneliness. The existential loneliness that hits us all at one point or another: it hit me there and then, setting out down Taipei's busy Renai Lu.

Some days later, my parents appear at the door, home from the hospital with my new brother. My father immediately encloses me in his arms and my mother, weary and stiff, bends slowly down to show me the baby in hers.

The servants, too, are at the door, standing in a line, to greet the arriving trio. My mother rises from greeting me and passes in front of them holding my little brother, wrapped in his blanket. It is like she is a queen in a parade holding the newborn heir. It is, indeed, almost like a royal pageant since Americans are royalty, at this historical time, in Taiwan. As she proceeds from amah, to cook, to housemaid, the servants chime "boy-child" over and over again, in both English and Chinese. The Chinese clackers are banging and the whining music is blaring, and I am forgotten. The prince every Chinese family and every 1950s American family requires for completion has arrived.

After this, to pile on the insults and to drape with rubies the crown in which he arrived, there was my brother's cute smile and merry chuckle. He was, by nature, a jolly child, while I was a shy and pensive one. At least that is how my mother had it in her magazine of life, to which we all subscribed. He came out of the womb making motor sounds, and when he was two, would happily spend hours pushing his always-revving cars along the floor. He could entertain himself with his singing and *vroom-vrooming* and the stories he told out-loud to himself, and though he was stubborn, he was little trouble. After all, he was the prince. And "boys will be boys." I don't think my parents were unique in this view of things—and, in fact, my father adored his little princess too—but the truth is, back then, boys were favored. For the mothers, mostly deprived of careers and power, sons were—since husbands were never quite the men their wives would have been—their most magnificent male selves.

Everyone thought my brother with his tousled hair was so cute when he plopped his diapered bottom, grinning, into the housemaid's wash bucket full of grey suds-water and when he wore his little sailor suit with the blue grosgrain ribbon outlining the white mariner's collar and the short pants revealing his chubby little legs. My mother loved that he prattled on about turtles and tanks and guns and donkeys. And when he returned home from his Chinese nursery school, she always lit up like a Chinese lantern.

The amah walks into the house, holding my brother by the hand as he prattles to her in his baby Chinese. He is wearing his little blue smock with the Chinese embroidered characters designating his school and the hanky pinned to the chest.

My mother, just home from the orphanage and still in her white physical therapy jacket, kneels down and folds him into her arms.

"Oh, you delicious little skunk!" she says.

She smells his hair. "Mmm. Did you have that garlic soup for lunch again?"

He nods and squirms as her kisses land, smack, all over his face.

She finally lets him go as he pushes away from her body to go play with one of his trucks on the floor, but while she holds him, squirming in her arms, I can see that she is filled all the way to the brim with happiness. And I know I do not make her feel the same way. For my mother's eyes aimed toward my brother are shining and dancing, while when aimed toward me they have in them always a flit of darkness.

This sort of thing frequently occurs in my daily Taiwan life with my mother.

My mother and I are walking down a market street smelling of fish and oranges and screeching with music, and a strange lady bustles toward us from up the lane. Because it has happened before, I know what she is about to do. She will put her face up very close to mine, tug on my hair, and pinch my cheeks. Still touching me with her strange, heavy hand on my head or body, she will say something very fast in Chinese to my mother.

When I see the lady coming toward me, though, instead of letting her touch me, I whip around behind my mother to hide and cling to the back of her legs.

"Oh, Sara," my mother says, in an exasperated voice. "This lady is just saying how pretty she thinks you are with your blond hair. Stop pulling on my skirt. Just come around here and say hello to her."

But I can't. I keep clinging. I don't want that lady to touch me.

The lady eventually goes away, and my mother peels me off her legs, grumpy now. "Oh, Sara," she says again as she grabs my hand. "This is a bunch of stuff and nonsense." She gives my arm a smart pull as we start off again down the street to buy tangerines and Chinese buns.

When one child fits a mother's needs and dreams better than another, no one can be blamed, but the truth is, my bashfulness was a thorn in my mother's bubble of happiness. She wanted me to take the caresses and pokes in stride, to laugh and giggle at my admirers, bask in it all. She loved the attention I brought to her, but I frustrated her full enjoyment of this attention——the attention she yearned for with all her being and that being with my brother filled up. I was never the outgoing little chap he was, the self she wanted to be, and *was*, really; for he was, by nature, more like her while I was more like my father. But maybe that is what my magazine of myself says and my brother's of himself might have a different article in it.

I knew my mother loved me but I did not make her feel light or give her Impressionist pink-and-blue-cloud happiness as my brother did. He was the sunny, red-cheeked swain of a Renoir. I was the pensive girl of Mary Cassatt's *Child in a Straw Hat*.

There was also a one-line story my mother always told about my greeting to my new brother. She would be sitting at the head of the table and my father at the opposite end, and other couples would be positioned along the sides. She would be urging upon them fragrant dishes of mapo tofu, mu shu pork, dumplings, and rice brought in by the cook, while entertaining her guests with a rip-roar of funny family tales.

"When Andy was a baby," she would say as she plopped some dumplings on her plate, "Sara tried to give him a stool!" And then she would be off and running with the story that made me squeeze up inside.

Apparently, I had, indeed, one day tried to plunk a wooden stool down inside the basket where my infant brother was sleeping. As my mother told her guests this entertaining story about me and the wooden stool, she would toss her bobbed hair and laugh and, reliably, this would stir the other women chopsticking-up their rice to jubilantly recall their own children's sibling rivalry.

My mother would sometimes also recount the story at a

dinner with just our family—as my stomach clenched again. I did not find the story humorous at all, as it was clear in these renderings that my mother considered that I had been intently trying to harm my brother and this interpretation stung my heart. My mother didn't seem ever to gain perspective on this stool-giving as the natural inclination of a jilted toddler, or—who knows?—maybe even an altruistic gesture of help to a shorter being. Perhaps she knew the murderous feeling all too well, having been the ninth and last child, and not having had the luxury I enjoyed of being *displaced*, because she had never even been *placed*—that is *seen* as an individual—in her offspring-overloaded family. She probably knew what it was to be on the receiving end of an older sibling's jealous resentment but may have been blind to the plight of an older child.

My mother didn't laugh when she told the stool story *en famille*. Nor did I. Her version of the story cast me as the murderous rival, set against the unwanted younger brother, and over time the story hardened in her mind. She thought of me forever more as consumed by this selfish wish. As for me, the story fanned the burning flames of jealousy. I frequently felt like a small, insignificant bird when my brother was in the room with my mother and me.

"You tried to give your brother a stool when he was a baby." It is astonishing how a single instant, a single casual comment from a mother, can stamp a child, can grow like a stain, and can, despite any efforts she might make to fight against it, define her life and become the lens—a lens of inner badness such as the one I came to have (and, by no coincidence, my mother had), for instance—through which she sees the world. There is no cleanser that will remove the blotch. Once, as an adult, one understands such a moment's arbitrariness and lack of intentionality, one scrubs and scrubs, and it fades a little, but it will always be there. It is indelible, a delectable little dessert of obsession that one could spoon up and eat all day, and the only possible answer is to turn one's attention to other things until one day, hopefully, one hardly ever thinks about it or knows it is there.

# MEANNESS GLANDS

My mother beckons. "Come here, Sara, let me feel your glands." She says this on an almost daily basis. In Taiwan, children, including my brother and me, are often sick.

I go and stand before her and watch her concerned eyes as they focus on my body. The routine feels holy, like a sort of communion. I feel a reverent patience as I halt before my grown-up mother, and a runnel of love trickles through me as she gently palpates my neck and behind my ears with her competent fingers that know just the signs they are searching for.

"Yep. Swollen glands again," she often pronounces with a kind of victory in her voice.

My mother was a person who loved glands. My mother was a person, to go further, who loved the insides of animals; she was the sort who would have willingly put her arm inside a cow to turn a calf around. She sewed wounded birds back together when she was a girl of eight. She loved dissection class during her physical therapy training at Washington University, and she adored muscles.

Watching the Olympics or seeing a man with well-defined abductors was ecstasy for her. When I rode in the car with her as a little girl in Taiwan and later, she would see a limping woman out the window and say, "Ooh, her plantar fascia hurt, poor thing." Or she would say to one of her friends with a sore shoulder, "Shoot. That's that darned arthritis of the glenohumeral joint. I see it all the time. Alternate ice and moist heat on it and it'll feel better tomorrow."

My mother was the kind of person who, if a friend had a painful hemorrhoid, would probably go right over, tell them to pull down their pants, and push it back in for them. She loved to eat the insides of things too—not just the ordinary flesh, a steak, for instance, but liver and blood sausage—anything bloody, really. I see her mashing up the hamburger for meat loaf with her hands, her fingers coated with pinky-red blobs that made me gag. She loved massaging and she loved mush—especially bloody mush—of any sort.

When my brother and I are sick in Taipei, she goes straight to the source. If we have stomach complaints, she inspects our productions for worms, which, living in the tropics, are sometimes squiggling right there in the pot full of vivid life. If we have earaches, she is right beside us with her flashlight, pronouncing, "It's infected, all right." If we fall down and scrape our knees, she appears with a rough washcloth and cleanses us with a vigor far more painful than that produced by the fall itself. Yellow soap is her best friend.

As a physical therapist who had worked with all variety of sick people, my mother had seen every sort of bedsore, vomit, diarrhea the world could produce. Since her dream as a little girl had been to be a doctor, all of this—pus, crooked legs, piles—gave her the nearest thing to her ardent childhood guts-and-blood dream.

I was a sickly little girl with nonstop tonsillitis. I had incessant, searing ear infections and sore throats, and one time my ears were so ill that I couldn't hear at all. That's when the doctor finally took my tonsils out in the four-room American Embassy dispensary on Yang Ming Shan Mountain.

Throughout all those first seven Asian years of my life, the truth is, my mother was constantly feeling my neck. She'd say, "Sara, your eyes don't look good. Let me feel your glands." I'd been trained to expose my neck to her—it was one of those mother-child refrains that are part of a family's song—so I'd go over and she'd press her sensitive, slender fingers against my upper neck and around the back of my ears. "Ooh, Sara, there you go again. Swollen glands," she'd say with satisfaction. My mother loved glands: pituitary, adrenal, endocrine, she adored them all.

During these early childhood years, as I say, I was at the height of brother-jealousy, in the middle of the pitched battle to secure the favored spot in my mother's heart. My brother brought my mother such pleasure that I frequently went around feeling less than charitable toward his cute face with its irresistible grin. I once put chewed gum in his ear when he was sleeping, and whenever he did something wrong like touch my toy, I was quick to tattle, which did not elicit the hugs and praise I imagined. I knew my mother was basically glad to have me, but it was always my sense that he was the child she'd wanted most—perhaps because he was the male child she'd have wanted to be so *her* mother would have loved *her*. These various things—my jealousy, her preference for boys, combined with her penchant for body parts—perhaps explain how she came up with notion of "meanness glands."

Alternatively, perhaps the term was an expression of the meanness my mother herself felt and couldn't own—projected onto her daughter. In any case, from the time I can remember, I was the person in the family who had them. "Sara has meanness glands." It was just one of those indisputable facts of life.

# THE PINK DRESS

*She pulled the thread and bit the thread*
*And made a golden gown,*
*And wept because she had dreamt that I*
*Was born to wear a crown.*
— W.B. Yeats
  "The Player Queen"

"Oh, Sara, you look so pretty!" says my mother.

We are now ensconced in a small house tucked within a high wall along a dirt street. A plain, concrete dwelling with water buffaloes lowing in the lane. Scents of dung and rice and jasmine waft in and out of its open windows. The gauzy curtains in the living room flutter in the breeze.

I am wearing a gingham dress my mother has smocked for me—stitching with white thread through gathered cotton, held just so with her nimble fingers—over evenings in this house in Taipei. My mother has sewn into this beautiful rose dress she has made for me, the garment she had never had as a girl. When she was herself a little girl, her dresses were hand-me-downs from her five older sisters: simple frocks with round collars hastily assembled by her own mother, every single dress the same, year after year. By the time they got to her, they were grey, limp sacks.

Flaring out the skirt of my new dress, I look up at my mother, in her plaid shift, smiling at me. My hair is in a headband. I have on the anklets and patent leather party shoes my mother bought for me. I give a twirl.

"Come here," my mother says. "Come here, Sweetie."

"Sweetie" is an ice cream cone. I taste my mother's delight. Her delight in *me*! Not my adored and adorable brother with his cowlick and his cocked face—*me*!

I stand before her and she pats her lap. "*Here*," she says, and she pulls me onto her knees.

She hugs me close against her bosom. I can feel my mother's arms tight-wrapped around me, squeezing hard, squeezing hard from enjoyment of me and just me. The love-delight is delicious—lavender honey, cream pie.

I remember with lush pleasure my mother's pleasure in me. But then again, looking through a telescope at this mother

33

embracing her girl, who is who here? Was my mother's delight in a little girl in a dress, delight in *me*? Might it actually have been delight in herself—her would-be little girl self that she was holding? Was this long-craved love for herself, or was this what the ancient Greeks called *storge*, familial love, love of me? And if the sewing and the hug were perhaps unconsciously delivered by my mother to give herself love, is that still love? If she did things that were good for her daughter out of a need for self-love, does that count? What about if she handed forth these offerings half for herself and half for her daughter, or in a 75:25 ratio? Can such a thing be measured? Indeed, is a mother ever fully signed over to her child and should she be? And regardless of the ratio of self- to daughter-love, mightn't a mother's love be love simply if a daughter experiences it so? And at the beginning or the end, one wonders, does any of this matter? Where does a mother end and a daughter begin?

# MOTHERS TURN THE WORLD

Our family of four is taking a walk through Taipei's downtown. The streets are a messy, spewing jumble of bicycles, pedicabs, taxis, and tanks—with rattling donkey carts and loose water buffaloes jostling through. As we wander down the cluttered shopping lanes, women with baskets are bargaining with peanut sellers, their babies tied to their backs with dingy cloths. Old men are slurping noodles and squatting along the walls, while younger men dressed in army fatigues are strolling in twos and threes, guns sharp over their shoulders. Urchins are dashing every which way, jolting to a stop now and then to beg for coins. The air reeks of open sewers, steamed fish, and garlic, and from every corner, jangling music blares.

I hold my mother's hand, and my father holds my brother's. We are five and three now. Headed home, we approach the part of the big, main road where the pedicab drivers gather. They are all very skinny, drawn-faced men in singlets and shorts and zoris, with stringy, muscled legs and arms, leaning against their carts and smoking.

Two men rush up to us out of their caucus, pulling their cabs. My mother and I start to climb into one but the pedaler of the second cab rams up beside us and insists we mount into his cart instead. My mother immediately pulls me out of the way of both pedicabs and yells something in angry Chinese at the second man. Her voice is scarily dictatorial and sharp and makes me quake in my stomach and along my arms.

The pedicab man's Chinese reply is pushy and shrieking and furious. He yammers at my mother and then starts pushing at the shoulder of the first driver.

My father, meanwhile, is hailing replacement cabs with a big sweep of his arm. Hurriedly we clamber into the two arriving vehicles. Our drivers speed us away, their naked legs pumping furiously as we bump and swerve down the big noisy road.

As I peer back from my lurching chariot, I see the first two pedicab drivers whaling at each other with their fists. They are slugging each other's faces, chests, and arms, out to do damage.

My belly careens with the men's fury. I think, in trepidation, "Mom caused those men's fight."

Mothers are all-powerful. Mothers cause the world to turn. Mothers ignite tempers and set off explosions. Mothers are to blame. This is what small daughters wrongly, and rightly, conclude from watching their mothers in operation on a busy Taipei avenue at midday.

# HER CUP OF TEA

I stand watching as my mother's hand glides along the little girl's leg. The little motherless Chinese three-year-old has the biggest, roundest, ebony-blackest, shining eyes I have ever seen.

She is a light of small beauty and gazes up at my mother with utter love and trust. And my mother's hand—the hand that briskly passes me my morning blouse, and fetches me my afternoon cookies and plunks the plate of them in front of me—now gently massages the little girl's leg.

As a child, my mother felt she was worth only as much as she could work, but still, life at the forestry offered her a sense of purpose and determination, and sometimes even moments of triumph and thrill.

One day, when she was about six, my mother, in a wash-worn, hand-me-down frock and dirty knees, was playing with a stick doll outside the family's log house, surrounded by deep forest. Her father, dressed in his faded forester's green, approached from the woods, carrying the family collie, limp in his arms. Little Lois looked up.

"Shep broke his leg," her father said, looking very sad. "I'm going to have to put him down. It's no good."

"No, Pop! You can't." She began to cry.

Her father fondled her head. "Sorry, little one. We can't let him suffer. I'm going to get the shotgun."

He laid Shep gently on the ground.

My mother wept over the dog for a moment, then fiercely smashed out her tears and dashed behind the barn. She called out to two of her sisters—seven and nine—and the three of them hauled the big dog toward the barn. There, with an older brother, they half-carried and half-shoved the dog up the ladder to the hayloft.

When her father returned with his gun, the dog had vanished, and Lois stabbed the dirt with her toe as she told a fib—an ability that would come in handy later in her life, as the wife of an undercover spy.

"Oh, Pop! Shep ran away," she said. "I couldn't stop him!"

"Oh well, probably for the best."

By later that day, word had gotten out, and the eight siblings gathered around Shep, tucked way back in the hay. The little girls had splinted the collie's leg with some sticks and a rag, and Lois, the stalwart and commanding littlest, held court.

"We can save him! I know we can. We just have to stop him from licking his paw and getting the splint off!"

Her oldest brother engaged with her plan and proposed everyone be assigned two-hour guard duty. This thrilled the little girl.

"Just like in the army! Give me the midnight shift!" she insisted. "I can sneak out quiet as a rabbit. I really can!"

For the next two weeks, Lois, plucking her courage, rose at midnight and curled up beside the dog in the barn's murky darkness. As she struggled to stay awake, she patted him quietly, admonished him when he tried to lick his paw, and whispered into his ear, "It'll be okay. It'll be okay," as she did to herself when she ran through the woods.

When Shep bounded out of the barn at the end of this weeks-long clandestine operation, her father, rather than being angry, wept for joy and her mother's face snuck a grin. These— her father's pleasure and her mother's reluctant praise, and her own sense of satisfaction at a mission accomplished—galvanized my mother for life. Righteous defiance, a belief in "Where there's a will, there's a way," and a dedication to healing implanted themselves in Lois' young fibers. She also came then to the conclusion that, though she might be a rat to be chased out of the way, if she did something to help others, to help the world, she would be worthy of being kept alive on this earth.

When she announced to her father one day when she was in high school that she intended to be a doctor like Albert Schweitzer, the doctor who'd set up a hospital in tropical Africa, her father replied, as though it was a rock-bottom fact, "No one will go to a lady doctor." Since her beloved father knew all there was to know, she gulped down her ardent dream. However, determined little cuss that she was, she didn't entirely give it up. When she got to college she chose, with dogged practicality, what she thought would be the next best thing: to become a physical therapist.

Now, in Taiwan, it was as if my mother had been infected by the clang and push of this Chinese city so eager to improve itself. Its pace matched her own fervent forward drive. A place of boundless need—for food, shelter, medical care—this country was her scalding, black cup of tea. The minute she scanned the lay of this beautiful, rugged island with its murky rivers and glinting sea; its teeming capital; and its overload of diseased adults and crippled children, elation flooded through her. "I can be of use!"

As soon as my mother found a good amah for my brother and me, she telephoned a Chinese doctor, put on her white P.T. coat, and, with him, set up a polio clinic. She contacted an orphanage sponsored by Madame Chiang Kai-shek, pled "Put me to work!" and initiated physical therapy with abandoned children besieged by rickets, polio, and dislocated hips. After that, when I entered kindergarten, she got herself an additional job as a part-time math teacher at the Taipei American School. It was as if she couldn't use herself enough. Determined to defeat the world's miseries, single-handedly if she had to, she was a one-woman rescue squad. As she pushed through the thicket of Taiwan's troubles, she was scraped by twigs, pricked by burrs, and tripped by fallen logs, but she didn't even notice. She would save the lost children. She would save the people of flailing arms and legs. She would plant math and science into the brains of American young.

My father, on whose outlook my mother's depended, loved the Chinese language—his pockets bulged with flash cards—as well as the back-slapping Chinese men he worked with. He, too, was jet-fueled by youthful idealism. As time went on, he would be more and more clutched by moral doubts about some of the covert operations work he was asked to contribute to, but, for now, he was cleaving to the conviction that he and his country would relieve the forsaken of tyrants of all sorts: fascists, communists, dictators such as Chiang. The U.S.A., with the help of clandestine operatives like himself, would save the world.

Into this mission, too, my mother threw her strong and vigorous body—to support her country and bolster her husband's career. And when she wasn't serving her clientele, she served his. She had Chinese ladies for tea, she attended twenty-course banquets with him. These two Midwesterners heartily toasted their Chinese hosts with "Ganbei!"—"Bottoms up!"—and downed shots of the Chinese white liquor, baijiu, as if they'd done it all their lives.

As I watch my mother at the orphanage, it is as if she knows just what an orphan feels; and, as I watch, with my eyes I see, and in my own legs I feel, my mother's hands transform from brisk, efficient commanders of a household into patient, loving, skillful maidens of healing.

# THE PERFECT LIFE

My mother is talking to her friend, Jen, in the living room. Age six, I am drawing a picture of a house and a water buffalo while lying on the floor of my room just on the other side of the open door. Jen is the friend with whom my mother feels the greatest kinship because they both work, rather than just being housewives. Jen teaches science at the Taipei American School.

Their sentences fade in and out as I listen and color.

My mother says, "I just love it here. I love my work at the orphanage and the polio clinic—I feel like I can really make a difference...Don't you just love your work?"

Jen says she couldn't live without it.

"Of course, it's only possible," my mother says, "because I have Mary to look after the children. She's a gem. No one could love them more...I'm just pinching myself. I just can't believe how lucky I am..."

They talk now about going to "functions" at the ambassador's residence.

"They're kind of fun," my mother says, "but isn't it awful how so many of the women priss around and fawn over the ambassador's wife? Instead of standing around chatting, they could all be out there helping the orphans that get dropped full of oozing sores on the orphanage doorstep every day, or feeding those hungry old men."

Jen says, "At least the food's good at the Residence."

"Sheer delectamy," my mother says. And then they rhapsodize about the dumplings and the mu shu pork.

My mother says, "You know, Jen, some of those women just hate it that we work. One of them—that Lucy—actually told me I was neglecting *my representational duties*!"

"I know," Jen says. "Some of those women are something else!"

"Well I say, what kind of American women do we want to represent? That Lucy's one of those spoiled society girls. She and those others like being frail little flowers and putting on nail polish and complaining about the toilet paper. That's all a bunch of hogwash. They're lucky they *have* toilet paper. All we had was old Sears Roebuck catalogues in the outhouse back at the forestry."

But my mother then says she feels sorry for some of the ladies. Some of them, she says, barely leave the American compound and they're scared to go out without their husbands who speak Chinese. "I'm so glad we got out of the compound and live on the local market. And I'll be damned if I'm going to be dependent on Charlie. You've got to fend for yourself in this world. Heavens, my Chinese is dreadful too, but I just plunge in. I just laugh at myself, and the Chinese do too. The other day with that fish-man I almost wet my pants I was laughing so hard...

"Forget being scared...Look around and find something to help out in this world. It's as simple as that, I say. Lord knows, there's awful poverty and sickness everywhere. It doesn't matter how *you* feel. Think about someone besides yourself. Just get out there and do what's got to be done."

Even at this young age, as I listen to my mother talk to her friend, I am learning to peer through artifice. That American lady in red high heels and red lipstick—who looks like she commands the world and I think looks so pretty—apparently doesn't like my mother's helping orphans who have no mothers. Maybe she might not be as fancy and nice as she looks. I ingest my first instruction in defiance of female city hall.

# THE BEARS

*Je est un autre*
– Rimbaud

I am sitting in the dining room with my breakfast. A water buffalo lows leisurely in the lane.

My mother has had Bik, the cook, make cream of wheat this morning. A bowl of sticky, lumpy glop fragrantly steams before me. There at the wooden table, the whole, luxurious morning stretches ahead. My father is off doing something like reading a weeks-old *Newsweek* shipped in by sea, and my brother is already playing with his Matchbox cars on the living room floor. My mother and I, though ostensibly in public, are actually in a private mother-daughter bubble. These little apparently transparent mother-daughter spheres can turn mushroom-shaped in a flash.

When my mother, who wears her hair in a practical pixie cut, first set the navy Taiwanese bowl before me—she picked out these dishes at a local pottery and loved them, as she wasn't of the background or the kind to have had a wedding China pattern— things were friendly and fine. She was in a pert mood, and I was cheerful enough. There was no school, and I was looking forward to my book about Raggedy Ann.

But sitting look at my bowl, I couldn't understand why my mother specially bought cream of wheat from the base commissary for us to have for breakfast when cornflakes were better and easier. It seemed a complete waste to me. Maybe this particular hot cereal reminded her of her childhood; this can solve many inexplicables in life. Furthermore, my mother liked her cream of wheat with lumps. She couldn't stand hot porridges with smooth, silky textures. Something about her being from hilly southern Indiana maybe: she liked a certain amount of topography in her mouth. But I didn't like cream of wheat at all; lumps were a problem for me, and I really didn't want to eat any of it.

My mother could never get enough food when she was small, even though there actually was enough. Her family was lucky during the Great Depression because they lived where they could have a garden, and so they had big Sunday dinners of roasted meat and arrays of vegetables and home-baked cakes, and only slightly smaller dinners the rest of the week. My mother was also lucky enough, at ten, to have a job at a little grocer's where she was allowed all the baloney she could eat. But still, my mother—always hungry for affection, for which food was the next best thing—never quite got enough. I, however, never felt short of food. One of my mother's many adjustments in her adult life—we all make these small or large corrections to our mothers' ways—was that, during my childhood, we always had an abundance of food. No matter what country we landed in, there was more than enough and we could eat at any time.

I, contrary to the plump little girl my mother had been due to her fondness for fresh-baked bread, was a very skinny girl, a runt of a thing in early grade school—so much like a starving Calcuttan did I look that my mother wouldn't send photos of me home from Taiwan to her mother. To her despair, for a couple of years of my childhood, I lived on two Nilla Wafers and a glass of milk at bedtime. How she worried—in that urgent way some mothers have of fretting too much about things they needn't.

On this particular day, my mother's worry about my eating took her a long, long distance. Perhaps she was seeing too many truly starving children at the orphanage and thought if I didn't eat more, I would end up one of them and die on a doorstep. Or perhaps Dr. Dawson, the doctor at the U.S. military dispensary on Yang Ming Shan, had told her I was underweight and she ran with it; she was always an excellent student and did all the extra credit assignments. It must have been a Saturday, because I recall it as a leisurely day, if, in retrospect, "leisurely" is the right name for it.

I take a sip of milk, and just sit there, dreaming a bit, looking around the room, ignoring the bowl with its steaming white mound. After a while, I kick my legs around and my mother says, anticipating me... "No, Sara, you cannot get up from the table. Take five bites and you may leave."

I take a nibble, say an eighth of a teaspoonful, and manage to get it down.

"Bigger than that, young lady." She has taken up a position

kitty-cornered across from me by now, at the head of the table, as I sit in the middle of the long side. I feel like Oliver Twist in the play, but with the opposite agenda. Mom is my workhouse mistress.

I sit a while longer. Ten minutes or so.

"Sara, *take* another bite."

I spoon up another eighth of a teaspoon, chase it with a glug of milk.

Her voice turns shrill. "Sara, I'm ready to wait here all day. Take a real bite this time."

Hearing the fury building in my mother's voice, and seeing her torso rise, I know I have to lower the stakes, or else—for my mother's voice and posture do not just issue from her and reside in her. They shrill and rise inside of me as well, for her body is mine just as mine is hers.

Head down, summoning my bravery—a girl's equivalent of girding for battle, or a spy's preparation for a chancy clandestine meeting—I resignedly plunge in my spoon and raise up a full round of the snowy cereal. It looks bland and innocent, but hides a toxic charge within. Already feeling like gagging, I close my eyes, open my mouth, and stick in the spoon. Strange, this business of sticking things into yourself... I manage to part the food from the spoon, and it sits there now in the back of my mouth between palate and tongue. Each stage in this maneuver—for it does feel like a spy's cautious maneuvering behind enemy lines—is an eternity, and a measured and careful and excruciating thing.

"Swallow it," my mother says, her voice now one big and dangerous sound, like the oncoming booming of explosives. I can sense naught but one thing now. I am just my own full mouth.

Heaving my body up with the effort, I duck my head down and back and push the glop backward with my tongue. It should have gone down, but this is theoretical. I have down the French theory but not the American practicality. Instead of slithering down the food pipe, the glob stays there, poised as a missile, until, as I've known it would from the very start, the gagging begins, I feel like I am going to choke to death, and my throat takes over, and does its ejection trick—right, splat, onto the table beside the bowl.

I didn't have to say a word. This was a nuanced film, in which much is conveyed through the child's face and body.

But my mother was on it, right there, like a military sergeant.

"Sara, don't be absurd. Eat it!"

I am silent, gulping, heaving, trying to recover.

"I expect you to eat three more bites, and I expect them to go down!" My mother's voice had changed again now, from emphatic to verging on hysteria. There was that high thread in it—the vocal equivalent of nails on a chalkboard, and also the siren of an all-points-alert emergency. She'd turned to pure reflex. Fear inside her had swelled like wheat in water. If I didn't eat those three bites, I think her mind was telling her, her daughter might die. Maybe like the only-bones orphan who'd arrived on the orphanage steps one day.

I could feel this. I could feel in my own belly my mother's ever-mounting, pitched desperation. The maternal command was loud and clear, hulking and indomitable. But so was my, or my body's, response. My throat refused.

I dare a sidelong glance at my mother, whose face is like a bomb ready to go off. I look at the bowl, and I feel my body go limp. Tears start. I whimper.

"Alright, young lady." Then I feel my mother's body, as if it were my own, stride toward the kitchen.

Soon she is back. "Look at me. If you don't eat those three bites..." She holds a tall glass of ice water in her hand, ready to throw it at me.

My mother's jaw was clenched now. Her eyes had flashed dark. She was in the hands of something other. Something resembling a towering bear had taken her over and assumed her shape.

When my mother was no more than four, her job was to take a lunch bucket through the woods to her beloved Pop, Charles Guernsey, at the nursery where he was head forester. This was to her a daunting job, and each day, as she faced her task, she would pause a moment at the pasture's edge.

Blond ringlets bobbling down her back, with the slab of roast beef folded between two thick hunks of homemade bread, an apple from the orchard, and the jug of milk all tucked into the galvanized bucket, she stands still and sucks in a deep breath before she sets into the trees.

Gulping hard, holding back her small but strong shoulders, and fixing her determination, she bursts into the woodland. Heart galloping, propelled by terror, she hurtles as fast as her short, sturdy legs can carry her. As she runs along the path, she chants to herself, "It'll be okay. It'll be okay," but her eyes dart back and forth, looking for the bears that she is sure lie in wait for her.

In her mind, the bears, hidden behind trees and crouched in grottos and poised to lunge, are large as trucks and brown as mud and black as shoe polish, and have white fangs as big as eggs. Their claws are knife blades.

She hurtles and slaloms through the rising trunks and grabby, green undergrowth, one great pumping heart of terror, until...at last, she spies the patch of light at the end of the path, which leads into the open yard surrounding the nursery office, at which point her throttling heart finally begins to slow in her chest.

Each day, my mother's assigned errand was a test of her young mettle, and every day, through sheer pluck and determination, she won, but each day, it was as if the task was brand new.

My mother never met a bear at the forestry, but, it seems to me, she spent the rest of her life prepared to meet one, and

46

that terrified but dogged little girl stayed inside her, always. The daily terror of those woods-crossings lodged inside the very atoms of her body, and forever after, at unexpected moments, it would rise up inside her, itself like a bear arching onto its hind legs for a kill, and yowl and slash at anything in her path to stay alive. It was always a question: would the bears win?

Most of the time my mother was a solid citizen: practical, sensible, to the point. But sometimes she would make a jailbreak. It was like a prisoner part of her jiggered her way out between the bars and beat it, wholesale, for freedom—we have so many selves inside us. At those jailbreak instants, fear, or a strand of craziness and wilderness that resided deep inside her got riled up and tore free and streaked around for a while, shrieking and flinging. You never knew when this might occur. She'd suddenly just do something that made no sense. It seemed as though something in her brain got triggered. A hidden match ignited, the panic response suddenly shot off, or the mother mammal, on an instant sensing her young under threat, awakened and charged—and all thinking was lost.

This escape of thought and takeover by fear may well have had its source in those daily trips she took, as a lunch pail-lugging little girl. It seems possible the ordeal set in her small body a hair-trigger propensity for terror. She came away with a conviction that she was a lone operative in the world, and with a surly sense that she must suck in fear and fight like a wildcat for anything she ever wanted. Bears could pounce from anywhere in any form; one had to be prepared to do battle.

In a way, my mother's and my relationship paralleled and was just as touchy and perilous and underground as my father's covert maneuverings were with the Chinese. He, as an American, was conducting all sorts of activities—the equivalents of holding glasses of ice water before a child's face—designed to make the Chinese swallow something they had no inclination to swallow, in fact something that, perhaps, made them gag.

Here at the Taipei table, my mother's altered face was suddenly now a mask of terror and fury and pure, distilled determination. This wasn't your everyday mother badgering her daughter to eat. This was something bigger than both of us. This mother-child face-off was a test of wills a mother must win and a dog-eat-dog test of survival. I *would* comply or she *would* explode.

But my small and skinny seven-year-old body had its own strength, its own distilled something, and it refused to comply. It couldn't. *It* was bent on survival too.

So there we sat, my mother and I, for the whole morning. My mother red in the face, her hand trembling around the sweating glass in its grasp, me feeling whipped and limp— trembling uncontrollably inside too, but utterly unable to do what my mother said no matter what or how dreadful the consequences might be. It was a death grip.

This is the first scene I remember in which my mother's mind took flight, when it traveled somewhere, in theory, it shouldn't have. Some strange force, some covey of invisible beings had taken possession of my usually calm and comprehensible mother. I could hear wings flapping in the air, furling her away.

Some positings to account for this childhood interchange with my mother…All of us experience trials in our lives. Some are small, some are large, and there is great range in the blows that may bolt out of the sky. My mother would undergo many sorts of buffetings in her life. My less-fraught life—I would not marry a spy—would deliver me fewer strains, and the ones I was hit with would be less varied. Many of the upsets in my life, instead, would come from a single source: my multiply stressed mother.

Shocks and blows seem to self-spawn. This moment at the breakfast table was one example of a small but indelible ordeal bestowed upon me by my mother. A clawed, wild-eyed being could rise up out of her.

Whatever the provenance of that moment, I feel sorry for my mother, stressed beyond capacity. These aggressive-giddy take-offs, these scary maternal flights injected a slow, leaking poison into our particular mother-daughter bell jar. A poison that, as more such episodes occurred, would become more and more potent.

How sad, I now think, that a girl who loved cream of wheat could turn into a woman who would try to force it down her daughter's throat, but this seems to be how psyches work. It might seem upside down but people's insides have their own logic. If my mother hadn't done this, according to her insides I might have died. On the other hand, her comportment might have arisen from a mad, engulfing need for control in the guise of concern. It might have been an obsession to keep me healthy that could make me sick in the process. It might have been demonic hatred. Or a rogue neuron in the brain. Or strange, unidentified forces in the world making off with her…Who can figure this out? The one thing I know is that it inserted a choking glob in my throat that would congeal at times throughout my life to come…But this urge to force me to eat a repulsive bowl of porridge might also have come from love.

# INDOMITABLE

One morning when I rise and shuffle, half asleep and in my nightie, to breakfast, my father is looking at my mother. All frowsy, she is shrugging her shoulders and grinning at him over her toast, while he shakes his head. "You are indomitable, Lois Taber."

My mother, lying in the tropical heat beside my father, had heard a noise deep in the night. She lay stock-still, listening, on rigid high alert like a forest creature. Fear shot through her. Her heart banged wildly. Someone was riffling around the house. He might be after Charlie! He might hurt her babies! The fear shrank back. Thought evaporated. An iron-hot, protective fury slashed through her. And then a calm.

She rose from the bed, her body both sweating and cold. Careful, silent as a trained operative, she crept into the living room. She looked around. She could feel someone there. She noticed a strange motion in the living room curtains. She marched over, swept open the drapes, and found a strange, perspiring man in front of her. A thief.

Instantly, the man tore out the front door of the house. Just as instantly, my mother tore off after him. *Streaked*, actually, for my mother was stark naked.

Without a single thought of clothing, my mother chased the man around the compound until the guards finally wrested her quarry from her.

This was not the first time that my father had scratched his head at my mother's instinctive bravery. She was one of the few among the wives who had learned to parachute when they were back in Japan. She was not going to be left behind when the men air-dropped into China to save it from Communism. She was going to save it with them. And when my father had gone on secret dead drops in Hong Kong, she had sometimes insisted on trailing my father from two blocks away—ostensibly to provide a second pair of eyes, but secretly, in her mind, to fling her willing body in front of any assailant who might threaten her brave husband doing the world's work. Once, when an anonymous person had threatened to toss acid in the face of an American spy the next time he crossed the Star Ferry, she demanded to go with my father on his next ferry crossing, and was like a twitching German shepherd, guarding her prize, the whole way across the waters.

At any smelt threat to her loved ones, my mother became a bare-naked, one-woman security service. Her hackles rose, her eyes flashed dark. She became ferocity.

# LIFE RINGS

The rhythms of daily life always resume. Chickens cackle, water buffaloes bellow, the cook clanks a pot. My father reads his Chinese newspaper, my mother shoves medicines into her sacky purse and leaves for the orphanage.

One morning, romping with my brother while our mother was at work, I fell off the couch and felt a startling, shrieking pain in my arm as it split in two. Mary, our beloved amah, immediately hoisted me piggyback and rushed me to the American neighbors down our dirt street and around the corner.

Now I am lying on the examining table at the little clinic at the base on Yan Ming Shan Mountain with Dr. Dawson leaning over me. Dr. Dawson is telling me, "Don't you worry, little precious, we'll fix your arm as good as new." Dr. Dawson is from Texas. I am whimpering from the pain but I trust this tall, rangy cowboy who has treated my earaches and tonsilitis and sties and boils and measles and mumps and chicken pox and many other hurts and diseases over the years. Because I can feel the calm emanating from his high male body and shining out from his intent eyes, I feel calm too.

Then my mother rushes in. "Oh, Lois, good," my calm savior looks up from me and says. "She has a compound fracture but we can deal with it." Then he sees her face. "Oh, don't you fret, honey. She'll be fine," and he starts over to her to give her a hug.

But my mother is quick. She takes one look at her skinny little seven-year-old lying on that stretched-out table, and at her daughter's arm, completely distorted with a bone poking through the skin. She has seen every sort of disfigured child, every sort of crooked and cracked bone, but this is her daughter, and she, her little girl's mother, hadn't been there when it had happened.

So she throws up.

Both Dr. Dawson and the nurse rush over to her as I lie on the table and watch.

This was often how it was to be. I would be hurt, on a part of my body or in a part of my heart, and my mother would be the one people would rush to tend. It was like I would tip over the side of a boat and be treading water in the waves, and my mother, in the boat, would be shrieking and the life ring would be tossed to her. At least this is how it seemed to me.

# MY MOTHER IS IRON

The driver has pulled the car to a stop on the road next to the field across which I can see the building of my new school.

"You just get out there and do it!" my mother says.

She and I are standing beside the car, the driver sitting behind the wheel smoking, the engine idling, the mountain rising up behind. I am weepy and have been pleading. "Just a few more minutes. Just a few more minutes. Please, Mom."

I am so afraid and worked up I am nearing hysteria. My belly is heaving up and down. I'm starting to bawl.

But she is iron. Iron. Iron. My mother is iron. "This is for your own good. It hurts me more than it does you," she says, her brows scrunched, her hand gripping me by the arm.

She pushes me onto the playground of the new school, sprawled out in the vast padi at the foot of the mountain slope, and, after she gets back in, the car pulls away.

There is no excuse. A girl must be brave.

# CHEESECAKE LOVE

I am at my friend Lisa's for my first sleepover. Lisa's mother is showing me the specially made-up bed I will sleep in, in Lisa's room. I look at the strange bed in the strange room and I am suddenly abandoned on a cold, grey island of loneliness. I think of the frayed, comfortable couch in the living room at home, and of the Sara Lee Cheesecake, my favorite dessert, thawing on the dining room table, and I can't bear it. My insides judder. My eyes well.

Lisa's mother takes me to the telephone and has me call my parents.

"...and I really want some cheesecake." I finish my plea.

"Oh, Sara," my mother says over the phone, irritated at how ridiculous I am. Nevertheless, perhaps in a flash of empathy, for she would have dropped everything for a hunk of baloney when she was little, she sends my father to pick me up and has my cheesecake waiting for me on a plate.

# BLACK COFFEE

I am sitting at breakfast, eating my Cheerios—thank goodness my mother has stopped trying to make me eat cream of wheat.

When my father comes into the dining room, my mother, cigarette burning between her fingers and her yukata askew, gets up from the table and bursts out "Why the *Hell* did he come here, Charlie Taber?" She rushes toward my father and pummels his chest, and half-crying, half-roaring, says, "How the *Hell* did you let him put our babies in danger? Who knows what would have happened if those government thugs had found him here? It's bad enough having to worry all the time about the kids being kidnapped, but to have one of your men come here with Chiang's security men after him, that's just beyond the god-damned pale."

"Oh, Lois, Lois," my father says. "We had to help the poor man. He's a good man, a journalist, and he's working for us."

"I don't give a damn. Your work is a bunch of hogwash. We should just god damn go home this minute!"

My mother's voice makes my insides shrink. Why is she being so mean to my nice father?

The night before, I had been roused by a bustling in the middle of the night. I had tiptoed down the hall from my bedroom and discovered a strange Chinese man huddled over a cup of tea with my parents in my father's study.

When my mother spied me at the doorway, peering in, in my embroidered Chinese pajamas, she dashed over and shoved me back down the hall to sleep in my brother's room, saying the Chinese man had to sleep in mine. As she pressed me down onto a straw mat she hastily unrolled for me, she put her finger over her lips and hissed, "Just get in the pallet and be quiet, Sara. It's very important."

My mother's whole body had been buzzing, and when she hurriedly tossed a sheet over me, I could see a shining, crazed, fierce look in her eyes like she could see a monster. Immediately she rushed out and locked the door behind her, bolting me in like a prisoner. Her quivering body left mine quivering too. For a long time in the monster darkness, I couldn't close my eyes as I listened to hushed spurts of Chinese and tiptoeing in the creaking hall.

When I get home from school, my mother is crashing around the house, pulling out the plaid suitcases and the big metal trunk and piling clothes on her bed. When my father finally gets home

54

from work, he goes into their bedroom and tries to hug my mother. She shoves him away and then he closes the door. I hear my mother's high, crying-yammering voice and my father's calm voice, trying to soothe her for a long time. Finally they come out of the room, my mother's face red and blotched and my father's arm over her shoulder.

We have a very quiet dinner of soy sauce-y chicken and walnuts with rice during which my father repeatedly pats my mother's hand as she stares off at nowhere.

As I sit stealing glances at her, I can almost hear my stiff-faced mother's brain whirling. Both as little girl and as writer, the words of my mother's mind run stark and nude through me. It is as if she and I are one and the same—both in body and mind. My mother's words are my own; my words are my mother's. Thus they swirl:

*What on earth are we going to do? Charlie's in such a state, torturing himself, saying that damned chief of his, Buck, is requiring him to do something unethical. I don't know what to think...Charlie just thinks too darned much. I do know that. Why can't he simply just do what the boss says? Buck has been at this business longer than he has. He must know something. But Charlie is the most moral person I know. Maybe he's right...*

*Oh golly, I don't have a clue...But sometimes poor Charlie looks like he's the walking death. He's so wan and pale and he keeps saying he feels like he's compromising himself. He says he's putting his Chinese contacts in danger just by associating with them. He says that man Chu who was here last night is publishing anti-Chiang stuff, going way out on a limb for us. He's scared to death he'll be imprisoned by the Gimo's security thugs, or worse. I keep telling him, "You have to get your hands dirty, Charlie, to do good——it's right to support democratic people to challenge Chiang." Of course, he pretends he's fine and holds it all in and brushes it off like all the men do, but sometimes he looks like he's on the verge of tears ...*

Another day at breakfast time, my mother is drinking black coffee and smoking a cigarette instead of eating. My father is standing up, eating a piece of toast before he heads out the door to work.

My mother says, "If you want to keep doing this business, you'd better the heck just mind your *P's* and *Q's*, Charlie Taber...

"I *had* to say something, Lois. It just isn't wise what he's asking," my father says.

"Well, you'd better watch out. You know what Buck's like. He doesn't give a damn about ethics or the safety of the men you cultivate or all those other things you care about. He doesn't care that one of your men is being tortured in that jail. He'd sell his own mother to get a Communist...And he's a strongman type. You know that as well as I do. He'll toss you to the wolves if you keep crossing him.

"Besides, he's probably just following orders from Headquarters. They must know what they're doing. You just mind your g. d. *P's* and *Q's,* Charlie, or we'll all be in big trouble."

My father says not to worry as he kisses her, but my mother, rather than kissing him back, just sits there, smoking. Her mind wrests my own again.

*Oh Lord, what on earth are we going to do? What if he really offends Buck? That man would fire anybody in a second and then where would we be? He's a nasty son of a gun, I can see that. But why, oh why can't Charlie just do what he's told like the other men do? They don't worry about the welfare of their Chinese contacts. They just do what they've been tasked to do. He's oversensitive and he stews too much...*

*But it does seem like something bad is going on. Charlie looked positively shaken when he came home the other day after Buck called him in. I don't know what to think. The bosses have to know what they're doing, don't they? They know what's best for America, for the world...Oh heck, what do I know? I'm just an Indiana farm girl...*

*Well, one thing I do know for sure is I can't let on to the other women that Charlie's having trouble with Buck. They'd all go gossip and gloat and that Patsy would use anything to help her Brian get ahead. She'd throw Charlie under the truck in no time flat...*

## "IF YOU CAN'T SAY ANYTHING NICE..."

I am in the bathroom, trying to find the red towel to take to the beach. I can't find it anywhere. In a fit of annoyance, I grab a ratty tan one and shamble to the door, my bucket and shovel and bathing suit tumbling from my arms as I rush. My mother is yelling from the living room. She uses Japanese when she is trying to pretend not to be mad. "Hayaku, Sara. The Hannons are almost here, Sara. Get a move on."

My brother is standing at the door, all ready and smug, beside my mother. He is holding my favorite red towel rolled up under his arm. I go up to him, elbow him, and say, "Stupid. That's my towel."

My mother's words are instant, as though they have been poised, like a boa constrictor in a tree, just waiting for their chance to wind around me. "Sara, if you can't say anything nice, don't say anything at all."

"Oh, hi, Gloria!" my mother says, all cheery and nice, as she opens the door.

If you can't say anything nice. If you can't say anything nice. My mother says that a hundred times a day. As if being nice is the be all and end all. Be all and end all—that is another of her phrases.

Nice, nice. Rice rice. Mice Mice. Nicey nicey stupid nice.

My mother is sludge. She is that grim, that straight-line mouth, those thin, turned-down lips. She is those slitted eyes. She is black and brown and pungent and thick. She is sticky and stinky and blobby and blunt. She is viscous and curdled. She is gummy and muck.

My mother is stuck. To my arms, to my legs, to my lips she is stuck. My mother is tar. She is tar. She is tar.

On the long car ride to the beach my mother hands me a pack of gum. She never lets me chew gum. She says it's vulgar. But here it is, a whole yellow pack in my hand.

My mother is buttercream. She is buttercream. She is pale yellow butter whipped into a delectable froth. I scoop her on my finger and lick and grin.

I am happiness. I curl. I ribbon. I twirl. I dip. I flit. I am girl. I am dancer. My mother is music to which I am dancer.

## "A WOMAN HAS TO DO WHAT A WOMAN HAS TO DO"

My father has just returned from his day at work. We have been in Taipei for four years now, not counting a year in the middle when my father studied Chinese at Yale and we went with him.

My parents are sitting in the living room beneath my mother's brush painting of a Chinese mountain with a tiny hermit's hut tucked high up its slope. She has been taking painting lessons with her good friend, Anne. My mother and father are drinking my father's favorite Chinese beer and shelling and eating peanuts.

"Oh, Charles, I love it here," my mother is saying. "I have such good friends, and such good work. I love my work with the orphans...Oh, Charlie, those little faces! And Mary is so glorious with the children...I've worked so hard to make a good life here..." Her voice turns pleading now, and weepy and soft, and she is looking down. This is her sad, not her mad kind of crying.

I have seen my mother this kind of sad other times. One day

when I peered into her room, my father was holding her close and she was saying, "Oh, Charlie, I can't believe Pop's gone. And I was way across the damned world," and then her voice went very high and she sobbed. My grandpa Guernsey, her father...

But now it is like a dark shape suddenly rises up in my mother. She sits up straight and her voice shifts to something hard and stiff. "I love it here, but if you must, we must," she says, plunking her hands in her lap. There is strength and bravery and resolve in her sound now, but it is like a taste of bitter lemon peel has gotten mixed in with her vanilla ice cream, trying-to-be-good voice.

Putting his glass of beer down, my father leans toward my mother, reaches out his hand. "I just can't do it, Lois. I can't live with what I'm being asked to do. I just can't ask for an extension of our tour here, even though I know it would be best for you. I've got to get away from this."

"I know, I know," my mother says. "It's alright. We've got to do what's best for your career."

My father hugs her, saying, "Thank you, Lois. I promise. It'll be alright."

But later I heard her say to her friend Anne over the phone, "You know how it is. A woman has to do what a woman has to do."

# THE PEARL

*More than gems in my comb box shaped by the God of the Sea
I prize you, my daughter.*
— Otomo no Sakanoue

"This pearl is for Taiwan," my mother says, handing it to me, cupped in her wet palm. My mother's voice has a softness in it, the caressing love within which she enfolds me at unexpected times—along with all the many other wildly varying emotions she bestows on me.

Earlier in the day, we had gone to a place, somewhere on the outskirts of Taipei, somewhere far out of our normal circuit from our walled home-to Taipei American School-to the Naval Auxiliary Communications Center compound where my father worked and we ate hamburgers at the Officers Club. This place we went was an odd place, one I'd never been to before, a sort of swimming pool complex with palm trees, long-long rectangular ponds of water, and a tiny, street-side stand displaying a few tins the size of tuna fish cans in a small pyramid pile. My mother was full of confidence and spoke her Chinese with surety as she bought two of the cans from the goateed Chinese man in a pair of baggy shorts and zoris.

We drove a long way through the stinking and clamorous streets I loved on our way back home, and when we got there, my mother plunked the two tins on the dining room table and fetched a can opener from the kitchen. Unusually, she and I were alone. Not even the servants were around, and there was a hallowed silence. The air parted as she screwed open the cans. The moment was packed saturated mystery. By the time she stopped her screwing, sitting in each of the cans was a craggy oyster, a single crustacean in its own little pool of water. As my mother returned to the kitchen to fetch a knife, I could smell the sea as I bent over to look at the clam that held, possibly, a jewel worthy of a princess.

With a paring knife, and the competent fingers I'd watched care for sad and wonder-eyed children and old, smelly men, my mother expertly sliced open the first oyster's shell, and, to my utter astonishment, nestled in the curl of translucent gelatinousness, pert and like it belonged there in that ugly place, was a single white pearl.

This is when my mother says it: "This pearl is for Taiwan."

By this sentence—this scene which is like a crystal globe in my mind—I think my mother meant more than I knew and perhaps even she knew, for soon we would be leaving Taipei, the home I had known for most of my childhood, and she, I think, intuited that the way onward would be neither pearly nor easy.

"Oh, Sara," my mother says, there at the table. "We'll make this into a little ring for you. You'll have it always." And this is just what happened. I ended up with a tiny ring in a little red velvet box to take with me into my life, onward into the rollercoaster life with my mother, the Indiana farm girl turned spy's wife, and beyond.

3

# HOMESICK

I am sitting tucked in the green armchair where my father sits after work, in our new living room in Bethesda. I listen to my mother talking on the phone in the kitchen. Gloria, the friend she is talking to, used to live near us back in Taipei. My mother's voice is free and wild and she's going on and on and up and down, and it sounds now and then almost like she's going to cry. She doesn't know I can hear her. She isn't being careful like she is when she talks to me.

"Oh, Gloria," she says, "it's so good to hear your voice!"

Bethesda, where we've ended up in 1961, is full of fathers in seersucker suits, mothers in shifts, and backyards with barbeques. It's a land of families in three-bedroom brick Colonials and frame Cape Cods where, as my mother said, "a woman is judged by whether or not you can eat a fried egg served on her kitchen floor." My mother would win the contest. The president now was handsome John F. Kennedy—my mother said 43 years old was young. People had huge cars like fifteen-foot Buicks parked in their driveways. Beehive hairdos were in.

Bethesda had all sorts of smells, different from the soy sauce and shrimp and sewer smell of Taiwan, and there was an olfactory regularity to the year. Every weekend during the summer as I waited for school to begin, the air lifting from the backyards smelled of hamburgers and hot dogs sizzling on the backyard grill. In the fall ahead, the air would turn smoky and my nose would fill with the wafts from piles of burning leaves. Winter would bring meaty fragrances of Chef Boyardee canned beef stew and Sloppy Joes, and in spring, the air would turn a floral mélange of daffodils, azaleas, and honeysuckle as families tumbled outdoors again.

Conformity was the country's middle name, and both TVs and Americans were viewed in black and white. At this instant—post World War II but just before the storms of the Cuban Missile Crisis, the Civil Rights movement, and the colossus of Vietnam—most Americans were reading the same book. Walter Cronkite kept America abreast of the news, and America was the greatest country in the history of the world, fighting passionately for freedom and pursuing its noble mission of expunging the world of the evils of Communism.

Most of the time, ripped from Taipei and dropped into this America, my mother kept her feelings well hidden. An optimist by nature, and dutiful, she was going the distance to fit into this girdle of a place. Spending money on lipstick and elastic underwear seemed a waste to her, but she bought each, and respectively and determinedly smeared and tugged them on. Keeping up appearances like the best of them was just another item to tick off her list, the to-do list of the impeccable, unimpeachable, perfect spy's wife and government servant. She'd show those Talbots women what a Guernsey from Indiana could do in a perfectly pressed shirtwaist dress from Sears.

It was impossible for my mother to be a stay-at-home housewife, even when most women revered the role and though she hadn't read Betty Friedan. As soon as she could, after disembarking the ship, depositing my brother and me in school, and moving into the Colonial on Wilson Lane—my parents' first purchased house—my mother got herself some part-time physical therapy work and also drove herself down to Georgetown University and found herself a place teaching English to foreign students. My father went to work every day at "the State Department," as he called it. Though he hadn't received the promotion he wished for and thought he deserved, he, too, was dutiful. He worked late at the China Desk, but the Civil Rights movement inspired his passion. He rattled the pages of the *Washington Post* each morning, reading aloud to my mother the latest on Martin Luther King while she poured

Cheerios into our bowls. Though she was actually Albert Schweitzer, my mother was trying her damnedest to be June Cleaver. Giving it the old college try.

My mother is telling Gloria about getting the house settled, and her P.T. job and her teaching. I listen to my mother's spurts between the lulls when Gloria is saying things.

"It's all going fine, Gloria," she says, "but I miss Taipei something awful, don't you?...Yes! It's like losing an arm. Everything about it...Is this how it's going to be after each post? This terrible homesickness you have to hide from everybody who doesn't have a clue that Taipei could be home?...I know. Some days I miss Mary so much I could die. And I don't even know how she's doing. Her sweet, kind face, helpfulness, and of course how she loved the children, almost more than I did...And yes, of course. That delicious food!...And I miss my work something awful. Those little bouncing children at the orphanage in their white smocks, little bodies running up to greet me even though they had no one to love them. How on earth can the world be so unfair?...Oh sure, the teaching is fine. I like my Arab men here struggling with their English, but they aren't like those little scamps clambering all over me when I arrived on hot afternoons in Taipei..."

At this I hear my mother's voice crack, and I feel a scrunching deep down inside. I miss Taipei something awful too, and I grab the fuzzy, white stuffed kitten I got in Japan on the way "back home," so I don't cry.

# WILSON LANE

*I felt—therefore I was.*
— F. Scott Fitzgerald
  "The Crack-Up"

It is soon after we moved back to America from Taiwan.

I hear my mother's voice at the front door. She screeches, "What?" and then she rushes into the living room where I am standing, stiff and shaky, looking out the back window to our green square of Bethesda lawn. Eyes flashing a frightening dark, a flush of wild flapping in the air, she flies across the floor spurting, "Sara, how dare you!" and immediately starts hitting me. Hitting and hitting me like a mad woman.

Half an hour earlier I had walked up the aisle of the springy yellow school bus, waved good-bye to my friend Jane, and descended the three-step stairway. As the bus rumbled down the road, I set out across the street toward our small brick colonial house.

Then…There was nothing…Except a horrendous screeching as the driver of a car slammed on the brakes.

Next, everything was blank, but my whole body was trembling on the other side of the road and a woman was talking fast, standing beside her car—stopped in the middle of the lane. Wilma, our housekeeper, was soon running at full speed out of the front door of our house. She grabbed my hand and pulled me toward the house. She was large and panicked, and both scolding me and patting me as she hurried me down the walk and into the front hall.

"You bad girl. You bad, bad girl," my mother says.

I stand there cringing while she bats at me, her face crumpled, eyes darting and wild. I'm crying, but it is as though she's utterly forgotten that she's my mother, that I'm her daughter. I've become something other. With the strange flapping, my everyday Bethesda mother has been swooped away and replaced by another. Everything is mixed up and blurred and savage and terrorizing. My mother is a furious and ravenous bear, and I am not a victim, but a rival bear to be defeated with her bare hands.

And now, afterwards, I crouch in the far corner of my room upstairs, facing the wall, pressing my head against the hard vee of the corner. As I crouch, I am shivering like a mouse in a cage. I shiver and whimper, knowing I have done something dreadfully, dreadfully wrong.

I hear my mother's voice shrieking to my father over the phone, "Oh, Charlie, Charlie! How could she?!?"

In a little while, her footsteps on the stairs. She comes into the room. I can feel in my body that her body and her eyes are different now. They have switched back. She sees me crying in my corner.

"Oh, Sweetie, Sweetie," she says, and she takes me onto her lap, holds me desperately in her arms, squeezes me so tight it hurts.

It is perhaps understandable to a grown person that a mother might become deranged at the thought of her child being hit by a car. Perhaps, though, even another parent would view my mother's reaction as extreme. In any case, a child doesn't have such perspective, and may store in memory, as I did, only the smarting of the mother's blows, not having any sense of what might have spurred them. The shiver crouched inside me, the sense of having done something deeply bad.

Years later I would learn that when my mother was small, her own mother used to spank her when she was injured. It was her responsibility, as one of nine children, to take care of herself. What long-term effect would this have had on an afraid little girl? If a child is to have a sense of safety in the world, repair after rupture may be crucial. Perhaps mothers improve upon their mothers' mothering tactics generation by generation, smidgeon by smidgeon——or don't.

When my father was transferred again in two years, my

mother did not want to rent out the house on Wilson Lane. She insisted they sell it.

# MOTHER-DAUGHTER
# TWINS

In Bethesda, most of the time, my mother and I walk down the street, dressed in Villager blouses with round collars in complementary floral prints—blouses my mother has picked out for us at The Next to New. Hand in hand we walk—in and out of Bradley Drugs, the A & P grocery store, and Bruce Variety—in our close-to-matching outfits.

These two grade school years in Bethesda, my mother's body is mine and mine is hers. We inter-live each other. We are merged, two pieces of tissue paper overlaid on a screen. I am a smaller version of her, but we are the same. My mother is so, so happy with us this way, and I am happy to be her smaller match walking in step with her.

Could it be that there are times when the question as to where a mother ends and a daughter begins matters not at all? Could it be that sometimes a mother and a daughter are simply quite content to be each other's middles?

# SHE CAN READ ME
# LIKE A BOOK

I trudge up the front walk, open the door of our brick house, dump my fourth grade Radnor Elementary School home-work on the floor.

My mother, in her pixie cut and her old plaid shift, takes one look at me. "So, what did Kathy say to you today?"

She says this before I say anything, just by glancing up from the *Washington Post* she is reading.

A mother *knows*. She reads the dull gleam in an eye, the slump of a shoulder, the sound of a pore opening.

When I tell her that Kathy ignored me when I asked her to play jump rope with me, and went off to whisper to Polly, she says, "Oh, Sweetie, this too shall pass."

# LESSONS

*With a little hoard of maxims preaching*
*down a mother's heart.*
— Tennyson
 "Locksley Hall"

My mother is sitting on the flowered armchair with her legs curled under her, reading a mystery story while I am lying on the floor, leaning on my elbows, reading one of my own. The air around us is cool and fresh and pleasantly hums.

My mother had her Agatha Christies to get her through. These homey stories of puzzles solved and problems reliably overcome soothed her as she, once in a while, clad in her old flannel nightgown, stretched out on her bed or curled up on a chair as today, in her worry-plenty, ever-moving, spy's wife life. Like mother, like daughter, it seems, for, at nine, Nancy Drew mysteries were my own comfort reading. Nancy discovering the hidden staircase that leads to her captured father. Nancy, gagged on a cabin cruiser, finding her orphan friend's stolen inheritance. Nancy and her chubby friend Bess sharing milkshakes as reward for a job well done. Stories of girls who could do anything, brave as boys, mischievous as monkeys, buoyant as butterflies. I could feel Nancy's omnipotence flowing through me as I turned the pages. My mother and I both thrived on the cookies-and-milk tales of powerful females outsmarting ne'er do wells and laying conundrums to rest.

"You can do anything you put your mind to." "Where there's a will, there's a way." "There's no such word as 'can't.'" "Nothing ventured, nothing gained," my mother always said. Over and over, I heard these aphorisms, as though my mother were my family's own private Benjamin Franklin. She was a true believer—in her red gingham blouse with the Peter Pan collar in Bethesda, later in her old grey Dutch sweater in The Hague, and later than that in her batik shift and sandals in Borneo: a believer in "If you don't at first succeed, try, try again." As if stored up down-home wisdom weren't enough, my mother had studied with Frank Gilbreth, the time and motion efficiency expert—and author of *Cheaper by the Dozen,* when she was a student at Purdue University. An ideal student and born disciple, she became the original multi-tasker, believing no one should ever do just one thing when two or three more could be accomplished at the same time. On her best days, 25 tasks were ticked off by the time she let herself go to bed.

When she became a co-leader of my Brownie troop, my mother added yet another tenet to her creed, seizing the Girl Scout motto, "Be prepared." Sitting on the basement floor on homemade sit-upons with us girls, she and Mrs. Finch guided us in making first aid kits for our fathers, milk cartons of emergency sand for our family cars in winter, and sewing kits for our mothers. No one in our families would lack supplies for any emergency, if my mother had anything to do with it.

She was the great American pioneer woman: pluck, hard work, efficiency, and preparedness win the race.

While all this belief in enterprise was active in her, there was another disconcerting and contradictory side to this woman of will, another set of idiosyncratic, equally powerful refrains that issued from her—refrains arising from a potent, broiling brew of love and fear. These life lessons, too, my mother deposited in me: Refrains, when I was young, such as, "Don't go up that slide. It's too high." "No, you may not walk to Charlotte's alone." "Don't go to that party. You're too tired." And when I was grown: "Don't cook dinner. You've done enough for one day." "Don't quit your job. You're lucky to have one." "Don't drive tonight. It's too foggy." When it came to her own daughter, this woman—who once parachuted onto beaches and believed in willpower over all—couldn't help but protect and huddle in a corner, curdled with fear. At any change or possible risk to her offspring, she became a cave woman, clutching her brood to her, feeling exposed on the beach with an incoming sea. Miss Marple and Nancy Drew reduced to cowering tears.

Nighttime, my mother sits next to me in her worn, flannel nightie, our sides touching, on my bed. I nestle against her soft bosom, her strong, smooth arm loose around me as she reads me a story. When she closes the covers of the book, she says, "Now think about the two best things. What were the two best things today?"

I say things like, "Playing jump rope with Kathy," or "Twinkies after school." If I start by saying, "But it wasn't such a good day. Jane chose Vicky to go the cafeteria with her," my mother says, "Oh, there are other girls to go to lunch with. Just remember *The Little Engine that Could.*" But it doesn't really matter what I say during these conversations. What my mother is trying so hard to do, with her two incantations, is to install in me a pattern of mind—to suffuse me with an inner sense of hope and safety and anoint me with self-sufficiency and self-protection. Something better than "When I lay me down to sleep," the only bedtime prayer I know, and which sends through me a tremble of fear. "If I should die before I wake?" "My soul to take?"

Even though she'd go before a firing squad any day of the

week for me, my mother knows she might not be able to save me. So, she gives me the secrets she knows: hard work and eyes trained on the goodness in the world.

## "WOMEN ARE BETTER AT THAT"

My mother's voice is in and out and smothery, like she's trying to whisper but she can't since she's on the phone. She's talking to Gloria again. I'm sitting in my father's living room chair again, keeping my eyes aimed down on the biography I'm reading, but I'm really listening because I can hear the upset in my mother's voice.

"I thought it would be better here but Charlie's still not happy," my mother says. "He didn't get that damned promotion, Gloria."

Gloria talks for a while. Then my mother says, "Yes, you're right. Charlie says the same thing. The office is a stew pot. But Gloria, you have to be happy where you are..." Then she adds, "Women are better at that than men..."

Gloria says something in reply and my mother laughs. I feel happier then——I can hear my mother's body unclench as she laughs with her friend, so I settle back into my book about Florence Nightingale.

But then, after they hang up, my mother goes into the kitchen and starts banging pans around. I can tell she's back to being upset. I know her thoughts from what she talks about with my father when they don't know I'm hearing.

*I thought it **would** be better here but Charlie just stews. He stews and stews about that damned promotion. I keep telling him, "Oh, don't be a worrywart, Charlie. Next time for sure," but why the heck Terry got a promotion and Charlie didn't is beyond me. Charlie's so much sharper*

*and more dignified and professional...Who knows how things work in*
*this world...He always says the office is like a Chinese market, there are*
*so many different things being sold. He's brave of course, and dismisses*
*its importance sometimes too, and when the men get together they all*
*laugh about the ridiculousness of everything and then he seems lighter*
*and fortified on the way home. And he always emphasizes how he still*
*loves the China work and the Chinese, but maybe, really, he should get*
*out. After all that mess with Buck. I'm not sure these are really his kind*
*of men. I can feel the tension in every muscle in his body at night...I*
*told him the other day that he should go to law school, like he wanted*
*to do before we were married. But he keeps saying the job is fine and you*
*can't do better than a government job, and he assures me that when we*
*go abroad again he'll be happier again...Okay. But, if he's going to*
*stay in, he'd better play the g.d. game...*

## CROSSING THE LINE

We are eating beef and green peppers, the Chinese dish my
mother makes that we all love. My mother hurries down her
rice and beef with her chopsticks and then shoves her blue and
white bowl with the Chinese fish pattern away from her. She
launches right into something, as if she and my father have been
in the middle of a conversation. Her voice is yammery like when
she's mad.

"Why do you have to pour oil on the fire, Charlie? Why in
the devil do you think *you've* got to be down there at the
Washington Monument? I believe in Civil Rights too—Lord
knows I want to cut the gizzards out of those men who call
people who just want to ride the bus those awful names, and I'd
like to snip the you-know-whats off those men who violate those
sweet little girls with those beautiful brown eyes down south,
and those KKK-ers who hang people in trees and burn those
awful crosses should be burned up in the hell they want
everyone else sent to except their foul chicken house selves—

but why tempt the powers that be, for God's sake?

"I've got the right to express my opinion, like every other American citizen," my father says, "especially when I'm in Washington and not having to speak for the government…" He's calm and his voice is quiet and clear.

"But why tempt fate?" my mother says. "Who knows what the other men at the Company will think. None of them are going to be down there at the mall. What if one of those bigoted Wallace types happens to be passing by and sees you? I wouldn't put it past that Joe to report you to the boss…

"And what if some of those John Birchers from Mississippi go down there to the demonstration and decide to shoot people? Or what if the police start fire-bombing the protestors like they did down south?…Oh, I know what you're going to say." My mother waves her hand so my father can't talk. "I know you're setting an example for the kids, and you have to stand up for your rights or it's not a democracy, and Medgar Evers said, 'You can kill a man but you can't kill an idea.'"

"It's important, Lois."

She shifts in her seat and slows her words down and her voice gets sad and soft. "Oh, I know it is. Lord knows, I try to help the world too—in my own way. All my patients down in those bad neighborhoods who don't have a prayer of getting P.T. if people don't cross the line." Her voice goes soft and wending now for a minute. "I just love that Mrs. Johnson and all her little grandchildren. She's had no treatment for that stroke for so long…I don't know how I'll do it, but I'm determined to get her back on her feet again…"

But energy seems to balloon up inside her and she shifts back to her yammer again. "Of course we've got to do something in this country to make things better for people who are basically still in slavery." Her voice pitches even higher, and she leans toward my father looking like she might spit at him. "I respect all the things you think about, but for God's sake, Charlie, why on earth put yourself, us, the kids at risk? I'll die if something happens to you. I'll kill you if something happens to you. And it'll be your own god-damned fault."

My father reaches his hand across the table, over the bowls of rice and sauté, and pats my mother's hand, looking her in her sparking hazel eyes with his soft brown ones. "It'll be alright, Lois. You'll see."

# THE GLORY OF BREASTS

I am in the fourth grade, nine years old, sitting on the bath mat on the floor beside the pink tub in our Wilson Lane bathroom, watching my mother bathe. One of the wonders all through my childhood is watching my mother wash her breasts. I look on mesmerized, from my skinny, flat body, as my Renoir-round mother soaps her chest, slops her big blobs up and down, and sloshes water over them. Even though she seems quite matter-of-fact about hers and even to like them, I await, with mostly dread, my own pair.

I want my body to stay just the way it is forever, and I want to stay for always just where I am. I want to be here, just here in this cozy pink room, and be my same self, safe forever in my familiar, just-like-any-old-kid's body. I want to keep my even chest, and my belly smooth as a tambourine, and my reliable, skinny legs like a deer's that can run so fast—and stay forever right in this Bethesda house.

But my father has told us we are being transferred soon. Even though it is the middle of the year.

**4**

## PATATES FRITES

My father's transfer, it turned out, was to the royal capital of The Netherlands.

I now enter a time—during the fourth, fifth, and sixth grades—when my mother and I walk in rhythm down Dutch cobbled streets. My days are melodies with the refrains supplied by her.

On this day my mother and I walk along the promenade at Scheveningen, The Hague's seaport. The walkway is a swath of old bricks. There is the strong smell of fish. Gulls swoop and cry. We are bundled in our woolen coats, hers camel colored and mine navy blue. My mother hugs me against her and pounds her mitten on my back, to keep away the cold. As we stride toward our favorite *patates frites* stand, I spot Dutch girls and mothers along the way.

A mother and teenaged daughter, in identical woolen coats of two green shades, walk briskly arm in arm. They wear hats that mash down curls peeking from underneath. Their thick cheeks aflame beneath squinting blue eyes. They talk in loud, emphatic voices, nodding and gesturing to each other with their free hands.

Another mother in clogs and a baggy, ribbed sweater chases after her toddler daughter and a small brown dog. She yells, "Kome hier! Kome hier!" as she whirls around, laughing, lunging to grab them.

A girl in a long purple and pink striped scarf flies a kite, her portly mother calling out instructions from a bench. The kite rises higher and higher in the blasts of wind. When it seems to rise above the elegant old Kurhaus Hotel, the mother goes to stand beside her daughter. Her hand on her daughter's shoulder, the two faces lift to watch the paper wings swoop in the air.

At the *patates frites* stand a girl my age wears a navy blue coat like mine, ordering *patates* with her mother. Feeling a sudden communion with Dutch girls, I say "Dag." The girl says "Dag" back, and grins. Our mothers, too, exchange greetings. We four stand together, holding our paper cones of French fries.

I look up at my mother. Her winter weed hair whips around her dusky green eyes. Her eyes smile at me. I toss my braids to keep them out of my potatoes.

Huddled under the small canopy of the stand, we munch contentedly, dipping each patate in the dollop of mayonnaise before we put it in our mouths.

Oh, the savory tenacity, the sense of utter completeness and of having discovered the answer, of a moment with a paper cone of frites!

As I peer into these past years, each of the recalled moments between my mother and me—and each recollected moment between any mother and a daughter—seems its own microcosm. The moments of mergings and bumpings between us are a series of overlapping transparencies, each carrying its own vitality and life. And a remembered scene, whether gleeful or troubled or triumphant, resembles an insistent child desiring to hold sole power, to claim the whole story for herself, to assert "*This* is what this mother, this daughter, this relationship was." This insistence perhaps reflects an irrepressible, inherent, biological human yearning for absolute certainty, but it is a patent falsity. And yet each successive interaction seems also a dewdrop of truth—each wavering image, perhaps, as true as another.

If I had a choice, this moment at the patates frites stall is the one at which I would pause the film forever. For why not halt altogether at this happy scene, if we truly have freedom of choice, and select this view into memory's porthole as the way my mother and I were, out of them all?

*Mightn't* we, or even *ought* we, choose a story that makes us happy or helps us to flourish?

# MOTHER-DAUGHTER SONG

The mother in the fluffy grey cardigan and the girl in the tan V-neck sweater sit at the farmhouse table in the kitchen in The Hague, laughing at something. Laughing and laughing. They laugh and laugh until their stomachs hurt, their eyes flashing merriment back and forth, my mother's squawks and my high-pitched giggles infecting each of us into more and more uncontrollable fits.

The joy of mothers and daughters. Nothing else is ever so fine. No connection is ever as close to song as this. They are a carousel. They are inside the music.

## *LEKKER*

"Isn't Holland delectamy?" my mother says, despite the foul weather, as we explore the lanes and pastures of our new country.

It was 1964 and we lived now in a world of wet brick. From dark skies, rain cascaded and hurled outside the windows of the row house we rented on a street of dignified old residences in the heart of The Hague, where my father was assigned now for the next four and a half years. He was serving as American liaison to the Dutch national intelligence service, a job that had put thrill in his voice and sent him jauntily bicycling off into the rain each morning.

My mother's heart galloped as she beheld her new domain. She loved the feel of the aged Dutch town with its narrow, canal-side rowhouses and portly burghers' homes, and the romance of the turreted thirteenth century palace around which the town hummed. She loved the city's smell of sea and horses and carrots, the touch of rough stone on her fingertips, the tolling of ancient bells, and the bite of aged Dutch cheese. She fell for the whimsical, trapezoidal Deux Chevaux and gumdrop-shaped Volkswagens that rattled, and the hard-working trams that sneezed down the rainy, cobbled streets. She revered the stately mounted policemen who stopped, like the cars, at the downtown streetlights. Her Indiana heart thumped in tune with the earthiness and work-a-day purposefulness of the Dutch: the striding housewives in stout shoes toting baskets of root vegetables and hyacinths; the men pedaling their bicycles, transporting children or fishing poles on their fenders. And she loved to see the boys and girls with bare, winter-chapped legs dodging along the sidewalks, skidding in dog droppings, and shouting the way healthy children should. She was a little sniffy about the scraggly-haired Dutch teenagers toting their U.S. Army ammo bags, waving "Ban the Bomb!" signs and ranting about "Amerika" like it was a dirty word—but she laughed off youth's foolishness.

There are no orphans or polio victims to heal or even African students to teach English in The Hague, but she finds a harness into which to click herself. This time it is translating Dutch for the Embassy. She's taken Dutch lessons at the Foreign Service Institute before arrival and will continue avid study throughout our stay. My mother adores the guttural sounds of *Nederlandse*. One of her favorite words is the onomatopoeic word for "tasty." The Gouda cheese, the pea soup, the raw herring, and Holland itself: all are pure *lekker* to her.

# NAPPING WITH
# MY MOTHER

*I will say it is so: My mother's voice is a lullaby in my cells. When I am still, my body feels her breathing.*
— Terry Tempest Williams
*When Women Were Birds*

"Mom? Mom! Where are you?" I yell out when I arrive home into our large, looming house from school.

In Holland my mother pursues her own life apart from me—a fact that is new in my awareness and slightly bothersome to me. While I pass my days at The American School of The Hague starting in the middle of fourth grade, she translates her Dutch on the rug-covered table in the music room, books and papers in three shuffled piles, around an overflowing ashtray. She chats and eats *boterhams* with her friends in downtown *koffie* houses. She goes with my father to parties several nights a week, spinning out the door on his arm in fringed hot pink wool, or a tailored leather skirt. Fiercely, I always watch her gone.

Afternoons, in the dark living room, with the heavy velvet curtains and the long burgundy sofa near the picture window, my mother entertains ladies, tea things on the coffee table. The ladies sit and drone on and on, as I wander by, back and forth, back and forth, out in the hall, wanting them to stop talking. Wanting them to yield up my mother, to give her over to me, so that she can attend my wishes. I interrupt my pacing to check on my guinea pig or to have a quick snack of Cheerios and canned whipped cream in the kitchen, but, always, my soul is bent on watching her.

When the guests have gone and I have her back at my beck, I am mired. I sit at my mother's feet in the shadow left by the ladies, simultaneously claiming her and longing to quit her. I am flooded with relief that she is all mine again, and yet I squirm. I want to escape. I want to get away from her smell, I want to escape the heaviness her nearness inserts inside me, but I am unable to move. My limbs and all of my body are underwater, sluggish, lodged.

"Oh, Sara, put on your white and blue shirtwaist."

My mother insists, when I am to go downtown with her that I wear a dress she chooses—instead of my favorite Lee jeans—and I seethe as I change. She says that, as an Embassy family, we have to look nice when we go out, but I know the dress is just what she prefers to see me in. As we set off in our Volkswagen, I don't know how to set my face. Inside I am half proud, half sulking.

Some days I watch my mother's eyes flicker as they pass over the pages of a book. As she reads during these years of my life, she smiles and laughs. Sometimes she reads books to me and my brother, long ones like *The Hobbit*, or stories about Miss Bianca, an elegant white mouse who commands her followers from a white pagoda, but I like it best when I catch her reading to herself. When she is reading, I feel free.

Some days, my mother suggests we take a nap on her bed. I cuddle up to her on the bed, dim-lit by grey light coming from the large, square window to the front of the house. In the pool of cool, wan light, I move up near her, keeping my hand touching her arm, to assure that she doesn't move, to assure that she'll be there when I wake up. But when I do, she is always gone.

# MY MOTHER, MY BROTHER, AND ME

Upon our arrival in Holland in the middle of the school year, my brother and I were plopped willy-nilly into the tiny American School of The Hague. I spend my days imitating and flattering the other girls with all my might, trying doggedly to make friends with the seven other girls in the fourth grade.

After handing me a special donut from the P.X. one day after school, my mother says, "You be extra nice to your brother, Sara. It's hard being the new boy. Pretty is as pretty does." My mother is asking me to summon my older and ladylike self and to appreciate and understand the fact of male vulnerability—and she expects me to go all out to protect my brother as she does, but I bristle. She thinks it's not hard for me to make friends?

When my brother joins us for after-school snack, I snatch the donut I know he'd like best and I flounce by him and knock him accidentally on purpose so his milk spills on the table. "You be nice to your brother," my mother says, "Or go to your room."

And so it continues: all the troubles my brother has, that my mother worries about, that necessitate my being extra nice.

Other afternoons, I hear her talking in a hushed voice over the phone to her friend Phyllis:

"He's so smart, Phyllis. Why oh why does he get those D's??"

"He's so unhappy, Phyllis," she says.

"He's alone every time I drop by the school," my mother wails.

All of this makes my mother sick with worry. She gets my brother a tutor but the tutor says he's reading at a tenth-grade level even though he's in second grade. She finds him a carpentry class with Dutch boys. She does anything she can think of to make him happy—though, to me, he seems quite happy enough, replicating the Battle of the Bulge with his thousands of soldiers all over his room or reading his history tomes on his bed. To me he seems as happy as a general winning a war.

All of my mother's overheard worrying and all of her pleas for kindness from me have the opposite effect. Instead of empathizing with him or trying to make his world a kinder one, I do mean things like pinch my brother's arm when she isn't looking, or hide the encyclopedia he is reading, out of pure chartreuse and scarlet jealousy.

This may be true, or maybe these memories come from my mother's magazine, and maybe I am not remembering— because my mother didn't notice them—the moments I was kind to my brother and we bounced and flopped around, having fun together like baby rabbits. Could this be?

## MOTHER PLAY

Sometimes my mother is a kid.

"I'm gonna get you!"

My mother rushes after my brother and me, laughing and chortling, arms stretched out in front of her, fingers reaching and wiggling out to grab. Her voice is light and happy, "Better watch out, I'm gonna lick you!" she says, running all around the creaky, old Dutch house with its worn-out Oriental rugs, upping the ante and flicking her tongue.

My brother is playful, too, and goads her, standing in the way, saying, "Oh no you won't, Mom!" and bolting when she's almost got him. I, on the other hand, am filled with a giddy panic. My heart is hammering inside my chest, and as my mother nears me, I blast out of the kitchen, take a right into the dining room, hurtle into the living room, swerve around the wing chairs, weave into the library, feint into the hall, and hurl myself onto the wide-open staircase—a place of safety. I can race upstairs if need be.

My mother bounces into the hall now, laughing, the game ebbing, my brother laughing too. Both of them are panting, and she grabs my brother in a hug. My mother is being silly, and I know that she is herself harmless and I can tell that she is just a silly kid inside, and it is almost fun, but not quite. My mother is comfortable as a cow in her body, and doesn't mind any kind of touching and isn't repelled by tongues, while I am sensitive in my body, and to me the game is a little like too much tickling.

# COWS

One day after my riding lesson—which my mother has arranged for me because I have a fantasy of myself as a fearless American cowgirl cum sedate English princess posting in her smart hacking jacket—my mother takes me and my brother, who also takes lessons, to a Dutch farm to visit and milk the cows.

Cows are important to my mother. She grew up milking cows back at the forestry, and she's told us about how she used to go out to the barn when she was mad at her brothers (who teased her all the time) and sit with the cows. She'd just lean against their smooth, steady flanks and steal drinks from their soft teats. Cows are also significant to her and to us because her maiden name is Guernsey. Furthermore, her mother's name is Daisy Bell. The silly family story about Grandma is that she had to think hard before she consented to marry Charles Guernsey.

We walk down the long middle aisle of the wonderful, old, reeking barn, tromping through the hay in our riding boots, skirting the behinds of the cows with their flicking tails, until the farmer, leading us in his woolen cap and wooden shoes, brings us to the cow he has chosen for us. He has an old hand-chiseled wooden stool in his beefy hand—a kind of tripod made of three chunks of wood the width of my arm and a wooden seat like half a dinner plate.

We halt at the lovely black-and-white Holstein, the farmer

utters some tender words in Dutch to the cow, sliding his hand along the top ridge of her, and invites me to sit down on the stool, which he sets beside her long, flopping udders. He briskly shows me how to pull on the udder, using a flick of his fingers that brings a vigorous squirt of milk into the galvanized pail. I try, at first squeezing the end of the teat and nothing comes out. The farmer wraps his hand around mine, like a roll around a hot dog, and gently moves my hand inside his to execute a gentle curving movement that brings forth the milk in a steady stream. With this tutelage, after his paternal hand withdraws, I enjoy the inimitable satisfaction of mastery. With glee, I shoot squirt after squirt of creamy fluid into the pail.

My brother, too, quickly catches on. After we've had our goes, my mother, in her old tan canvas skirt, plunks down on the stool. As if she's done it all her life, with expertise she milks the cow empty.

The farmer laughs a rich laugh and says, "Oh, *ja*, M'vrouw Taber!" pats her on the back, and sends us off with a jar full of milk with a two-inch frosting of cream at its top. It seems as if she and farmer are best friends.

We depart the farm via a path which wends through the wet, green pasture of grazing cows. "Oh, wouldn't it be marvelous to be a cow?" my mother says, wistfully, green delight in her voice. "Wouldn't it be delectable to live in a pasture and eat grass and give all the children your milk? Oh, I'd love to be a cow…" Her eyes gaze far off; her face looks dreamy and contented and this makes me feel dreamy and contented, and my brother and I promptly start a hay fight, laughing and at first tossing grass at each other and then trying to shove it down each other's shirts. My mother laughs too, as she watches us and cradles the jar of milk in her arms. She promises us *chocolade melk* when we get home.

During this Dutch sojourn, my mother is bountiful and lusty. She's plump and healthy, adores milk and adores food. She feeds us Dutch stroopwaflen and cups of overflowing milk, and she would eat hunks of *Gouda kaas* or *Leidse kaas* all day if she let herself. She never eats desserts, though. It is cheese for her. Cheese with a little hunk of bread is her favorite thing. It appears as though cheese is not only *lekke*r to her, but her way of cultivating her own milk. It seems clear. My mother is in her true heart and bosom, a cow.

# MY MOTHER'S HANDS

*Why did no one ever model or paint or carve that hand of Sido's, tanned and wrinkled early by household tasks, gardening, cold water, and the sun, with its long, finely tapering fingers and its beautiful, convex, oval nails?*
— Sidonie-Gabrielle Colette
  *Sido*

My mother has a knack for finding baby birds fallen from nests. The park with the kingly trees at the end of the block is where she spots them. It's like she's a magical bird nurse and can sense baby birds with her pin feathers. We will be wandering through the twiggy, fragrant, wet woods and she will notice something in the undergrowth. She will quietly bend down and scoop the something into her palm. Sometimes we take the floppy, scrawny feather-beings home and put them in shoe boxes filled with grass and leaves. My mother feeds them watered-down egg from a medicine dropper. As my mother feeds a chick, she makes a cup of her hand and holds the baby bird so, so tenderly, so, so lightly. I can feel her gentle fingers in my feathers, holding so cherishingly my weightless body.

On Thursday afternoons, my mother goes to her pottery class with her friend Mrs. Tucker. Mrs. Tucker is a real artist. My mother adores Mrs. Tucker and she adores her pottery class. She says it does her soul good to sink her hands every week into some "good, thick, red clay." She comes home with objects and statues she's made. First, she arrives with a candlestick which she poked all over with a stick so it looked like bark. Once a boy in my class in second grade made one like that. But then she starts bringing home sculptures of people. She shapes one of a baby, and one of a mother holding a baby—the mother looks like she's an angel singing with joy looking at her child—and then she makes one of me lying on the floor crying, or maybe "having a fit." She always says I was good at having fits when I was little—but maybe it's just of a girl sad and crying. Even though my mother's not a real artist, her sculptures are actually pretty good. And she comes home so happy, after the firing day, with her clay children in her hands.

An unexpected moment. I step into my mother's room to ask her something but instead, I suddenly go quiet. My mother's usually-in-constant-motion body is tranquil. She is peering intently at the table in front of her, her hands shifting cards from place to place. As she will do everywhere she will live—Borneo, Japan, Vietnam, Germany, America, and other locales from now on—my mother is playing solitaire.

Observing her from the doorway, her moving hands strike me, the way they always do, as surprisingly lovely. They seem to me the ideal shape and size, with smooth, conical, clean nails, and somehow inspirited by a perfect, perfectly calm confidence.

As she focuses on her cards, slapping down the last card, with the satisfaction of completing a round, I can feel her body quietly thrumming inside my own. What you watch your mother do to comfort herself becomes your own source of comfort—your vision of warmth, safety and contentment, your inheritance, your solace always at hand.

# ROWING TO LEIDEN

It is late spring. My mother and Mrs. Tucker have decided we are going to row to Leiden, a town about fifteen kilometers away. The Tuckers' yard backs down onto a canal, so we have brought our bathtub-like fiberglass rowing pram to their house and are starting out from their grassy bank. Mrs. Tucker and my mother have packed sandwiches of Dutch Gouda and ham, and cans of Coke, and Dutch stroopwafel cookies into a plastic washtub we're going to pull behind us.

Before we leave, as the mothers are getting everything we'll need, I wander around Mrs. Tucker's house. There is a lot of rich cherry red around, and the clay sculptures that Mrs. Tucker, who has vivid red lips and dark hair, has created. There are also the oil paintings of Melissa, Mrs. Tucker's daughter two years older than I, and of her son Mark, my age. Those paintings, like the furniture and like Mrs. Tucker, are rich and luscious in reds and purples and pink cheeks. The rich colors make Mrs. Tucker's kids look like they're Renoir's children.

We're in the boat now. There are six of us—four children and the two mothers—and the boat is wallowing, really, rather than floating. There is just about one inch of freeboard. Just as we set out, the Tuckers' high-strung Airedale leaps into the canal, intending to accompany us in the boat. Mrs. Tucker almost capsizes us, with her arm-flinging and exhortations to Tim to "Go home!" My mother has to grab her with one arm so we don't tip. Afterwards, with Tim barking from the bank, we all laugh so hard we have to clutch our sides. The boat rocks dangerously back and forth, and Mrs. Tucker hee-haws and my mother hoots like I've never heard her hoot before.

We row past the backs of lots of houses. There is washing hung up in yards, and buckets and fishing poles and old boats flung around. The grass is wet and comes right down to the water. Trees reach out over us. It is so funny to see how low we are riding in the water that we laugh constantly, and every time we change rowers, the boat almost turns upside down. We dangle our fingers in the mossy green canal, and watch our stick and string fishing lines trail behind us. We load and re-load them with hunks of old bread, which the mallards, instead of the fish, grab. We have a whole flotilla of ducks parading behind us.

Eventually—probably at the most four kilometers from the Tuckers' house—we pass the last house and find ourselves rowing between farm fields. Cows nose along the banks, coot families drift along the reedy edges, fishing. We can see straight over a wet, green flatness for a long way to where it ends. The sky is the kind of blue that looks as if it's been diluted with cloud. Shortly after we come into this open country, our mothers start joking about Leiden. We aren't sure if they're serious or not. "Do you think we're in Leiden yet?" they ask each other every few yards, and each time they ask it they burst out laughing.

"Are you sure this is the right canal?" one asks.

"I'm sure I see Leiden up there," the other says. Then they kill themselves laughing.

Our mothers seem strange—a little hysterical, a little too giddy. Their hilarity is theirs alone—coming from their lives as mothers somewhere off in another land. We kids are taking each minute as it comes—watching fish, urging baby ducks to return to their mothers, grabbing leaves from the trees. Our mothers' strange laughter is vaguely irritating, but we children have implicitly agreed to forgive them.

"This must be the outskirts of Leiden," my mother says as we come abreast of an old stone windmill. "Let's have lunch here." We all agree, Mrs. Tucker pressing her side as she climbs out of the boat. We don't see any sign of the town, but we're happy. The mothers plunk down on the grass beside the mill, rubbing their arms, and we dash off, dodging cow pies, to gallop around the field and throw clumps of grass at each other. My mother's face as I glance over at her sitting on the green bank, talking to Mrs. Tucker, is pure and shining and contented happiness.

I drink from this tableau, this wash of slow canal, green banks, laughing mothers, and children trailing their fingers in the flow, a refreshing draught of my mother's unadulterated happiness. Perhaps some of the most sparkling treasures a mother can give her daughter are unintentional: moments when she catches her mother in unself-conscious, flat-out expressions of vitality and joy. Moments when she beholds a mother happy in the world, happy with herself, a mother, yes—happy with her daughter, but possessing a happiness all her own. An independent happiness that inadvertently but crucially grants her daughter, like a congratulatory glass, the right to her own.

# LAND MINES

One weekend day in Holland when I am ten, we wend along a country road paralleling the North Sea. The dunes rise to our left. To the right: a hedge and then scruffy pastureland stretching flat to a horizon of farmhouses. My father pulls to a stop on the left-hand side of the route and we walk up the hump of land toward mid-winter's chill, green-pounding, foam-crashing sea.

We straggle up the dunes between two wind-sagged wire lines of fence. Single file, we plod up the tussocked slope, a family of four—father, brother, mother, sister—heading for the breakers. We are bundled against the cold, my father a long staff in his narrow ski parka and tweed cap, my brother a square in his wool schoolboy jacket, my mother a fat triangle in her thick, tan coat, and me, a cross scurrying at the tail, pulling on my hat and gloves. A damp and frigid wind slashes our cheeks, whips our hair.

Suddenly I realize I dropped my scarf over the fence a little way back. I backtrack, struggling against the wind, spot my scarf, which has already been blown up the dune. Hurrying, I clamber over the fence in my baggy corduroys, ripping them on the barbed wire as I cross over.

As I stand there, taking in the rip with the wind beating at me, my mother suddenly rushes up to me and shrieks, "Sara! You get over here, this minute!" My mother's voice is black—scarlet and harsh as rusted barbs, shrill with hysteria. Her face is frightening. Her jaw is clenched. Her eye is dark. My everyday mother has departed. Some other being has taken her over. In her military-tan coat, flapping, heaving, huge, and fierce, my mother looks like a giant man-woman.

Instantly, with her mitten that is like an iron claw, she grabs me by the arm and hauls me over the fence, batting at me maniacally with her other gloved fist. It is that day in Wilson Lane again, only more intense. Like cream of wheat thickening over the burner, my mother's panicked fury is, with each successive eruption, more concentrated.

My body whirls with panic. My chest heaves, my tears are spurting now—tears of outrage. What is Mom doing? I was getting my scarf—my pants are slashed!

My father is suddenly beside us. He has his arm around my mother. He says, "Sara, there are mines in these dunes. Leftover mines from World War II. That's why there are barbed wire fences."

I glance at the innocent-looking dune, tufted with coarse grasses. I picture setting the toe of my boot down and being blown to smithereens.

A fog of shame fills every niche of my body—charcoal shame laced with bright pink fear. I understand the reason for my mother's yank now and am mortified at my mistake, my badness, but my mother's face was hideous as a Chinese opera mask. Her terror was maniacal fury—jagged, ripping, huge as the sky. This terrible fury shudders through me. My mother's reaction is far more powerful, far more indelible, than my fear of what might have transpired on the dune.

In my deepest place, long afterward, I feel the tolling chill of stone.

This day is when I first know the truth: Rather than let me set a toe in front of danger, my mother will kill me.

# MY MOTHER, THE BULL

"Sara, you get down here this minute!"

I am in the midst of my English homework, writing a story. I dawdle.

By the time I reach the kitchen, my mother is steaming, pawing the ground. "Sara Taber, when I say get down here, I mean *this instant*. Do you hear me?"

I shudder. I can feel it. She despises me in this moment, and she is all male animal power right now. Her nostrils flare, her barrel chest heaves. She would charge me and batter me to pulp with her hooves if she could.

I go over to the kitchen counter to help my mother mash the potatoes, but as I do, I feel weak. My stomach caves in. I sense her itchy hooves.

Is there actually unconditional, unwavering love? Can a mother love a whiny or angry or dawdling child? Tantrums, acts of passive resistance, I know from experiences with my own children, are an extreme test of patience and affection. Maybe—to say the unutterable—maybe sometimes a mother's love flies off and takes a spin on the up-drafts. Maybe this recollection holds, indeed, one of those moments when maternal love makes a break for it, and my mother was truly internally snorting and seething, ready to paw me to the ground. Or might my eleven-year-old sense of my mother's fury in the kitchen have been merely a child's fevered, overimaginative, oversensitive exaggeration of a mother's feelings? Or—groping for truth—is this bright enactment in the portal perhaps not at all an accurate representation of straightforward maternal anger, but rather a memory of my child self's unconscious maneuver of projecting my own bullish fury onto my mother?

What is real in memory's glinting, glassy, gauzy maze of clicking cameras and flashing slides and reflecting mirrors? What is true?

# CHEERLEADER

I bang through the door of the brick manse on Duinweg.

"Mom, I got it," I yell. As of today's vote, I am a cheerleader. It is a wonder, a satisfaction, and a joy. I am a pink and glowing bubble scalloping in the air.

Through sheer willpower and fighting all my natural tendencies—Thank you, Mom—I have made my shy self into a girl with pom-poms, and now, I can see in her delighted eyes and the open arms coming toward me, my mother is happy. This is what a happy daughter, a daughter who assures her mother that she is happy, does: She bounces and bounds. She jumps and cheers. She sings and prances and shouts.

I am almost the right daughter for my mother now. I am almost my mother's happy *herself*.

When there was air, you could…
Curl up on your bed and read, play jacks, rough up the dog and throw her sticks, make sundaes of ice cream and peanut butter or gulp frozen hot dogs straight out of the freezer, draw a horse, run faster than a motorbike, shout and leap without a care, and stride home, slam the door, and shout out in sheer reckless glee, "Mom! I'm home!"
When there wasn't, you could…
Curl up on your bed, pull the covers over your head and then

scrunch there like a hermit crab, heart pounding, fury spurting firecrackers in your chest, fury so propulsive it could shoot you like a rocket into the black sky. Or you could stretch out, crying angry tears, pound the bed, vowing never to go downstairs to dinner, yet captive—flattened—with nowhere else to go. And then you'd have to descend, take in your mother's grim and relishing face, and eat the Salisbury steak she'd fixed, despite your strictest vows.

# THE THUMB

One day when I am eleven and Andy nine, my mother drives the two of us to the affluent outskirts of The Hague to visit some kids from school. In the other family there is a girl my brother's age, and a boy a little younger, and when we arrive at the other family's rambling, low-eaved, brick house, the mothers send us upstairs to play. What occurs then is both sharp and vague for me. I am inventing names for the family members. I have blocked out the real ones.

While the mothers, in their wool skirts, are downstairs chatting, we kids, dispatched to our second floor exile, come up with that classic, unifying game of children who don't much know each other—*Boys against Girls*.

The game starts up in the spacious square hall between the four large bedrooms.

Cathy and I toss the first gauntlet. "No boys allowed!" we say as we gleefully head into her airy, girl-flounced bedroom. "Girls are better than boys."

This, immediately and effectively of course, rouses the boys' dander. In instant mutual understanding, the two boys—Tommy, skinny and platinum like his sister, and Andy, honey brown-mopped like me—rush into the room, saying, "We can come in if we want to!"

"Can not!" sasses Cathy.

"Can too!" says Tommy, the pink rising in his face.

"Can not!" "Can too!" goes on for several rounds, ever-more heatedly, with me and Andy joining in, our faces steaming up to tomato like the others.

With each rousing repetition of the taunts, I can feel my body expanding ever-fuller like a helium balloon. Oh, the exhilaration of annoyance and a good battle!

Finally, Cathy and I, with much windmilling of arms, manage to usher the boys out of her room and close the door.

"Go play army or something," I say as we bid them adieu.

Cathy and I happily sit atop her high, canopied bed, whispering about nail polish and hairdos and how dumb boys are, and get a good round of girl-talk underway. I assume the boys have calmed down and are, indeed, contentedly tucked away in Tommy's room playing with plastic soldiers or something, like my brother always does. There are no sounds from Tommy's room. After a while I've almost forgotten about them.

Then, suddenly, the two boys do a sneak attack and rush into our secret chamber.

"Gotcha!" they say, holding the wooden swords Tommy made in carpentry class.

Startled, Cathy and I shoot up from our bed-top commiseration. Pumped with righteous outrage, we lunge at the boys, and proceed to flurry and shove them out of the room. (At some point, for me, the playful boy-girl rivalry has transformed into something fiercer.) As the boys are evicted, I feel a glorious spurt of triumph. But then, as I give the door a push to shut it, there suddenly bursts from the other side a scream of pain.

At the sound, my bright exhilaration instantly evaporates, and I jerk open the door. There I find Tommy sitting on the floor, holding one hand with the other. Blood is pouring down from the hand he is cradling.

The two mothers rush upstairs to Tommy's wails. Mrs.

White hurries to her son in a panic and wraps her arms around him.

My mother takes one look at the little boy and his hand and gently says to Mrs. White, "Take him downstairs, cover him with a blanket, and call the ambulance."

She instructs Cathy, Andy, and me to go down to the kitchen and wait, telling us, "It'll be okay. The doctor will help Tommy." The other two kids obediently descend, but I am in too much shock to move.

I then watch, cowering in the hall with my heart clamoring, as my mother begins hunting around the door-frame. She soon spies what she is looking for, goes into the bathroom to fetch a tissue, returns, and calmly picks up what she has found. I can see in the little nest of tissue that what it cradles is the top third of Tommy's thumb.

When the ambulance arrives, just a few minutes later, my mother calmly hands the emergency technician the little package. In quick order, the emergency doctor stitches the end back on Tommy's thumb and he is okay, luckily for Tommy and for me.

It is on this day in Holland, that it becomes shockingly clear to me what my mother is made of. And what I am not. She is a fixer, a person who can't but rush to the rescue in response to any call for help. Whatever human problem arises, she will be there in its hazardous, messy, bloody midst. I can't begin to name this yet, but I am something more along the lines of a poet.

I am relieved by Tommy's repaired thumb, but the incident also leaves me with a steaming stew of feelings about my mother. She is inspiring—that unhesitating bravery!—and yet I cringe. I feel shamed and daunted as well, for my mother's way of living is unmatchable. So often an act on my mother's part elicits in me fraternal twin responses: awe and a kind of shrinking. As with most mothers, her example is impossible to live up to. I, being made of other stuff, love her, but will forever be in the shadow of her heroic, pus-and-blood grandeur.

# "LE DÉJEUNER SUR L'HERBE"

My mother has a mink stole. Oh, how beautiful she looks today at the door, poised to go out with my father, in her sleek Jackie sheath and her high heels—with her mink stole draped around her shoulders. Above the soft fur, I can see her neck, with pearls shining there.

When my parents get home from their party, my father beams. He says, "Your mother was magnificent."

Tonight my parents are giving a party, as they often do for my father's diplomatic work.

Eleven years old, I peek into the living room from the dark, tall hall with the looming paintings. The guests—foreign officials and my father's colleagues—have glinting drinks in their hands. The fire crackles.

My mother stands by the fireplace with Mr. Munro, her breast brushing against his arm. She is twinkling up at him, twinkling. She is too happy, too sparkling. My mother is sparkling too bright.

My mother is lamp-lit in her grey tailored dress, her fluffed up hair. She is too happy. My father is over there, trim and glowing handsome in his suit, talking intently to Mrs. Robertson—while my mother has her hand on Mr. Munro's arm.

My mother doesn't look like the naked, full-breasted, round-hipped lady sitting with the men in suits having a picnic in the Manet painting, but she quaffs, she exudes something intoxicating, something giddy, something seductive. Her eyes sparkle, her breasts swell, she whispers in a man's ear.

*My mother* is flirting with a man. I can't say it out loud: *flirting*. My 38-year-old mother is a coquette. My 38-year-old mother is flirting. I will throw up. My mother wants to kiss Mr. Munro.

I hate her, I hate her. I will pretend I am sick and rush into the room. I will ram her with a tree trunk. I will claw her face.

# APRICOTS

This is a day I remember distinctly. I am somewhere in the precincts of eleven and my mother takes me to see our Dutch doctor at his nineteenth century curiosity cabinet of an office in the Wassenaar suburb of The Hague.

The office is in his house, which is stone and beautiful, with ivy on its outer walls and surrounded by a luxuriant treed lawn. I don't know why we were going to his cabinet today; usually he made calls at our house. This was for a physical—not for sickness; perhaps that's why. Anyway, I remember his asking me to take off my clothes, including my blouse. The Dutch aren't modest, so there was no covering gown.

Dr. M is a kind man. He uses his stethoscope gently, saying before he does each thing, "First I will check your back," "And now I will check your chest." I shiver a little though, as the metal sphere touches my skin, and I am not Dutch, so I am uncomfortable showing my newly developing chest.

At the end of the exam, Dr. M asks me if I have any questions or worries.

Apparently, according to my mother who remembered this part of the scene forever as though it were yesterday, while I do not—I've suppressed the trauma, I suppose—in response to Dr. M's question, I asked if it was possible for a girl to get only one breast. One of mine was bigger than the other, I explained.

According to my mother's report, Dr. M got out of there quick. He'd rushed out into the waiting room, told my mother what had happened, and the two of them howled with laughter. He then returned, face sobered, dignity restored, to give me the hard and serious facts.

I do remember the end of our consultation: Dr. M is even more solicitous than he had been earlier, and gives me a tiny, very tender pat on the back as we leave. The truth is, my mother would always be more confident about breasts than I would ever be. Hers were ample, the size of grapefruits, while mine were apricots at best. She was soft to hug while I would think of myself a bony board with a couple of hard fruit lumps partway up.

# PEEING IN HOTELS

It's been a terrible day. We are visiting Paris. Our parents wanted us to see Versailles on our way to Spain, so they got us up before dawn, drove the endless roads to the chateau, hurried us out to get tickets after a lousy car-lunch of peanut butter and crackers, dragged us around all those boring velvet rooms of mirrors and gold—Sure it was impressive and fancy and sort of cool, but why did adults like to see hours of *furniture*?—and now they have finally started to look for a hotel.

We drive around and around rainy-ugly streets and nowhere has room, and finally, book into what my father laughingly calls "a two-hour hotel." We can't find a good restaurant either, and have to eat onion soup for dinner, and my mother is grumpy and tired, her hair all frizzled from the rain, and when we get to the hotel and she sees the one tiny room where we will be sleeping, with my brother and me on sleeping bags on the floor—What does she have to complain about?— she tears off the bedsheets to check for bugs, and then, like she always does in European hotel rooms with just sinks and bidets and the real bathroom way down the hall, she pees in the sink. My mother is the most repulsive person in the world.

# MULBERRY RIBBON

*I have never seen anyone as radiant, as gay as she was, forever admiring the pine trees, the sea, the meadows, the trees, the flowers that surrounded us...*
— Nathalie Sarraute
  *Childhood*

We are in Rosas, a Spanish seaside village composed of gleaming-white children's block houses tumbling up the hillside from a gently-lapping, delphinium sea. We are renting one of the little white lookalike abodes. It is an economically designed structure with a small, plain, stark-white bedroom each for my brother and me, and a slightly larger one for my parents. There is a kitchen and a living and dining space, all small and cube-cornered, and spare and efficient as the inside of a boat. It is a place of perfection and delivers a perfect happiness.

Every morning of this perfect week, my mother, dressed in a faded madras shift and zoris, waggles the straw baskets and hails us all to get into our swimsuits and to grab our beach towels for our day at the sea. As we depart the little house, she positions on her head a new straw hat with a mulberry ribbon, as if a valiant proclamation to herself and us all.

We troop down the steep, narrow lanes of the hillside, cross the sleepy boulevard that parallels the beach, and with our striped beach towels establish our encampment on the sand. Then each of us sets to our customary pursuits.

My father reads his book on Spanish history for a while, then lifts his head and gazes far out to the sea. In a few minutes, he takes off for a long stride down the strand.

My brother immediately blows up the little inflatable boat my parents promised to buy him when we crossed the border from France, and, dragging it bouncing behind him, heads for the water. There, he frolics for hours like a seal pup, clambering onto the float, lying flopped atop it for a while, paddling around in spurts, accidentally-on-purpose falling off, losing the raft in a swell, splashing after it, climbing on and riding astride it again like an admiral. He is all happy, unthinking boy-ness and easy triumph.

I slather my body with Coppertone, and turn myself like a sausage on a spit, hoping for a tan to rival my Texan friend's perfect caramel. Who is to quash a girl's futile, ardent hopes? As I roast, I read, for a spell, my latest Enid Blyton adventure about four children and a dog finding hidden treasure on chalk cliff or moor, and then decide to join my brother in the ocean.

There in that perfectly cool sea, for a time stolen out of our regular routine of school and home, my brother and I have the best fun there is in the world, fighting over possession of his plucky vessel. He basks atop its puffy tubes, baiting me with "Ahh! This is so nice," then happily flops out as I, swooping like a rival seal, upend the raft from beneath. I, then, take up the realm, relishing a pretended languor, as he devises new assaults, each one craftier and more splendid than the last. This continues on and on, as we shout in only half-feigned outrage and burst with authentic laughter in a perfect sibling synchrony.

My mother, meanwhile, slathered with the Coppertone too, holds the fort at Taber territory, handing up bottles of Fanta or handfuls of peanuts when the sea warriors need a snack. Whilst my brother and I, and our father are busy with our various affairs, my mother settles back, her head propped on one of the baskets, her body calmer than at any other time in my life, and turns the pages of her Agatha Christie.

At lunchtime, my mother summons us all in, like a pioneer one room schoolteacher, with a hail and a beckoning of her arm. When we arrive all sopping to plop down in the sand, she spreads before us our repast. There, seated like a seal queen, she fishes into one of the baskets. From out of its towel-y recesses, she produces a jar of Jif, a rare American treasure back then in that Europe of old, a cucumber, and a loaf of new Spanish-white bread. With my brother's precious Swiss army knife, for which she requests a lend, she first chops the crusty loaf into serviceable chunks. She then slathers each with an ample blob of American wonder-jam, and crowns each concoction with a slab of cucumber. In her straw hat with its mulberry ribbon, purveying this perfect lunch, she provides, as no one but a mother can, perfect happiness.

"Isn't this perfectly marvelous?" she says. We all, munching, mouths crammed and lips peanut-buttered, noddingly agree.

# THE ALPS

We are driving in space. Below us, just over my shoulder, not a foot away, is an open drop to the earth. Miles below, through open air, I can see little make-believe toy Swiss villages with chalets and steepled churches and mountain farms. The dots are cows. The land forever-around is green and rumpled with patches of light green pasture and darker green blocks of forest.

But I take this all in only in tiny glimpses, when I dare to risk opening my eyes. When I do open my eyes, I try to look upward toward the blue and the clouds—while at the same time, avoiding thinking about Heaven.

My father says not to worry, but he has his eyes plastered to the road in front of him, carefully maneuvering the car around the wide loops of the hairpins which take us way out into space to the one-wrong-move-and-it's-all-up outer rim of the mountain. There is not even a low railing to keep us from slipping over into oblivion. We are in our Volkswagen squareback, which usually feels so blithe and sturdy—a *Little Engine That Could*, but now feels like a will-o'-the-wisp—and the Swiss drivers wheel around at top speed in their Triumphs and Mercedes, and swerve past us as if they're racing on a football field. Now and then, too, as we're approaching a blind curve, a car coming from the opposite direction suddenly appears out of nowhere, coming at us head-on in our lane at top speed, heedless of our tentative grip on the earth, ostensibly passing a truck that irritates it, and my mother shrieks. "Oh my God, Charlie, get out of the way!" As if there is anywhere to go but over. Her voice, an accusing, electric jolt of terror, spins through me like a top and then whirls off the cliff—which is where I can feel my body would fly in a twirling missile but for our little vehicle's four thin metal walls.

After the third of these near-collisions, my mother yells "Charlie, stop the car this instant!"

"Where?" my father says, calm as the Buddha, still not taking his eyes off the road.

"At the next pull-out, for God's sake!" she says. "Don't be an idiot!"

My father complies; my mother's voice is half dictatoress and half madwoman, so he stops the car in the next little oxbow, which takes us right out onto a sort of car diving board seemingly designed for cars with chronic depression that have decided to throw in the towel.

My mother edges out of the car. Keeping her eyes averted, she creeps the foot and a half along the outside of the right side of the car, opens the back door, and commands, "Sara, put your feet up," in a voice hysterical and harsh, like a mesh of barbed wire thrown at me. I curl my feet around me on the seat and my mother dives in. She squeezes herself onto the tiny aisle of car floor between the back seat and the front, and lies there, wedged, eyes clamped shut, as if readying herself for execution.

"Okay, Charlie, go!" she yells—half muffled because she's so scrunched. "Get us off this god-damned mountain. This was your god-damned idea to drive through the god-damned Alps. Now god-damn finish it."

My father keeps his cool. I don't know how, with my mother like this. "Don't worry, Lois, we're fine. Look upwards. The mountain is beautiful," he says, but Mom is way past beauty. Heaven is not a concept for her. Only Hell exists.

My body chock-full of my shrieking barbed wire mother, I

am dying-grateful for every word my father speaks. I want to sit in his lap and turn into him and drive with him like his smaller self, a baby kangaroo in his pouch. I am so grateful for his calm voice and his calm body and his calm sense that a person has some control and his calm confidence in the goodness of the world that I could cry. Our mother is our demise while he is our savior. While she has us hurtling toward the pyre, our father has us picnicking on sheep cheese and wine in mountain meadows.

I try to will myself into my father's calm kangaroo body, but we still have a long way to go—my brother, who is sitting on the safe side of the car, has established this on the map and returned to the history book he is reading—and, I cannot deny it: I am terrified too. I try to open my eyes and will myself to look at the view and feel brave, but if my eyes veer from their fix on that city-shaped cloud, my insides pitch and cataract and my fear morphs into an even larger and more likely and more looming fear: that of turning out like, of *being* my mother. I would rather torpedo off the mountain than turn out like Mom.

Dismayed at my failure to prove my valor, I promise myself I will work on it. Surely if I practice, and as I get older, I'll master looking fearlessly off mountains.

Now, though, with my knees resting on my mother's back—there is nowhere else for them to go—I am simultaneously filled with disdain for her cowardice. *Mothers should be braver than their kids*, I think, and I press my eyes shut, enduring the sense of free fall in my belly every time we round a curve. As I whirl into space, I silently chant to myself, "I am not Mom. I am not Mom. I will never be Mom. I am Pop. I am Pop. I am Pop."

# BAD PENNY

My mother is in the hallway where the phone is. The entry hall has a three-story ceiling, since the wide-open staircase goes up and up past the three bedrooms on the second floor to the four on the third. It is dark, with towering, looming paintings of gloomy landscapes on the walls. My mother is standing out there twisting the phone cord around her hand. I watch her from the dining room where I am doing my math.

My mother is talking on the phone long distance to her sister Marge. They only do this about once a year, and they have to talk fast since it's so expensive. I know my mother can't talk to her friends about my father or his work since it might get her or him into trouble—even though my mother herself can't know very much about his work since it's secret work for the government, but with Marge it's safe to at least talk about my father a tiny bit. My mother is smoking as she talks, tapping her cigarette into the pewter ashtray she has carried with her to the phone.

"Oh, Margie, it's shades of Taipei…It's like a bad penny. Charlie's in a mess again. He's fretting about the office—he's got that worried face all over again…"

I hear the windings in my mother's mind:

*It really is like a bad penny. That wince in Charlie's brows and that worried face again. Every time a Chinese man, any Chinese fellow he's worked with, runs into trouble he can't sleep and all he thinks about is how his work is all wrong and he shouldn't be doing what he's doing, and who do we Americans think we are, anyway?…*

*I tell him these Chinese men are making a choice to do what they do and Charlie's simply helping them do what **they** want to do. They're both—he and the Chinese—trying to bring China democracy. God knows, the people in China would be glad someone was trying to, with these rumors of intellectuals being sent to work camps and thousands of people starving to death…*

*But now with this dead Chinese "welder," Charlie's back in the stew.*

*I don't know what's gone on but it's got to be something connected with us, with what Charlie and Whit have been doing. I know they've got that Chinese mission wired up and Charlie's always working on defections. Maybe that "welder" was trying to defect, and maybe it was Charlie who was cultivating him. Who knows? I'll probably never know…*

*It's just awful. Charlie has that awful look—pale and like he's sunk so far inside himself I'll never find him again. It's like he's hunched in a foxhole, or a deer in someone's sights, and about to die…*

*Charlie just thinks too derned hard about everything. I'll try to get his mind off it all in bed tonight, but who knows if I can even raise a little interest. He's been so tired…And why the hell hasn't he gotten that promotion he deserves? I know that's plaguing him too. He breaks his neck for his work, staying up to all hours, fretting about his people. But it's out of sight, out of mind in that place—back in Washington…*

Decades later I'll find out that, while my father was in The Hague and up to his usual work of spying on the overseas Chinese and recruiting Chinese who might serve as informants, there was a highly charged incident surrounding a Chinese man who had either been pushed or fallen from an upper story window in the residence of the third secretary of the Communist Chinese diplomatic mission—and died. According to the Chinese, American officials in cahoots with the Dutch had been trying to force the man to defect, and he had jumped from the window in order to escape the pressure. The incident led to a five-month standoff during which the Dutch would not allow the eight Chinese technicians, to whose group the dead man had belonged, to leave the country.

Who knows how many troubling incidents my father dealt with over the course of his career—dilemmas which my mother then had to deal with in the form of a dismayed, ruminating husband. I know that my mother witnessed innumerable work-related debates, either overt or coded in so many words, among the men at dinner parties with my father's colleagues and their wives. Over and over, she and the other wives held the fort while their husbands plotted and gyrated, worried and argued.

Now my aunt says something and my mother says, "You're right. These men should all get awards for what they deal with. Some of them just laugh it all off—so many of them have those big egos along with those big guts—but Charlie breaks his neck, staying up to all hours."

Then my mother's voice gets higher and faster. "Hell, Margie, things were going so well. The Hague is so glorious. I could live here forever...I worry about Andy's underachievement but he's okay I think, and Sara is doing fine—sassy and mouthy, but fine...And I just love serving on the school board and the translating is fun. And Charlie was contented—up until now. I thought we were all Guernseys chewing our cud... Now Charlie has that awful look in his eye..."

Aunt Marge talks for a long time now. I can hear the twanging of her urging voice trying to comfort my mother.

When my mother gets off the phone, she comes into the dining room. She's carrying the ashtray, full of butts. "Oh, Sweetie," she says, "that was Aunt Margie. She sends you a big hug."

# WHITE LIES

My mother is on the phone in the hall again. The huge oil paintings are frowning down on her from the open staircase.

"Oh, Betty, how nice. I'd have loved to come, but Sara is sick with one of those awful sore throats."

I fume. My dumb mother is doing it again. I don't have a sore throat; I am about to go downtown on the tram with my friend Candy.

My mother told many lies—many small white lies, and by "many" I mean almost every day I heard her tell one lie or another. For some reason, the real truth was never quite legitimate enough to her when she had to cope with conflicting invitations. On the phone, she'd usually make up an excuse other than the real reason for why she couldn't join someone for coffee. "Oh, I have to take Andy to his carpentry lesson," she might say, or "I've got to take Charlie's suits to the dry cleaner's." Often, she used my brother or me to get out of things. Her goal was, in principle, to avoid hurting the other person—to avoid telling the caller that she had another coffee to go to, or was seeing a preferred friend, or simply didn't want to join the telephoner, but I was always bothered, and wondered why she didn't just tell the truth, or something closer to it.

Later in life, her lies became different. She began to make up personal history and facts to go with how she was feeling. These later lies, and my memory of them, will be so slippery I won't quite be able to pin them to the page.

But all through my girlhood, I hated my mother's fakery— the way she lied even to her best friends and feigned cheeriness when she was in a surly mood. Everyone does this—home is the place you get to be grumpy while everyone puts on a pleasant face and best behavior for the public—but I could never understand the extent of her dissembling. Perhaps it had something to do with the difficulty of her stories being believed, back in Indiana, as the ninth of too many children. She may have had to invent tall tales to be listened to at all or felt her truths would be refused. Perhaps, on the other hand, she was in the habit of casting up fog, of making replies just to the side of the truth, as the wife of a spy who was always having to emit little, white, fudging misdirections.

I'd heard one of the other mothers at a school meeting say

to my mother, "Oh, Lois, come on now, doesn't Charlie really work for a different government agency?" with an insinuating and mocking tone. My mother had played the innocent. "You mean MAAG?" She was referring to the Military Assistance Advisory Group, another American mission in The Hague. "Oh my lord, Sheila, do you really think Charlie looks like a military type?" Of course, I wasn't aware then of the fundamental pretense of my mother's life. I didn't know then that obfuscation was its warp and woof.

As for me, back in junior high rattling along on the tram to go buy fishnet stockings and lipstick with my friend, I vowed never to be like my mother. When I needed to save someone's feelings, I decided, I'd say something general rather than fabricating a story. If one person had invited me out before another, I'd say, "I'm so sorry but I have something else that day." I wouldn't say, "I'm sorry, I'm going out with my best friend Cindy," which would be hurtful, but nor would I say "I am taking my son to the doctor" when I wasn't. To the best of my ability, I'd save feelings without a lie. This seemed crucial to me, the difference between real and fake. The difference between being my mother and not.

# A DIFFERENT TRIP
# TO PARIS

One dreary Netherlandish mid-winter day, my mother and my mother's crazy friend Mrs. Tucker decide they will take us kids to Paris. "Let's just take off without the men!" Mrs. Tucker proposes, her voice fluting like a thrush. And my mother trills, "Oh, Mary Lou, what a grand idea!" And so, a month or so later, off we traipse through the Dutch drizzle to The Hague's train station, leaving the fathers to their M & M construction and spying.

We are a motley, loose-jointed crew: two boys, two girls,

two mothers, the same-sex Tucker kids each two years ahead of us Taber kids in age: Mark Tucker, a ready-for-anything, I'll-read-anything, lanky boy with black poodle hair springing every which way. My brother, with a cockeyed squint and a haystack on top of his head, talking nonstop about World War II. Melissa Tucker, a newly buxom teenager with tumbling chestnut-red curls, precocious and wisely skeptical about our trip, intuiting, through intimate knowledge of her mother, the mayhem ahead. Me, with my two Pippy braids, half primper, half scabbed-up-knees, agog at Melissa's hair-tossing sophistication. And then Mrs. Tucker, object of my fascination, vivid as a Renoir portrait, with her own set of black kinky curls, scarlet lips, and lean as a racehorse ready to head the pack. And last of all, my mother, Mom, in her tan raincoat, toting her bottomless sack of a purse, her face lit up with glinting, new-to-me mischief-filled eyes and a strangely independent, giddy smile which gives me a shiver of nervous wonder.

We heap our sacks and packs and cases—the boys have regulation army ammo kits—and our frowsy, sleepy bodies into the train compartment, and flop out on the facing banks of seats.

It is only seven thirty in the morning but the mothers are already moving into uproarious.

"Hey, kids. Look," Mrs. Tucker chirps, pointing to underlines in her *Michelin*. "We'll go to the Louvre and the Champs-Elysees and the Eiffel Tower and the Tuileries...It's so exciting!"

"What about Napoleon's Tomb?" Mark asks grumpily, sword out, ready to be denied.

"And the Bastille," Andy says.

"Oh, we'll do all the war you want," Mrs. Tucker says, flicking her artist fingers. She makes beautiful sculptures of children out of clay and painted her walls red to match her lips. She is scarlet—not in the trollopy sense—in the sense of ripping life out, like a poppy, by the roots and eating it.

"And what about the Champs-Elysees?" Melissa says. "I want

a French miniskirt."

"Yeah," I say, with her every word worshipping Melissa more. She is *so* mod. "What about French clothes?"

"Oh, we'll do it all," Mom says. "French art, French war, French miniskirts." Then she goes rogue. "French men, French wine, French cheese," she says. And for some reason, on "French cheese" she and Mrs. Tucker crack up.

"Who knows what might happen. City of love, you know," Mrs. Tucker says, lifting an eyebrow just so, and making my mother laugh so hard she has to cross her legs so she doesn't pee in her girdle.

We kids squirm for a split second, trying hard not to take in our mothers' tweetings, and then resume our discussions of war battles and fishnet stockings.

Midway through the journey, the mothers look at their watches, "Okay kids, time to go to the dining car." They discuss whether to leave the luggage in the compartment or lug it with us for safety, but the problem is solved when Mrs. Tucker says, "Oh, good riddance, if the thieves want it. We'll just buy new clothes in Paree!"

We rumble down the train for what seems like miles, bashing into conductors by accident, trying to keep our sweaters out of seated people's faces, leaping across the car couplings, our hearts in our mouths.

Finally we arrive at the dining car, a serene, white-tableclothed realm of dignity and elegance. At its threshold, before opening the leather door, Mrs. Tucker turns around fast and shushes us, her hands motioning downward, and we all try to assume an air of dignity as we enter.

The waiter, French and haughty, seats us. As we choose between the steak-frites or coq au vin, Mom says, "Mary Lou, how about a little wine?" and picks up the menu.

"Hmm, the half carafe is nearly the same price as the full bottle," Mrs. Tucker says.

"Oh, Mary Lou," Mom says, "Let's just get the bottle.

We're on holiday. Let's celebrate!" And their eyes meet in sheer glee.

At the end of the meal, as we kids slurp and gobble our silver cups of ice cream and saucers of tarte tatin, Mom says, "Oh my lord, Mary Lou. Look what we've done! We finished the whole bottle of wine!"

While we weave back down the train, bumping into people and seats as the train lurches, Mom and Mrs. Tucker keep leaning into and elbowing each other, saying "I can't believe we drank the whole bottle," and cracking up.

A friend of Mrs. Tucker's has lent us her home for the four days of our visit, but this is not just any old house. I am coming to think anything Mrs. Tucker touches turns into a fairy tale. Our lodging, it becomes apparent, is a fourteenth century converted chapel hidden away on a tiny lane in a Paris suburb. After a couple more trains and a taxi ride, we finally arrive at a dilapidated, hoary chapel like something in a Van Gogh painting.

Taking a huge key from her un-ample bosom where she's stored it for safety, Mrs. Tucker opens the huge Christian door. We file in and dump our bags in the foyer. Standing there, in the high-rising nave, Mrs. Tucker spots a marble font on the wall and says, "Oh look, holy water. Everybody take some!"

Always one for feeling holy since my family doesn't go to church, with secret solemnity while the mothers giggle and the other kids gaze around, and not having a clue what you do with holy water, I dab some on my forehead and lips, not realizing of course that the water can't be holy since this is no longer a church at all. Or rather, it is the Church of Mrs. Tucker, another sort of spiritual cult, one of high-jinx and hilarity.

While the mothers inspect the kitchen—I can hear my mother saying, "Oh, Mary Lou, how marvelous," over and over again—we kids troop up the winding staircase into the bell tower where the two boys claim one owl's eye room and we girls the other. I gaze out over the French tiled roofs, taking a moment of pause, waiting for the mothers to call us down for the next episode in the story they are making up as they go along.

For the mothers are in command. Like two W.A.C.s, the next morning they march us off to the train and, coats flapping, with us trailing behind—the boys talking Normandy and we girls oohing and aahing at passing French girls' hair—they drag us, lickety-split as though checking off boxes, through Notre Dame, the Louvre, and the Tuileries...And finally to Place de Clichy and Montmartre, back then grimy spots teeming with real scarlet women lounging in doorways—all languor and cigarettes, giant posters of the Folies Bergeres, and dark-looking shops that the mothers, squealing, tell the boys not to look at. The boys, though not quite of the age, are suddenly silent. The war talk ceases as they lag behind and surreptitiously eye the women and slide over toward the shop windows.

We spend a whole day doing war—Melissa and I groaning about yet another suit of armor—and then, our mothers finally acquiescing to Melissa's and my begging, we leave the boys at home to enact battles in the chapel and spend a day on the Champs-Elysees, traipsing from one fancy designer boutique to the next. The mothers all audacity in the face of the elegant Parisian shop women, ignoring the snooty whispering about "les Americaines," they urge us to try on tent dresses and tube skirts like those displayed on the pages of *Vogue*—any fantasy French frock we desire. The maternal duo have had us agree that we'll pretend we are rich (neglecting utterly to inspect their own give-away careless middle class American rags) and just try things on in the boutiques, and then afterward we'll go to the department store, La Samaritaine, where we can probably find something French we can actually afford to buy. In each elegantly appointed shop, after a while, Mrs. Tucker says, "Oh dear, we've got to get to our appointment, girls," and she flicks a finger at the increasingly skeptical shop girls, and says in French, as if we are very important customers, "Don't worry. We'll be back tomorrow."

Once out on the sidewalk, she and Mom double over with mirth, and say, "Hurry up, girls. We've got to get to the next place before they call ahead!" At La Samaritaine, I am miraculously allowed to pluck from a jumble on a table not one, but two pairs of shoes: a pair of green and white golf-style shoes all the rage, and some only-to-a-teenybopper irresistible beach shoes made of bright orange terry cloth with zippers up the front. Melissa buys a French outfit that makes her so happy she flounces afterwards with such self-possessing exuberance that a hundred French boys whistle at her as we piously make our way home to our chapel.

As for the mothers, they are a-flounce themselves the entire time in Paris—all modesty and propriety be damned—and receive their own allotment of male attention on the street. Whistles and beckonings—to our astonishment and partial dismay—are directed at the two mothers as much as at us two girls. It is as though our fortyish mothers have transformed into radiators of a sexy good time. "Aren't French men wonderful," they say to each other, exulting in the catcalls, while Melissa and I exchange raised eyebrows. Our mothers are full to the brim with some very non-holy water, full to the brim of themselves. We never say it to each other, but we both know our mothers are behaving more like teenagers than we are.

Maybe it is all those carafes of burgundy they consume at lunch that turn them outrageous and make them so sexy—the train lunch having set the precedent. At our repasts in cheap brasseries, the mothers order the house wine first thing, and have us kids get the cheapest items on the menus—tartines of jambon-beurre or croques monsieurs, while they sip their wine and fork their quiche lorraines. They tell us to eat lots of the bread, and then order extra, and just before the waiter brings the check, my mother dumps the extra bread, to be eaten at dinner, into her big slouchy bag, and we soon are off.

It is a giddy, happy time, a rare moment in which my mother is all and maximally herself. She and Mrs. Tucker are ricocheting around in the midst of their lives, cut loose, cut free.

What they could have been if they'd had independent incomes, men on call, and each other.

# MENINGITIS

The windows rattle in their sashes. The wind howls. Rain storms in torrents.

It is the middle of the night. Lying flat on my back, I am so limp I can barely lift my arms. I am in and out of delirium with viral meningitis—shuddering, both sweating and icy cold. The inside of my head glows with searing pain. My body temperature has spiked to danger level for three days in a row.

My world has become a small, closed dome of fire and darkness. The outer world is a dim shadowiness that makes its way into my awareness only at odd intervals, in vague, ghostly shapes and sounds.

The wind shrieks and rain clatters against the window-pane. Roused by one of the shrieks, I feel a vague sensation on my arm.

I squint my eyes open for a moment. I realize it is my mother's soft thumb making little circles on my wrist. She is reaching up to touch me from her pallet on the floor beside my bed where she has remained each night, a temple dog warding off evil from her beloved, ever since I fell ill.

# OH MY GOD

My mother is on the phone.

*Oh my God, we almost lost her. Dr. M said it was touch and go.... Yes, thank God, thank God...No, thank Dr. M, or The Fates, as Charlie says. Oh my God, oh my God. She was hot as toast and limp as spaghetti. I could feel her body struggling, like a bird flopping by the North Sea...I will never forget that feeling of her lithe body in my arms,*

*so desert-dry, drooping in my arms, unable to lift any of her own parts.*
*I would have killed myself if she'd gone.*

# MY MOTHER IS CRYING

I am recovering from my long illness but still weak. I hear something, a muffled, high, plaintive sound. I tiptoe to the source of the sound and stand at the door to my parents' room. It is open a crack. I can see the corner of the double bed, with its chenille bedspread hanging down, and a sliver of my mother's hunched back. My mother is sobbing.

> *I walked out in a summer twilight*
> *Searching for my daughter at bedtime.*
> *When she came running I was ready*
> *To make any bargain to keep her...*
> **— Eavan Boland**
> "The Pomegranate"

# BLACK WATER

It is a Dutch November late afternoon. The rain is a slapping and whipping and drenching madness—hurtling in waves so wild and fierce they could sink a ship. It is only 4:30. The world is already midnight dark.

As soon as I come through the door, my mother, silent, helps to remove my sopping clothes. Then she reaches for me. "Oh, Sweetie," she says. She holds me close for a long time.

Slowly, the story comes out. Her dear Dutch friend Riet Wandersee had come by that afternoon while my mother was out and left her bicycle by the front door. Riet herself, however, was nowhere to be found.

My mother, who could read her friend's signs, had taken off

121

into the wet-slashing afternoon darkness, rushed to the park up the street, and hurtled through the woods under the torrent. Tripping and stumbling amongst the undergrowth and fallen branches, her heart kicking in her chest, she had finally discovered her long, lanky friend lying on the black loam in the thicket beneath a cluster of concealing trees—with her life seeping out of her.

My mother had covered her with her raincoat, rushed back to the house, called the ambulance, and, in the nick of time, saved her friend.

My mother's hair is still wet against my face as she holds me tight, as though to never let me go.

"Mevrouw Wandersee has the falling of the leaves disease," my mother explains, using the Dutch name for seasonal deep sadness. "That's a sickness that causes some ladies to get very sad during the darkness of autumn and winter. They can't make decisions, and need to go into the hospital. Mevrouw Wandersee is in the hospital now; she'll be safe."

I picture beautiful Mevrouw Wandersee standing in her kitchen, unable to decide which pot to cook her potatoes in. I picture her daughters alone, waiting for their dinner tonight. Black water trickles under my skin, icy cold.

*How could a mother with three daughters contemplate leaving those daughters forever?* My mother is my arms, my legs, my belly, my heart. Life without her is desperate. Unimaginable.

# THE CURSE

Menstruation is blood and white walls and steam.

The water is running in the bathroom next to my bedroom. I am leaning against my bed, taking off my clothes to get ready for my evening bath. As I begin removing my shirt and then my skirt and socks, my room starts filling up with steam. The plumbing system in our house is so old, the hot water heated to such a high degree it bursts out of the faucet in jerking, shooting jets, so hot it is mostly steam. For some reason, we always let the hot water in, and then add the cold, so my bedroom becomes a steam parlor before my bathtub is full.

When I take off my underpants, I see the blood. I've been prepared for this to happen for a long time, but a cold fist clenches my belly when I see the red splotch in my snowy white bikinis. Immediately a numbness takes over me. I hold the panties limply in my hand for a moment. Then, on wooden legs, I walk into the steam, toward the plaid splotch of my mother's blouse. I can see nothing else of her, but I know she is there, monitoring the water. I hand out my underpants toward her body in the steam. Her hand with the wedding ring takes them. She turns off the water.

A face appears through wisps of vapor. It is my mother's face, only my mother's face—a face I can barely see, it is so familiar to me—but altered from its ordinary look. Its eyes have a new kind of sympathy in them. Immediately, I recoil. I want to block out that tenderness in her voice. "Okay, Sweetie," she says. "Let's go get the things."

I follow her, feeling like one of the condemned and also like an obedient dog, and listen, numb, while she explains what I have heard so many times before, from her and from the other girls and from the filmstrip at school. About the pads and the garter belt and the importance of keeping clean, and all that. I know it all by heart and I know it means something important, but all I can feel is that cold fist of dread. Part of me—no, almost all of me—wants to back out of the trap, like a little rabbit who licks the bait and decides he'd rather not, thank you very much.

As I lower myself into the bath, I don't look at the little wisps of hair that have appeared down my legs almost overnight. I write my name in the steam on the side of the tub. I think about Peter Rabbit. I try to force myself to think about Peter Rabbit all that evening, while I do my homework, while my mother puts me to bed, while she gives me an extra kiss and strokes my hair. I whisper to her fiercely not to tell anyone, but I know she can hardly wait to tell my father.

After I got "the curse," as my mother called it, I soon began to have monthly cramps. The only benefit of the whole affair that I could see was the chance to get out of P.E. Sometimes, though, the cramping in my uterus was so intense, my mother kept me home from school. Midol didn't work and I lay in my bed, curled and tense as waves of excruciating pain pitched and ebbed in my belly. My mother shook her head grimly when the cramps seized me, and brought me tea and hot water bottles, and drew me baths, and gave me pats along my flank away from where it hurt. Sometimes she rubbed my abdomen. After the bad time passed—usually in two hours or so—she let me read in bed, and brought me soup, and, in a while, brought me the homework she had gotten by phone from the teacher.

Each month, it seemed, when the cramps would seize me or my mother would see my period coming in my eyes or in my mood, her eyes would soften. At the same time, her eyes glinted with something else, something less detectable and less benign. I felt a kind of subtle satisfaction running through her as she ministered to my female pains. At last, it seemed, she had a companion in suffering. There was a tinge of "I told you so" retribution as she brought me my tea. Her bustling efficiency spoke. "Now you see what I've been going through," it said. But after I started menstruating there was also a deeper, third element, a new fear and an anger in my mother. Something large and dangerous, something that eked away at her soul. Something, somehow, close to death.

I didn't understand it. I kept on with my trips downtown with my friend Lizzy to try on eye shadow and listen to L.P.s, and I kept on drawing, and diligently doing my science notebooks. But something drastic had changed for my mother.

Her eyes flickered with darkness. She couldn't tolerate her daughter's descent into feminine pits she couldn't oversee.

# I WANT TO KILL HER

I am twelve now and something is going on. I don't know why things have changed. My mother was once my lamp. Now she is my darkness.

My mother makes me my favorite meal for dinner: Viking stew—mashed potatoes and spaghetti sauce. I want to kill her.

My mother puts away my underwear, she fixes the figurines of Little Bo Peep and Mistress Mary on my mantel, she buys me cream puffs, she talks to me about my friends when they hurt my feelings, and she buys me a new skirt to make me feel better, all with the best intentions, hovering and taking care of me like a guardian angel.

"Look. Look," my mother's kindness says. "Look how I love you. Just look. Look how I love you." But when I look at the chocolate-topped cream puff she has brought me, instead of feeling flooded with a warm-flowing of love and even though this is far from what she intends, I hear, "For this love you must obey me." I feel hands clamped down on my shoulders, hands clamped over my mouth. My senses clash. My ears and nose bring to me one truth, my skin another. My mother loves me so much, but I want to kill her.

My mother sends me off Saturdays on the tram to meet my friend Lizzy, knowing we'll buy silver lipstick and fluorescent tops, and when I return, she admires my purchases. She buys me vanilla ice cream cones, my favorite kind. All the same, I want to push her just a little bit so she falls onto her bare knee above the grey wool knee sock, into the puddle. I want her not to know what happened and come up, clutching her knee, puzzled. And my face to be innocent.

My mother was once my lamp. Now she is my darkness.

Sometimes I hate her with all my heart. Sometimes I love her with all my spleen.

I hate her I love her. I hate her with a hate like burning glass. I love her with a love like birds' nests. I love her I hate her I despise her.

My mother is a black hole through which I step into another world, transformed from a girl into a blade of shining fury.

Black night rain. Rain night black. Rain black night. In the blackness of night, steaming and wide awake at two a.m., when I should be sleepy, I am murderous, ready to kill, plotting in my pineapple-posted bed. I will stab her. I will pound her. I will push her into the sea when the waves are fury. She will disappear into the cold and roiling waters...

But suddenly I am wide awake, terrified, my stomach sick. I rush to the edge of the sea. I plunge in. I drag her out of the waves. I will hug her alive again. I will be her rescuer.

# RAIN AND SMOKE

My mother stands huddled under her hat, cigarette to lips, striking matches in the rain. Her snake is coiled within her, snug, while the scudding rain drills her body with exploding pellets. I stand beside her, eleven, twelve, and thirteen—shivering, resentfully hanging onto her pocket, waiting for what she'll do next.

I come home whipped and small at the end of a day when my best friend Candy betrays me by wearing, ahead of schedule, the outfit we both ordered from Montgomery Ward and had planned, for months, to appear in together. By one hasty act, Candy has broken a promise and dashed my dream of being a twin for a day.

My mother is chopping carrots at the kitchen counter. In response to my disappointment, her words snap like the crop my riding teacher uses on his horse. "You just bring this on yourself, Sara," she says. "Why do you insist on having that girl for a friend? She's a selfish waste of time. How *can* you let that girl hurt you? You're just too sensitive."

My mother has trigger-quick reflexes. Some people feel more intensely than others. They react instantaneously. Their emotions are pistol shots.

"I don't know why on earth you let that girl make you feel bad. You're so much smarter than she is," my mother adds, putting down her chopping knife to fetch my after-school Cheerios and shove them toward me on the table.

"Why on earth can't you be more confident?" she adds now, her voice shrilling with impatience. "I don't know why you can't just be more sure of yourself. You've got so much more than she does. Candy's cheap goods, Sara."

"She is not!" I scream back to her as I race upstairs to sit on my bed. I rock myself, holding my knees, in the large room with heavy dark wood trim and watch the rain slant down into the grey night off the balcony. High on my bedstead, I stir into my pot such fury at my mother that it weakens the hurt from my friend.

Why *can't* I be more confident? I wonder, stabbing at the bed. I hate myself for my weakness.

I am a shy girl fighting to gain social purchase and a stable psyche in an ever-shifting geographical and maternal world. How is such a girl to feel confident with a mother who criticizes her for not being so? And, simultaneously: What is a mother with an unconfident daughter to do?

These conundrums given, from this and similar comments from my mother, I ferry away a powerful message that if a conversation with someone upsets me, I am to blame and my emotions are not to be trusted. Feelings, wrong by definition, are to be thrust away as you saunter on, feigning indifference. I will determinedly take a different tack with my own children. Rather than to doubt themselves, I will teach them to identify, respect, and be guided by their feelings. I will try my very hardest, without fail, to have their backs.

Another seventh grade's afternoon exchange later in the month: "Why do you want to go to that party, Sara? You'll feel left out and make yourself miserable," my mother says.

That night, I set out, hoping for romance, in the special bell-sleeved dress bought in consultation with my friends. A few hours later, I return home in a dress so saturated with disappointment I never wear it again. I cry into my father's shoulder sitting on his lap in the big armchair in the living room. As he pats me and whispers soothing words into my ear, my liquid sadness suddenly curdles. Anger at my mother takes me over and my body stiffens to its hard ebb and flow. The heavy bell of her wisdom sounds in my head. "You see. I'm always right," it tolls, over and over.

At night I dream of my mother. Days, snakes, like guards, coil inside each of us, poised to instantaneously flick their black, venomous tongues.

A day when it's too grey and sloppy for us to go downtown, Lizzy and I climb the stairs past my mother's room, to the third floor, to the room crammed with all the unused furniture. We slip through the door and each take one end of the ancient, down-filled sofa, and, listening to the rain pounding the roof tiles, we light a cigarette and pass it back and forth in the damp, wild air.

# MY FRIENDS LOVE
# MY MOTHER

Gabrielle is sitting on the counter that wraps all around two sides of the kitchen. The cookie jar and the cast iron skillet and an array of other dishes are splayed around to her right, and the bird cage is on her left. Her back is to the window that looks out on the wet and leafy sunken back garden and she's happily swinging her sturdy legs back and forth. She's got on her miniskirt and her Dutch clunky-heeled shoes.

"But Mrs. Taber, what do I do when Maman tells me I can't go out with the kids on the weekend? She always complains that I haven't shown her enough respect, and says that, even if American ones do, Belgian girls do not go out with their friends all day on Saturday. They stay home and help their mothers prepare for Sunday dinner...

"It's so unfair," Gabrielle goes on, gaining steam. "If I see a friend after school on Friday, Maman always says, when I ask her if I can go out the next day, *Ca suffit, Gabi*, in her angry voice. That means 'That's enough.'" Gabrielle moves her hands emphatically up and down in that French way.

"She only said I could come here today because she likes Sara and says you must be a good mother."

My mother, in her old yellow gingham apron, is leaning against the sink, listening to Gabrielle with a sympathetic look on her face.

She says, "Why don't you try this? Next Saturday, get up right on time and immediately get the things your mother wants done, done. Make her coffee, and then ask her nicely if you can go out for the afternoon? She's probably just tired and needs some help."

"Okay, Mrs. Taber, I'll try it," Gabrielle says, dragging out the "o" in "okay" and the "y" in "try."

"Here, why don't you girls make a cake," my mother says, giving Gabrielle a little pat. "That'll make you feel better. I got a Betty Crocker yellow cake mix at the P.X. this week. And you top it with the can of chocolate frosting."

When my mother goes off to the library to settle down to her cigarette and Dutch translations, Gabrielle says, "Your mom's so easy to talk to. Maman doesn't understand me at all. You're so lucky, Sara."

I never consider this aspect of my mother. I experience a billow of pride chased immediately by a plunging wince of guilt.

# CIGARETTES

One morning my mother and father are talking in the kitchen. Just beyond them, outside the window, it seems like all the water in the sky is dumping down. The room is very dim, the sky is so dark, and my parents are huddled together at one end of the table in the center of the room, talking very quietly. I watch them for a minute from the hall.

My father has his hand over my mother's hand, which is resting on the flat of the table, and he is leaning very close to her. Her body looks rigid. He is speaking very intently. She looks into his eyes as he speaks. She says something back. Then she shakes her head sadly or worriedly or ruefully. I can't tell which. Then she looks down a minute.

When my father dons his tweed cap and rises to head off to work, she gets up too, grips his arms, and kisses him extra strongly.

After the front door clicks shut, my mother resumes her seat at the table, lights a cigarette. She inhales deeply. Her shoulders seem to release. She looks into the dim air.

When I return from school, my mother is bustling around the kitchen getting out the potatoes and meat for dinner. "Oh, hi, Sweetie, how was school?" she says. Her voice is perky but I notice that the ashtray on the table is piled with ash and stubs.

Suddenly a startling and new fear darts through my insides. At school the sports mistress has been lecturing us about the hazards of smoking. She's been cautioning us kids to never pick up the habit, but as I look at the ashtray it dawns on me that her warning applies to my mother. To think that my mother could be endangering herself, could possibly be transporting herself away from us, is a shock. It has never occurred to me that my mother could be vulnerable. She is invincible. To entertain this new notion is frightening.

"Mom, I think you should quit smoking," I say. "Miss McGhee says it causes cancer."

This is something brand new to issue from my mouth. It's like a new baby has been born. I am surprised by it, and my mother stops unwrapping the hamburger, turns around, and looks at me.

"Oh, don't worry, Sweetie. I'm not going to get cancer."

"But Mom, you smoke a lot. Look!" I say, picking up the ashtray.

"Oh, it was just a kind of worrywart day for me. I don't usually smoke that many."

"Mom, still."

"I know, I know. Charlie is pushing too," she says, shaking her head. "I'll try. It'll be hard. I love smoking, it helps me relax, but I'll try."

Alerted by that unexpected streak of fear about my mother, I bug her regularly about her smoking. Finally, in a fit of exasperation, she says "Okay, Sara, I promise. By the time we get back to the States next time, I'll quit."

Mostly I forget about my mother being a person who could die, but sometimes when I see her happily standing with a cigarette dangling from her fingers or sitting tapping one into a tray, I feel the pang, and then I grab the chance to scold her. I love having something to hold my mother to.

# MURDER

*Home is where the hatred is.*
— Marita Golden

"I'd like you to do the dishes *right now*," my mother says.

"You can't make me!" I spit back.

And my mother's face mutates. Once a regular mom with pageboy hair and an open look, she is suddenly an alien: arched up brows, a predator's narrow squint, red flushing upwards through her cheeks, steam gathering in her nostrils. And now she starts spewing.

"How dare you, you little brat," she says. "You'll do as I say, young lady."

My mother will kill me with her hate-flashing eyes. My mother despises me. She despises me.

I cringe and quiver like a mouse, but simultaneously I billow. At last, I have done it! I have made her hate me like I hate her. My insides quaver but also sing. I am triumphant. I feel a marvelous, clean defiance. I feel joy, a power-surge of exhilaration. I am despicable. My mother loathes me. I am selfishness beyond selfishness. I am evil beyond evil. *I will out-survive you, Mom,* I trill. I am free!

But.

But my mother's face remains there: a stiff, enraged mask, her eyes bulging, her claws poised. She will stop at nothing to stop me. I must do as she says—or die.

Her ursine glare penetrates. The air rushes out of my chest. My song, barely begun, evaporates. Panic explodes the rapture...For I see, in my mother's triumphant, dictatorial mask: my own face. In her clenched shoulders: I see my match. I am dismayed. I am she and she is me. The blood coursing through me is hers.

It is this same day, or another.

"She's sassed me one too many times," my mother says to my father the instant he walks through the door. "Charlie Taber, you'd better do something about it for once."

Looking tired, setting down his satchel, with dispatch he says, "You may not speak to your mother that way," and he slaps my cheek. As he slaps, I spy my mother's face looking smug behind him, and, in a silent tsunami of fury and betrayal, I tear up to my room, holding my burning cheek. I feel as though I've been shot.

I sit on my bed and pound my mattress, stabbing my hurt feelings and, with more satisfaction, stabbing my mother. But the more I stab, instead of providing relief, the more the need to stab grows. My father's words hurt like a knife plunged into the deepest, surest part of me; my knowledge of my rudeness smarts; and my fury at my mother rises into a rolling, roiling boil. The snake in me is reloading with more, even more potent, venom. Feeling as though my fury will grenade all the windows in the house, I finally hurl myself down on my bedspread with a shriek, and sob.

For a long time, I cry and writhe, feeling whipped, limp as a rope, the frigid stone flopping back and forth in my insides as I move.

When my mother calls us for dinner, I scrub at my face fiercely with a washcloth before I go down so my mother won't have the satisfaction of seeing that I've been crying about what my father did for her.

It is absurd how one other person, a single person out of more than three billion, can be another's lodestar, judge, and mood-dictator.

Why is a mother so powerful? Maybe we should demote mothers. Everyone would feel better.

# TULIPS

It is a day of grey and thrumming rain.

My mother comes up to my room. She is still in her dripping raincoat and her funny, floppy hat. In her hand is a bouquet of scarlet tulips wrapped in newspaper and string.

"These are for you, Sara."

My whole body suddenly floods with light.

**5**

# AEROGRAM

"Why did we have to come back here?" I demand after bolting my brown sugar pop-tart for breakfast—one of the only good things about America.

"Just work hard and the friends will come," my mother says, looking up from a box of dishes she is unpacking. It is the start of my second day at my new tony private high school in Washington. "You can do anything for a year. Just try to think, 'Wherever I am is best,'" she says.

"Wherever I am is best." Later I will be able to see that my mother was trying to give me a gift—a preserving, enhancing outlook, a key she had found indispensable in coping with her ever-shifting life. But I can't even begin to appreciate it now, at the start of ninth grade as a new girl in Washington.

I slump my book bag over my shoulder, trudge through the leafy streets of Chevy Chase bungalows and colonials to the bus stop, and spend the hours in the school hallway feeling like a lone sandpiper skittering down the beach around and behind and at the edges of caucuses of social creatures—seagull gaggles of girls and braying penguin troops of boys.

Acorns drop from the statuesque oaks and wisps of marijuana tickle through the air as I make my way home from school.

We had been away from the U.S. for almost five years now and the country had since turned into a powder keg, a fact it would take some time to take in. In the fall of 1968, America was still quaking from the death of Martin Luther King, Fourteenth Street in downtown Washington was a charred wasteland—a smoking remnant of the race riots of April following his murder—and the whole city was vibrating with the impact of the counterculture revolution and the draft and the upscaling Vietnam war.

After a stay in the Alban Towers, a Gothic apartment hotel on Connecticut Avenue like something out of the horror story *Rosemary's Baby*, my parents bought a Cape Cod cottage on Thornapple Street in the village of Chevy Chase. Its rooms had been outfitted by the previous owner with baby blue and pale pink carpets and matching princess phones. My mother would have rectified these appointments with practical beige if she'd had time for such things.

Chevy Chase was a modest place at this juncture. Simple bungalows and brick two-stories set on quiet and leafy lanes. Its residents were government workers at the Department of the Interior and the CIA. The middle class drove Volkswagens and the wealthier, Volvo station wagons. Fifties materialism had become uncool. The rich wore frayed cotton and concealed their assets.

Though the rest of us, upon arrival, were sluggish and still complaining about missing *patates frites*, sea air, and our rambling Dutch house, my mother declared "Put your best foot forward!" She urged us to think the same, and marched off to work. She'd quickly found herself a job as a physical therapist at nursing homes. My father, on the other hand, was not to be a happy camper. Frustrated at yet again not having received an expected promotion, he drove off in a tinny used Fiat to a gigantic white mausoleum of a building nearly exploding with the nasty accusations of the hawks and doves. He would begin now to question more and more the morality of his country's methods of promoting freedom as my mother held the *America-do-or-die* fort.

When I get home, obviously downcast, my mother starts into her irritating litany again. "Just work hard..." and I cannot endure it. I hurtle upstairs. I fling myself on my bed. Then, after a while, inspiration hits, and I rise and fish out a fresh blue aerogram. I date it and then write, "Dear Lizzy, I HATE MY MOTHER!" I write those same four words on it ten more times in capital letters, sign it "Love, Sara," lick the three edges, and pen in my friend's The Hague address.

How a mother suffers at seeing her daughter suffer cannot be calculated by a suffering daughter. But oh, what a grand resource a mother is: a dartboard for spewing emotion, a sitting duck to be blamed for any ill fortune. A mother is a pocket compact to be used for prettying up; she is a soothing chocolate bar.

# THE SOLACE OF
# A SISTER

"Sara's moping and Andy's not doing his homework, but Charlie's the worst, blast him," my mother is saying into the beige princess phone posted on the kitchen wall. It's the weekend. The house is finally mostly unpacked, and my mother is talking to Aunt Marge. She lets herself talk long-distance a tiny bit more now. It's still expensive and she has to watch every minute that ticks by, but it's a lot less than a trans-Atlantic call. She doesn't know I'm listening again, like a spy.

"There's something about Washington all the men hate," my mother says in her voice that sounds like she's hammering nails, "but it's already hit Charlie and we've barely been here a month! I know he didn't get the promotion again, and that's just plain wrong—something's going on, but why can't he just make the best of it like I do? How can the office be that bad? He says someone has it in for him, but he must be exaggerating. It's the Washington syndrome. It's like he's got the yaws or something. I'm getting so sick of that hangdog look. And God damn it, he's working for that awful Buck again. I know he's an S.O.B. but why can't Charlie stand up to him? I know he can't give him what-for—I'd like to give him a piece of my mind or kick him you know where—but there's got to be some way…And I hate having to be with all the women and pretend Charlie's doing great while all of them cluck around…"

All my mother does sometimes, it seems like, is complain about my father.

Aunt Margie says something and my mother says "Yes, please. Your cherry pie recipe is just the thing this family needs."

## "THIS TOO SHALL PASS"

Making my way along the shining white aisles of school, I am a shy, slinking, involuntary operative in a swirl of glittering, confident people whose fathers are famous journalists or secretaries of defense. The other students wear bellbottoms bought at expensive Georgetown boutiques. As they fling their bangs or pride-stroll down the hall, they ooze cool. In a stab at gaining some smidgeon of social purchase, I try to approximate coolness via miniskirts and strings of tiny beads, and to feign their impermeability, but I am one of those spies who naturally blends into the woodwork. Despite my efforts at affecting a chilly, regal untouchability, I am all ordinary longing, and watch from my shadows a boy with a golden-brown mop who drives a jeep, but he doesn't know I exist and never will, for I am invisible. My walk home from the bus stop on Wisconsin Avenue is that of a clandestine girl dodging even herself.

I open the front door and head for my pale pink-walled room, but I'm stopped short. My mother has seen my face. "Oh, poor, poor," she says, coming up to pat me. "You've got the mulligrubs, don't you?"

Unlike many afternoons when she's hassled from her long day of physical therapy work, her body radiates calm and her voice is gentle.

"Don't worry, Dear Heart, it'll be okay. It'll be okay. This too shall pass," she says.

Today, she goes into the kitchen, pours me a glass of cow milk, and spreads butter on a piece of bread and sprinkles it with sugar, like Grandma used to do for her at special moments back at the forestry. As I eat, she says, "Now why don't you take a nice bath and get into your pajamas and climb into bed?"

I melt.

I start to cry.

She puts her arms around me.

She draws my bath.

No one knows me like my mother does. She is able to comfort me as only one who knows my body can. This is only one person in the world.

# MIRROR MIRROR

I am not Snow White. In the floor-length mirror in the powder blue upstairs bathroom, I am straight lines and angles like the girl in "Puberty" by Munch, or maybe—at my very most optimistic best—like the young woman of Ingres' "La Source." But my mother is rounded and rosy, with red lips and big warm breasts and a plump bottom like a lady in Renoir's "The Large Bathers." My mother is soft and inviting like a warm hen and I am sticks. Am I sexy at all? Will boys ever like me?

# CHICKEN DROPPINGS

*She was a quick, energetic worker and the chores that gave her the most satisfaction were, strangely enough, the most strenuous ones, the ones she cursed, like washing the sheets and scouring the bedroom floor with steel wool.*

— Annie Ernaux

*A Woman's Story*

Now that we are in America, my mother has me on a schedule of household chores since we don't have a maid anymore. Every week, I have to clean the toilets with Comet and dust the furniture with Lemon Pledge and vacuum the downstairs.

My mother runs around cleaning all the time after work, and she has to iron in America. Every evening just about, she's ironing her blouses and my father's work shirts as well as her white P.T. jackets. She never stops cooking or ironing or picking up. And then she also has to call her patients. She just works and works.

One of my mother's jobs as the youngest child in her family was to look after the chickens, a job that, to her, literally, stunk. She always tells us how she hated the smell of chicken droppings, hated cleaning the henhouse, hated being sent out to wring a chicken's neck for dinner, hated seeing headless chickens scamper around, and especially hated having to run in front of the hay mower, driven by one of her lucky brothers, shooing chicks out of its path in the dusty heat of summer. It was sweaty, dirty work.

I can tell my mother gets satisfaction and pleasure in watching me wipe the Japanese table with paper towels and trudge around the living room pulling the vacuum cleaner. She wants me to learn the value of hard work, but more: She wants it to be a little stinky.

# A MOTHER SHOULD BE
# A QUEEN

*My splendors are menagerie*
– Emily Dickinson
319

This weekend my mother is preparing *huo guo*, Chinese hot pot.

Huo guo is a Chinese cousin to Swiss fondue: A large,

round, pedestaled metal pot, with an open tube in the middle for hot coals, sits in the center of the table. It holds hot broth which is kept warm by the coals, and during the meal, the diners drop meat and vegetables into the broth—which simmers to perfection while everyone chatters. Huo guo is the special, celebratory company meal of my childhood that requires a little extra preparation, so a huo guo day always has a festive air, and spending the day with my mother preparing for the meal is a series of hours that have their own set of prescribed rhythmic, sacred rituals. Somehow this meal miraculously, reliably transforms my mother, whose mood is often unpredictable, into a bouncing, gleeful cherub.

As we bustle around the A & P to buy the ingredients we need, even though my mother hasn't brushed her hair and is wearing one of her practical A-line skirts, she might be in purple velvet and ermine, for she sheds a regal glow. It is like she is wearing a halo as she selects the vegetables and as she rings the bell for the butcher and asks him very sweetly and pleasantly to slice her beef "very very thin, as thin as you can make it, please." Instead of hasty, for once in her life, she bothers to say "please"—huo guo is that important and pleasing to her.

Back home, my mother plunks the vegetables on the kitchen table, ticking off her list, "Okay, here's the Chinese cabbage, here are the spring onions, here are the rice noodles, here's the spinach, and the dried mushrooms are soaking over there in the bowl. I've put the meat in the fridge. We can get it out at the last minute." She stands tall for a second, then pauses, and breathes in the air as if it is suffusing her with a heavenly contentment, and then we get to work.

She brings us both aprons, and says, "Okay, Sara, you cut up the cabbage, spinach, and spring onions into pieces easy to handle with chopsticks. Then you can arrange them with the noodles and mushrooms on the big Chinese plate, and I'll get out the ingredients for the sauces."

As I chop all the vegetables, cabbage spilling on the floor

and spring onions flying, and then arrange the food on the platter—a large and beautiful and moss-colored Japanese one, with a dark grey floral motif—my mother hunts through the cupboards for mustard, peanut butter, soy sauce, sesame oil, vinegar, and ginger. She has collected lots of small bowls and saucers over the years for this special purpose.

"Okay," my mother says now. "You can fill them with the sauce ingredients."

I adore this job. I take a blue and white jar and fill it with scoops of grainy mustard. I hold a bowl brush-painted with fish, and spoon in the peanut butter. I pour vinegar into a small pitcher that looks like it is made of stone, and so on, and this, too, feels holy—like Easter, or the first sip of Beaujolais Nouveau, or a señalada, the Patagonian feast of the new lambs. The sauce made from these ingredients is delicious. I can already taste in my mouth the meld of vinegar and peanut butter and soy sauce. After all the sauce ingredients are imparted to their bowls, I arrange them on a round bronze tray.

Usually, I hate working in the kitchen with my mother. It is "Sara, put the milk on the table. Sara, get the tomatoes. Sara, hold this bowl while I stir," and I resent every minute of it. Usually my mother is imperious, and simply expects me to help, as her mother must have expected her to help, as is certainly natural and right for mothers to expect of daughters, but her tone is always grim and dictatorial, as though she considers me endlessly spoiled and too slow on the job, and she seems to expect resentment from me—which, like magic, is a self-fulfilling prophesy. This is not to deny that I am equipped with my very own homegrown resentment as well. It's just that her expectation of it doubles it.

But preparing the huo guo is different. When my mother makes huo guo, she slows down. The pace is leisurely. She seems to have taken a draught of the spirit of the Orient, to slip into the meditative slow of tea ceremony. She is still the commander, but every movement is caressed, relished. Her usually suppressed inner artist replaces the efficient drill sergeant; she's on her feed, focused and gentle.

Per my mother's instructions, I set out the dark blue Taiwanese plates on the round oak dining table, find the Chinese porcelain soup spoons, retrieve the funny little porcelain chopstick beds, rustle through the chopstick drawer to find those that match, prop each pair against its little stand, fetch the long serving chopsticks for seizing and placing the ingredients in the hot pot, fold and set out the napkins, and—the flourishing, special touch which allows me to let out my inner artist too— make little name cards for the guests.

When the guests enter the lamp-lit house—my mother and I now in our pressed dinner party clothes—they all doff their coats as my brother takes them to the T.V. room, and immediately exclaim, "Oh, Lois, you've made huo guo!" and the whole evening transforms instantly into a celebration. A ravenous and reckless pleasure seizes all. My father is a benignant, presiding backdrop and my mother is in her element, immediately the irrepressible little farm girl who used to charm her classmates into running in circles outdoors around the one-room schoolhouse when their teacher took an outhouse trip— turned into the mistress of ceremonies of the carnival. She is in command. Whenever she is able to make one of her artistic-social visions come true—she loves creating beautiful dinners and then finessing a matching conviviality among the guests— my mother is at her height, her fullest power. Her own ecstasy infects the company. She was meant to be a queen.

When everyone is seated, my mother stands with the tray of sauces in her hand and explains, for those new to huo guo, that each guest should mix his or her own sauce in the saucer beside his or her plate. She tells them what is in each bowl or pot, and then says, "Now Sara, show them how to mix their sauces," and, like a waitress, I take up my little side plate and demonstrate the mixing of the blobs of mustard, and peanut butter, and vinegar, and sesame oil, and soy sauce, and a tiny bit of pickled ginger, on my saucer with my chopsticks. Then she has me pass the huge platter of ingredients around, and has everyone pile some on their plates. "Now Sara, show them how you do the vegetables and meat and things," and I drop some cabbage leaves and floppy mushrooms and stiff rice noodles and wiggling slivers of meat into the pot. A delicious fragrance begins to lift from the pot, and after a couple of minutes, I retrieve them, swirl them in my sauce, pop them into my mouth with a mound of rice from my bowl, and everyone dives in.

Within minutes the men have doffed their sports coats and the women forgotten their good dresses, and everyone is hurling spring onions and cabbage and spinach into the swirling brew, and dipping out perfectly cooked bits of beef and vegetables, and mixing their sauces—some heavy on the vinegar, some big on peanut butter—and exclaiming and making a mess like in any happy, self-respecting Chinese family.

And afterwards, after the guests have slipped out the door, patting their satisfied midriffs, my mother gives me a pat and kisses my father and hugs my brother, and as my father and I clean up the mess and my brother sneaks upstairs to his book, she says, "Oh, wasn't it divine!"

And it was. For huo guo wrought miracles. For those few hours, my awkward school days vanished and I was restored to my comfortable, natural, Asia-reared self, homesickness, for the moment, at bay. And here, eating huo guo, was my family at its happiest: my mother at her happiest and most regal, and my mother and I happiest as a mother and a daughter. Happily, for once, I behaved just as my mother wanted me to behave: as her chopsticks.

# FEMININITY

We are sitting in the living room in Chevy Chase. It is spring, with bright sun beaming through the window. Daffodils are bobbing on their stalks on the front lawn of the Harveys' Tudor house across the street. I am finally feeling a little more viable, more tangible among my peers. I have adopted a hip-hugger skirt and Clarks Wallabees as my hippie uniform, and I wear a black armband most days. The anti-war movement—hating Nixon, hating war—is a pot I can pour myself into. I go to all the demonstrations, the shouting and marching and reverential silences ideal shunts for my longings. I also have a friend now, a girl named Pansy. She and I sit on the grass dreaming of boys and plucking daisies: "He loves me, he loves me not." And a couple of the black boys at school—as marginal as a new foreign service girl—have started flirting with me. This extends to me a twig of hope.

I am lazing with my parents on the overstuffed couch and chairs set around the fireplace. My mother has placed a pot of daffodils on the mantel. Somehow the conversation turns to the question of femininity. Which women my parents know are most feminine. My father says, offhand, "Well, your mother is more feminine than you are."

My mother looks at me, then to him, and says, aghast, "Charlie!"

I know my father is thinking of my unshaven legs, my chambray workman's shirt and fierce know-it-all-ness, my recently adopted pose of defiance. I know my father likes women's legs in nylons, women's bodies clothed in fine tweeds. An aesthete and artist by nature, he reveres women's beauty for itself, nude or clothed, as an eternal gift of nature. I am shy yet of that sort of embrace of the feminine. My father is usually the one who understands me, but this time my mother knows something more, something he doesn't. From her own body, she knows something about a girl's tentativeness, about clefts and pulsing wombs, and about still-tight but hopeful buds.

Later, in the evening—when I am out of my bath and in my nightgown, and she is in hers and we are both rosy and soft with post-soak warmth—my mother comes into my carnation-walled room and sits on my bed beside me. She says, "Sara, don't pay attention to what your father said. That's sheer nonsense. You're very feminine."

I rest my head on her shoulder.

# DUCKS AND GEESE

My mother can fix a toilet, hang a painting, unclog a bathtub drain, make a plant grow. I can barely open a window and I have a black thumb.

My mother loves funny movies like *The Three Stooges* and *Blazing Saddles*. I like what she calls "angst films." "How can you and your father watch all that angst?" she says every weekend. "I get enough angst all week at work."

My mother can add up strings of numbers in her head. I still count on my fingers. My mother loves chemistry and biology and anatomy. She can name all the muscles in a hand and knows how to heal a strained knee or a wounded leg. She can make a paraplegic laugh. I am afraid of bodies. I'm squeamish when I see a deformed limb. My mother is more comfortable with twisted legs than straight ones.

My mother wears clothes just to cover her body with. I wear clothes as an act of self-expression.

My mother likes to read Erma Bombeck. I like to read Hermann Hesse.

My mother is color-blind. She thinks green is red and red is green. I am color hyper-sensitive. If a red is not just the right red, I don't like it. If it is scarlet, I disdain it. If, on the other hand, it has a drop of orange in it to turn it russet, my heart trills.

My mother likes scrapple, which she orders whenever she gets a chance at a base mess hall—that or liver and onions. I can't stand scrapple. I tasted it once and gagged. I like granola or whole wheat toast.

My mother doesn't eat dessert. She always says, "Oh no," when the hostess offers her cake or pie, "I don't eat sweets." I live for dessert. My mother likes cheese after dinner like the French; "I'll just have a little cheese and bread," she says when the brownies come out. I think she's crazy.

Some researchers say people are predictable and patterned—we're all repetitive, one-note songs. Others say there is no steady self; we flicker with the breeze. A look at the list assembled here argues for the dominance of nature and character over mutation. Save for my budging with regard to dessert and cheese, all of the itemized proclivities and preferences remained true for my mother and me throughout our lives together.

My mother is standing in front of the full-length mirror in her good dress, patting her stomach. I am fourteen.

"I look like a goose," my mother says.

"Oh, Mom, you do not," I say.

Juliette—a friend I will make in my early 30s—is French. She is a radiant and beautiful woman wreathed in dramatic scarves, with waving blond hair down her back and a long stride, who headed up the Doctors Without Borders program in Afghanistan for a decade during the war with the Russians. Her mother was another radiant and beautiful woman, a woman also with waving hair but a little more russet, whose wrists tinkled with all the bangles she wore, a student of Buddhism who viewed all the world's creatures, from worms to yaks, as dear treasures to be cherished. The mother and daughter adored each other, but they were also different: the one leading horse pack-trains into the ravaging world, the other seeking to influence through softer, more hidden means such as nursing a sick fox or a bat. Each admired the other; theirs was a tender love.

I loved one thing Juliette's mother Madeleine would say,

with certainty, about the two of them—an aphorism to keep handy when considering mothers and daughters. "Oh, yes," she said, "I am a duck who gave birth to a goose."

From the time I was small, when I would stand beside my mother, or flop on her bed, or sit cross-legged on the floor watching her get dressed for a party, and I said, "Mom, you look so pretty," she would, more often than not, reply as she does today. She would take a quick glance at the mirror and say, "I look like a goose."

"Oh, Mom, you do not," I would always say. But the thing was, she did. My mother was frank with herself. She looked pretty, but she also looked like a goose. When I thought about this, Beatrix Potter's geese came into my mind, and to be goose-like seemed not at all a bad thing. A goose seemed one of the better animals to be.

Maybe my mother was a goose who gave birth to a duck.

# A TRUE FRIEND

She drives us way out into the far Washington, D.C., suburbs to visit Dora, the ex-wife of one of my father's colleagues. He has discarded her for a European woman he met on assignment, and she has become a wasting alcoholic. Divorce in this era is an almost unbearable, whispered shame. Dora's neighborhood is one of tiny, ill-kept, one-story brick houses, and though she's been there half a year, her house is still a clutter of half-unpacked boxes from her life overseas. The curtains are drawn and the tiny living room heavy with depression. Through the years she will become more and more ravaged, and, over and over again, my mother will visit her, carrying in cans of food so as to encourage her to eat—until she succumbs far too young to her disease.

Dora is just one of the multitudes to whom my mother gives succor and serves, variously according to what is required, as nurse, mother, and goad.

My mother will endlessly lend her ear to the woeful tales of a female spy who had made the mistake of falling in love with a foreign woman whilst at post—and been fired. Being a female spy was extremely rare in those days, to be a known lesbian in the CIA even rarer, and to be both, rarest and most suspect of all. While men philandered and were kept on, a woman such as this was quickly dispensed with.

While dear friends are posted abroad, my mother will first scold, then advise, then take care of those friends' son when he turns up on her doorstep in legal trouble for stealing drugs from the hospital where he works. And on and on.

My mother was a case manager for anyone rejected or neglected by society. About her friends, she always said, "I'd give her my right arm."

# DAUGHTERING

My mother takes me shopping for a new dress, just for a treat. She would never buy herself a dress, but she waits patiently as I try on six dresses and try to choose one. She says I look pretty in them all. I finally settle on a frock with an empire waist and a pattern of tiny flowers.

My mother never buys herself treats. She is saving up for my college, for her and my father's retirement. "Waste not, want not," she sometimes says, while prattling, for no apparent reason. "Oh, I don't need anything," she always says when I try to get her to try on a sweater from the stack at Woodies department store.

At home, modeling my new dress again, my mother hugs me and says, "Oh, Sara, you are perfection!" I can feel her arms tight-wrapped around me, squeezing hard from a burst of joy. Joy she almost never allows herself. Indiana Presbyterian girls are taught that joy is not good. Work is good. Pleasure is near to sin. Every minute of every day you must earn your way to heaven.

All her life, my mother gave to others luxuries that she would not permit herself. How much should a mother sacrifice for her children? How much should she spend on helping her daughter look pretty? At what point does sacrifice turn to resentment and come home to roost?

I longed to give my mother something on these outings, to assure she received small pleasures too and to try to equalize things, but she refused. There is mothering but there is also daughtering. I urgently wanted to be a thoughtful and loving daughter. Where was I missing my cue?

## "HOW *CAN* YOU SAY THAT?"

"Nixon and his war are anti-human," I announce while my mother is serving the rest of us Sara Lee chocolate cream pie.

"How *can* you say that, Sara?" my mother shoots back. "How *can* you say that about our government after all we've done for the world, after all your father and our young men have done for the world?" I know she is recalling the lamp-lit evenings she spent, as a girl of my age back in Indiana, knitting socks for the soldiers in Europe.

My father says, "Now Lois, it's okay for Sara to experiment with ideas...the times are different," but his words are lost in the blasts of my mother's vehemence.

As our time has mounted in Washington, the world has increasingly seemed upside down to my mother. The popular slogans of the day are no longer "Cleanliness is next to godliness" and "Things go better with Coke," but "Think different," "We shall overcome," "Make love not war," and "Bombing for peace is like fucking for virginity." The young people we encounter on the streets are restive and sloppy, wear peace signs around their necks, and carry banners of hand-painted doves. Even the hawks are beginning to get shifty about Vietnam.

My mother is appalled. Girls wearing skirts that showed their fannies? Mere children telling the government what to do? This was all foreign to the Indiana farm girl turned diplomat-cum-spy's wife who, for the sake of her husband's career, had trained herself to mind her P's and Q's and dress in tailored linen and, by turns, changed herself from Hoosier to sophisticate through native canniness and will—and who had recently been informed by her daughter and the world that America and apple pie and old-fashioned patriotism *were*, in fact, *out* and ranting boys with goldilocks and girls with bare fannies were *in*. All this while she was working hard all day as a physical therapist with old people and young people with real problems, not the so-called problems of the kids at her daughter's school who now wanted to not only wear miniskirts but pants to school.

"We should be condemned by the international court," I am going on while enjoying my cream pie. Heedless of my mother, I'm marshaling the arguments of the student body president at school.

"How *can* you talk like that!" my mother says, flinging her napkin on the table and escaping upstairs, sputtering with outrage.

Sometimes a mother *does* want to exile her daughter.

To my mother, I am completely out of line as of now, with my newly adopted, feigned private school confidence and sass. I am not serving my proper role as daughter. I am on this earth to be her best self and make up for all her flaws. I am meant to be all she has failed to be. I am to be her dreams. I am not to be a girl who questions the president or signs petitions or spouts heresies.

The relationship between my mother and me has always waxed and waned like the North Sea, waves of love billowing in, waves of fury crashing out. She likes me, she hates me; I like her, I hate her: That's how it has always gone. But the cycle has intensified since we've come back to America. Since I've turned fourteen, rather than just *my* hating everything she says, as was the case at twelve, now it seems something even more clutching and intense has come into play. Now, it seems, my mother hates everything *I* say. She doesn't want me to think, especially she doesn't want me to think anything that she doesn't think. It makes her want to scream, and she fumes and stomps, or withdraws, or spits verbal fireballs. I must agree with her, or vanish.

Where *does* a mother end?

My mother's insistence on agreement, on my being her, will shape my interior landscape and my relationships, especially those with women, as I move ahead through my life. I will be afraid to differ; I will be afraid of conflict—with females. I will fear other women's wrath—and expect the smallest and most unlikely thing to bring it on. If I express a varying opinion, an all-powerful, angered goddess will swoop down from Mount Olympus and slay me for the audacity of daring to *be*. Abject with friends when I was a little girl, I will put up with too much as a young adult.

There will be another upshot from these frigid rows with my mother. Excruciating as they were, I think it true that my daring to stick out my neck and defiantly express opinions opposed to hers, even ill-conceived ones, saved me. I adapted to her power by turning rebel and regarding rejection of any sort as a challenge. "Fury is the high queen of strength," wrote Aeschylus in *The Eumenides*. Fury and defiance allowed me to survive.

My mother's wish that I be her twin will have yet another effect. It will turn me into a writer. Since I can't express certain divergent things out loud, I will resort to the page.

Another day, I say at the dinner table, "I think people should sleep together if they're serious about each other. They should make sure they're sexually compatible before they get married." This is another pronouncement I make inspired by the cool older students at school. The ones in love beads and desert boots headed for the University of Chicago.

I don't have a boyfriend. I've never even been kissed. I couldn't possibly have a sex life. Somewhere in her, my mother must know this, but elsewhere my assertion fires off terror flares—which is part of what I was aiming for—and it's as if any trust she might have felt in me has never been. Fear is a match struck to her reason.

My mother doesn't look at me as she slams the platter of fried rice down on the table.

When she sits down, she utters two terse sentences, her mouth a straight, grim line. "You won't *get* married if you sleep around. Men don't marry used goods."

With hindsight, I surmise that, with this announcement, my mother considered that she was giving to me the facts of life— the ones that, to her, directly followed from the other ones— but her face was rigid. Marriage was to her, and in this era, still the all-important goal for a girl in life. In this moment, even though she could support the whole family, if necessary, inside a week, marriage seems to her *the* crucial factor in a female offspring's survival on this planet. In the sway of this conviction—at the thought of her daughter ruining herself and thus besmirching her own motherly pride—she turned desperate and angry and a despot.

Within my mother's 1969 actions seem embedded the very same concerns Mary Wollstonecraft expressed for her daughter, Mary Shelley, in the 1790s:

*I feel more than a mother's fondness and anxiety, when I reflect on the dependent and depressed state of her sex. I dread lest she should be forced to sacrifice her heart to her principles, or principles to her heart.*

My mother is silent after our exchange and chopsticks her fried rice into her mouth with the speed of a Japanese businessman on a train platform. Her silence is thick and contagious and frightening, and makes the rest of us say little, except "Pass the soy sauce, please."

Throughout this exchange, I act cool, calm, and rational, imitating my father's response to my fiery mother. Looking back, I wonder if perhaps this was wrong. Might we have connected if I had shown my own heat and screamed at her? Sometimes raw emotions are more generous, respectful, authentic—and truer than pinched, considered, "rational" thought.

When my mother's bowl is clean, she tells us all to get our own dessert. There's ice cream in the freezer. She got it at the A & P today.

Still not looking at me, she brushes her hand across her brow like she has a headache and says she's going to bed.

My poor mother, stuck in this moment with this goading daughter who is just playing with ideas new to her, while she, on a different plane, is dealing with the heavy question of her daughter's long-term welfare. The Japanese say that different generations are from different planets. Sometimes mother and daughters are aliens bleeping at each other.

# TO BE A WOMAN

My father is sitting next to me on my rumpled bed. "You have a right to your opinion, Sara. No matter what your mother says."

"Remember that," he says, giving me a kiss on the cheek before he goes downstairs.

My father's words are a fresh, pure spring to a girl crawling across a desert. But they are also troubling.

"You have a right to your own opinion," my father says. This helps. But then he adds, "Your mother is a little hysterical." Which doesn't. The adjective "hysterical" is attached to "female," which complicates the matter. I am implicated.

My mother preferred men. This was always a given, a known truth. People with Y chromosomes, in her book of life, as in that of everyone raising children at that time—she hadn't ever said this, but I knew it to be true—were superior: calmer, smarter than girls and women, and more fun for her. Boys made her laugh. Men flattered her, teased her, kept her happy, and thus pacified her ire. People with Y chromosomes were clean and dry. People with two X chromosomes were complicated, intense, a soup of moods and fluids. They were dangerous rivals who smiled at you at a coffee party and secretly criticized you to the ambassador's wife.

My mother would have preferred to have had a Y chromosome. Maybe she did. She was the more aggressive parent. She was the one who could have commanded an army.

I kind of wanted to have a Y too, so that I could be labeled smart and not be branded hysterical like my mother was, like females were no matter what they did, no matter how right or rational they might be. No matter what a girl said, because she had a high voice and a body lacking a certain part, she was seen as shrill, hysterical, not worth listening to. She made no sense.

She was worth just a pat on the head. *Just humor her. She'll calm down...*

It wouldn't occur to me to question the labeling, this strict bifurcation, until years later. I *believed* all women, especially my mother, were irrational, and men and boys were inherently superior. I believed hysteria was the exclusive province of females. I didn't know hysteria could be called something else, something respectful like emotional attunement, or be seen as something men might feel too.

The confusing thing was, my mother *was* hysterical. Her emotions could precipitously fly loose, and lash and spew and splatter us all with blood, or fog the entire house, from attic to basement, with gloom. Her emotions had no membrane around them, no body equipped to hold them safely in. To me, it was plain: My mother didn't have Y's calm. I didn't yet detect all the hysterical, out of control, rageful men—some of whom deceptively appeared to be paragons of rational calm. Or did I just see my mother as hysterical because that was how my father saw her? Had she been prone to strong emotions at the beginning or had she become that way due to the stresses of her particular life, or through a self-fulfilling prophecy, imposed by the oracle of our culture upon all girls, when she was born? Was it actually because expression of emotion was verboten, that women had to exaggerate their emotions to be heeded at all?

*Do I want to be a girl at all?* This is what I wondered, fuming up in my room after a row with my mother. It was so exhausting: this hysteria, this inferiority of females. Was there any hope for me? Might it be possible that my mother was hysterical and I was not, even though the men in my family, in my culture, would always see me so? Could there be differences, on this score, between women, between me and my mother? Or was I doomed to become a wild-haired, raging, scarlet-faced creature ranting in the road? At fourteen, I felt trapped by my society, judged only by my body.

# DAUGHTERS!

She trudges upstairs like a Christian martyr and I hear her ranting to Aunt Marge. I've heard it all before, but it's hard to concentrate on writing my D.H. Lawrence essay with her going on and on.

"Hell, Marge. It's like Sara's picked up her father's idealism and now *she's* got to be the one demonstrating on the mall. She's so bull-headed and so smart-alecky these days. Ranting about the Vietnam War and all the boys and Vietnamese being sacrificed for a losing cause...

"It was a big mistake to send her to that Quaker school, even though she's getting good grades and everything, and Charlie thinks it's good how they encourage the students to think for themselves. Yep, she sure thinks for herself... Thinks she knows everything when she doesn't have a clue how the world works. She doesn't know how pig-headed policemen can be—all those policemen assigned to keep the peace marchers in line. I know the types from the paramilitary guys overseas. They would mow down a thousand pretty little teenaged girls like they were a bunch of fleas on a cow pie if they thought they could blast a single Communist dead. I'll mow down the whole police department if they do anything to her...

"Darn it, Margie, it was bad enough when Charlie had to go down for the Martin Luther King speech back when we lived on Wilson Lane—and now I have to worry about Sara. And with Charlie halfway around the world—in Kuching, for God's sake. It sounded good in theory to go to a wild place and for him to go in advance of the family, but it's too hard without him, and who knows what he's really dealing with—there are headhunters down there!

"...I'm going to kill her. I just can't get out of my head a picture of her lying dead in a heap on the ground by the Washington Monument. That's all I can think of after her meningitis. I'd cut out my heart or lop off an arm or anything

159

else for that girl—even though she has such a mouth on her these days—and Charlie would kill me if something did happen to her. It would be the end of it all...

"But how am I going to stop her from going? All her friends are going. And if I demand that she stay at home she might kill me—or at least never speak to me for days. She can be so petulant and sniffy. I'd never have spoken to Mom the way she speaks to me. I'd like to wash her mouth out with soap. She doesn't swear or anything but she's just galling; it's that *tone*..."

# DAUGHTERS' SECRET MANEUVERS

*Inside her, my grit and timbre, my reckless.*
— Carmen Giménez Smith
  "The Daughter"

"No, you may not go to the demonstration," my mother says when I bring up an anti-war protest at the Mall. "It's not safe. The SDS are threatening to bomb the capitol. I heard it on Walter Cronkite."

I am instantly furious because I know my father would let me go—he trusts the world more than my mother does, but he has gone to Borneo, his next post, three months ahead of the rest of us. We are staying in Washington until Andy and I finish the school year.

When the day of the demonstration comes, I say to my mother, "Pop would let me go, so I'm going—with Pansy." and I fling out the door to meet my friend.

Pansy and I were actually cautious ourselves—we'd heard the scary rumors too—so, instead of going to the demo, we walked to the National Cathedral, one of our favorite places in the city. It was beautiful there, and had a spiritual generosity we couldn't name and didn't know we needed, but sought out, perhaps because both of us had tumultuous relationships with our mothers. In the hallowed dim, with the stained glass windows sprinkling in their red and blue and gold droplets of light, we lit candles for the soldiers in Vietnam. There, under the magnificent, towering, heavens-embracing arches of the cathedral, thinking urgent protective incantations for the safety of the young soldiers I imagined slogging through swamps—"If there's anyone up there, please save them"—I felt reverential. As a Unitarian, I didn't know how to pray and, as a young person, I didn't know how to help the world I was so fearful for. Should we be putting daisies in the barrels of guns like the hippie girl in the newspaper photo? Feeling utterly helpless, by lighting candles, at least I was doing something to express my concerns for the world.

Afterwards, walking round the cathedral, safe as I could be, I was less than reverential. I was relishing a secret pleasure in knowing I was causing my mother to worry. Her constant nervousness about demonstrations, her fretting about and trying to control everything, made me want to defy her any way I could. I felt superior, fattened with satisfaction. It was delicious to keep her in suspense while doing something indisputably good. My mother's inexplicable reactions had frightened me in the past. Now I could similarly frighten her. For once I had the power.

My mother is in knots by the time I get home. Her face is a teary squint of fury. "There was a scuffle near the capitol," she says, splintering terror and scarlet ire sparking in her eyes. "I was scared to death you were hurt. How could you have done this to me?" She sputters when I tell her we just went to the cathedral, and yells at me until I feel a cold, stony blackness deep down and I cry.

# THE CRUX

**Mothers and daughters can hurt each other by *existing*.**

**6**

# MOTHER OF ORCHIDS

"Isn't Borneo splendiferous, Sara and Andy!" We have been transported across the world to an enchanting and strange land, and reunited with my father.

It is as though we've swooped like lost, brown sparrows into a peacock realm. A glorious, steamy, floral place where orangutans swing in the trees, hornbills preside, and people yatter in 137 tongues, from Malay and Iban, and Tamil and Mandarin, to the queen's English.

Kuching, the capital of East Malaysia on the upper edge of Borneo where we'd landed, seemed a brave little city hacked out of the rainforest. A white mosque topped with gleaming onion domes oversaw its dilapidated river boats and cluttered streets of small shops and humble dwellings. One neighborhood featured elegant houses with verandas and lawns built by the latter day British rajah Sir James Brooke and his fellow expatriates who'd ruled over Sarawak until 1946. We were lucky, as the vice-consul's family, to be assigned to live in one of these.

Wherever we stepped in this new country, we were served a visual and gustatory banquet. Moist airs transported the scents of curry and coconut, and the downtown markets overflowed with all the fruits of the jungles, streams, and seas: fans of bananas; splays of chiles and spills of limes; droopy yellow chickens with stick-up legs; turtle eggs; fish with glaring eyes. As we wandered, poking and sniffing and sampling these enticements, fascinating peoples strolled from stall to stall. Malays in sarongs, sari-clad Indians, Chinese in epauletted shirts, Iban jungle migrants with betel nut-stained teeth, and helmeted Britishers leftover from Sarawak's Colonial days.

While the city was enchanting, the interior of Sarawak only

moments from the city center seemed a daunting realm. The vast territory, suffocated by trees and hanging vines and cut by streams, was accessible only by boat. It concealed within its nearly impenetrable growth anteaters, hornbills, orangutans, and poisonous snakes—and, until only recently, had also concealed bands of headhunters. Who knew if there were still some who maintained the custom? What was known for sure was that Communist insurgents from Indonesia to the south had infiltrated the jungles and lurked there, seeking to convert the rainforest-dwellers to their rigid code—and that overseas Chinese were scattered through the city. These two groups were the excuse for my father's presence: his assignment was to monitor the activities of the insurgents and try to exact information on Big Brother China from its Kuching diaspora— as yet another arm of the indefatigable American push to beat back the Communist menace. My father felt he'd been relegated to a backwater—which was literally true—but it suited him to, for a time, be as far from headquarters as possible, away from the competition, ceaseless moral quandaries, controversy, and fray.

Kuching's very beleagueredness, with its diseases and poverty, adds to its draw in my mother's eye. One look at the city and its challenges, and she dons a white jacket over her dress. Within days she is treating residents of the Cheshire Home, an institution for the disabled and incurable, and making regular trips to a leprosarium, one of the few such colonies left in the world, about an hour out of town. In her earthy, medical soul, she is flourishing like the orchids of our new country. Gone is the hassled Washington mother. Here is a mother quick of step with happy purpose in every move of her efficient body. Her plate is full of not only good works but of social engagements too. She quickly acquires an entourage, and coming over for the Italian dinners our Malaysian cook makes are every version of missionary, Peace Corps volunteer, social worker, or graduate student bent on bettering the world.

Afternoons, my mother arrives home gleeful of heart holding bundles of orchids, and she urges my father to flourish too. "Just enjoy it, Charlie," she exhorts him each morning as she heads off in a batik shift, her body thrumming with her day's mission. She is more than happy to be done for a while with the husband she had in Washington, the man with the pained look that flickered across his eyes whenever she asked about the office. She pats him on the shoulder of his khaki suit. "Ignore the mosquitoes and heat. We'll be back in civilization soon enough."

The only fly in the elixir of Kuching is that it has no school for my brother and me. My parents fret about this, but Andy and I have romanticized boarding school. We've read *Summerhill,* the portrait of the English free school, and are excited at the thought of dormitory living and weekends spent roaming strange places with our peers. My mother is tortured about whether it is the right decision, and whether a mother ought to send her children away, but they have at last chosen a school for us in Kobe, Japan, and, as she likes to say about decided things, *the die is cast.* The summer together in this exotic realm is to be relished. The change to occur at the end of August we put out of our minds.

Evenings, as coolness wrests control from the swelter of the day, my celebratory mother herds us into the Land Rover and drives us down to the market as the sunset splashes pink over the still-busy stalls. We choose plastic chairs at one of the tented tables and dine on chicken satay smothered in delectable peanut sauce, pineapple slabs, and crabs pulled fresh and dripping from the sea.

# THE SECRET TO MATERNAL TRANQUILITY

I stand on the veranda, fragrant air billowing inside my body, filling more of me than has ever been filled before, as I breathe in this new vista of orchid-festooned, fervid green.

By some change of scents from lawn grasses to fragrant fruits—and a two-day air journey—a spell has been cast or a hex broken. Something dire has been evaded, and, magically, my mother can again look upon me with kind eyes. And I, her.

The days in Sarawak unfold to a pleasantness pleated and pressed into place by my mother, by way of the family of servants that inhabit the quarters to the rear of the spacious, open-aired, sprawling British colonial-style consul's residence where we now reside—*reside*, rather than simply *live*, as we did back in America.

I rise in the dawn—always the first one up, along with the gibbon calling from the thick, tall, flower- and fruit-drooping trees—and step out onto the veranda. Even the air seems scrubbed during this particular and graceful dot in time. It's as if the servants spend the early mornings with their cold-rinsed cloths washing down the sky.

Standing in my fresh, white, servant-ironed, Chinese pajamas, I take in the world: the baskets of tiger-striped and magenta orchids slightly shifting on their toggles to the eaves; the jasmine's wafting fragrances; the balmy equatorial atmosphere's caress on my neck and arms; the cluck of the chickens across the way. I can almost taste the coming mouthful of freshly cut papaya waiting on its plate on the straw-woven placemat on the breakfast table. An anteater noses over the slope of the hill toward the lane below, where a man on a bicycle in a coolie hat rounds by, a pair of women with baskets chat along, a Land Rover of soldiers heads for some errand in the jungle. (These soldiers, the only hint of electric charges in the world.)

My parents are seated at the breakfast table in their yukatas, my father's nose in the imported, days-late *Herald Tribune*, my mother's face scrubbed with Pears soap, a congenial happiness in the air. My brother shuffles in, a tome in his hand, and plunks it down beside his plate, getting a bit of the jelly, from the blue and white porcelain bowl, on his book's rim. I join them now, gobble my lemon-drizzled papaya and then happily chew the cook's homemade toast slathered in his homemade pineapple jam, and thus commence my day. We speak of the plan to picnic by the waterfall or the outing to the Dayak weaving museum— for it is eternal summer these days, no school to interfere—and my father rustles his paper, and my brother crams toast into his mouth, and my mother rings the bell for more coffee as I push back my chair with my bare toes, and I proceed to my "chamber"—as it must be called, for I now live in a kind of fairy story. I pull on my bright-fresh white panties, choose my dress—a batik shift of floppy, large blooms, insert my toes in my zoris, and then, just before embarking on my own fresh-supplied day, last but not least—for this is a time when things are just-so and just so pleasant and nothing untoward has happened that I can discern, and all is right in the world, and I have it in me even to do things to please my mother—I fold up my pajamas, just as my mother instructed me to do when I was very small, and tuck them under my fresh, starched, embroidered-pillow-slip-sheathed, plump pillow.

I cycle now to the batik lesson arranged for me by my mother—a blissful tutelage held by the goldfish pool on the patio of my art teacher's family's compound. Miraculously my mother has known just what would suit me, and orchestrated for me this summer of magic. A line from Abraham Lincoln distills the rarified sense that occasionally flows through me as I intently work by the green and gold, gleaming pool. "All that I am or ever hope to be I owe to my angel mother."

After painting with wax and dyes on bolts of cloth for a trio of hours that slip by unnoticed, I return home at midday, to a beautiful and graceful lunch of greens and nibbles from the sea set on the gleaming table overlooking the vast and sloping lawn toward the flower-decked rainforest.

After "luncheon"—for this word, too, must be selected in these circumstances—I sit in one of the two, wide-open living rooms with the whisking ceiling fans, reading drowsily in the gleam. For all the surfaces of this world—sky, garden, and the surfaces within our abode—glow. This is so because, throughout the day, two graceful women, like silent swans, drift by with bottles of furniture polish and beautiful whisk brooms held in a single hand. Wearing flower and dragon-splashed sarongs secured with silver belts, they make the tables and sideboards and lamps shine with a regal lustre, and sweep the dust away. Indeed, Queen Elizabeth could have come for tea at any moment of the day to our current house without our experiencing a single ripple of embarrassment. The ashtrays are ever emptied and wiped, a fresh carton of cigarettes available on the coffee table, at the ready for any formal or informal guest. And often friends—my mother has so many—do drop by during these languid afternoons, or new acquaintances come, or my parents' diplomatic contacts arrive to leave their cards.

I might take a brief "kip," as the colonial British of this place say, after this midday replenishment, and then my mother and brother and I mosey over for a swim at the British club, followed by tea or spicy ginger ale, after which we stroll home for dinner through the wide residential colonial realms of large houses overhung with dramatic giants of trees.

Dinner time, like every other point in the day, is sprucely orchestrated by my mother. Hipni the cook standing by her with his earnest eyes and long white apron, my mother has planned out the dinners with him for the week, and they arrive at the table in tune with the hands of the clock without a drop of additional energy required of her. Except for the days when a dinner is being prepared for members of the local diplomatic corps or Malaysian officials, the dinners are luxuriously tailored to my family's preferences: "Hipni chicken" on Monday (a delicious Italian dish taught to Hipni by the previous consul's wife), hamburgers on Tuesday (to please my brother), a curry on Wednesday (any one of a number of Hipni's Malaysian specialties), beef and green peppers on Thursday (my family's nostalgic Chinese comfort food), fried rice on Friday (to please me). The dinner table linens are so pressed and starched they could walk on their own, their embroidered, embossed "T" monograms standing in their intended relief. Tabers now, indeed, are on their best American flag display.

And through the whole day—all these every days—my mother's arms are calm, her eyes have a happy shine, and her body moves with a secure and tranquil assurance. She likes me. She loves the world.

And what is the spell that has made my mother have patience for and even sometimes delight in the daughter who could be so irritating, and adore the life she owned? The answer is simple. Servants.

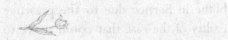

This question of servants, and the advantages associated therewith, is a squirmy issue for me at sixteen. I have become politically avid after my experiences at Sidwell, and attuned to power imbalances and human experiences of inequality. I am guiltily aware of the pleasures associated with having household help, and simultaneously deeply uncomfortable with my family's "use" of other people to prepare and serve our food and clean up after us. In the clutch of and trying to resolve this conflict, one evening I decide to make a stand and I refuse my mother's instruction to ring the bell to let Hipni know that we are ready for dessert.

"It's wrong to exploit human beings," I declare.

My defiance is committed—I am certain, like no one but an adolescent can be, that my logic is unassailable—but my parents' responses to my defiance complicate my simple view of matters, and dampen my thrilling righteousness.

My father tells me, looking me straight in the eyes with his sincere ones, that we are offering Hipni, his wife, and sister-in-law good jobs that pay them very, very well by the local market standards. He says Hipni and his wife feel extremely lucky to work for the American consulate. To this, my mother adds that Hipni told her that he has his own servant to help *his* family when they go home on the weekends.

As I chew on their words over the next few days, the idea drifts to me that I need to adjust my thinking. "Service," after all, is not a demeaning sort of work to engage in, so long as its providers are respected, appreciated, and decently remunerated. To go further, what could be of more value, really, than helping others? Helping others is really what my father does. He is a government servant, after all. And my mother does nothing but serve.

Returning to my teenaged sense that my mother was more blithe in Borneo due to the presence of household help, the reality of the ease that could arrive to a woman with such aid became crystal clear when I had children and a household of my own to single-handedly manage. The work of maintaining and nourishing a household, if it is to optimally meet the needs of all members, requires more than the devotion of one strong woman, especially if that one strong woman is to, herself, function at her best or have a chance at flourishing. So, back to the subject of servants—or helpers, or maids, or aunties, or extended family, or supportive spouses, or whatever you wish to call such household maintainers and carers, here is my conclusion. Every mother, every woman, every household in an ideal world, should have them.

My mother is a flourishing woman and I am a flourishing girl in the wild smells and fecundities of Borneo, but it is while my parents are stationed there that a dart fires out of the jungle to tangle with vines and creepers my mother and me.

# JOAN OF ARC

We are standing at the altar of a temple in Kuching. Gaudy, glinting statues of gods and goddesses are set in the dark recess, with pieces of chicken, durian and rambutan fruits, and assorted globular vegetables placed in a jumble on the bank at the front, all alive with flies.

In recent days I have visited my mother's stomping grounds, the organizations where she now works—the "home for crippled children" full of tiny children stumbling along on bent legs, the leper colony of crafts people weaving with stumped fingers. These are places ringing of hope for my mother. She is exhilarated by anywhere she can provide real aid through her physical therapy skill. "If, at the end of the day, I can say I made someone's life a little easier, then I've had a good day," she says, and says again. But my mother's favorite places are haunting grounds for me. I have no skills to offer. I feel only spoilt and helpless, and left with indelible images of suffering.

At the temple, I watch women in faded sarongs wander up and add their sacrificial food offerings to the array. My mother gives and offers sacrifices all day long while I paint pictures on a pleasant veranda. At a nearby stall, I buy some papaya to place on the altar, an offering that seems pathetic in this place of uncountable poor people (to whom the food will later be given) and compared to what my mother brings.

My mother stands, shoulders straight, over to the side, her hair a-toss but comfortable and confident in the swarm of sweating people. She catches the eye of a little girl in a ragged shift. She bends down to show the child the necklace she is wearing, made by someone at the leper colony. They grin at each other as the girl fingers the bright wooden beads.

One of the women praying at the altar now is draped in white garments from crown to toe. An image forms in my mind. *My mother is wearing white robes, bowing before an altar. A man approaches and leads her toward a pyre. I choke up. I whelm with horror*

*and admiration. She is strong. She is poised. She was born just for this.*
*How inadequate I am. I will never match her.*

# MY MOTHER LEAVES ME

*I gaze out*
*over the fields of Tadaka*
*and see the cranes that cry there*
*without interval,*
*without pause:*
*such is my longing for you.*
— Otomo no Sakanoue no Iratsume

Kobe, Japan.

My mother's face crumbles. The fated day has come. She grabs me in her arms, gives me a quick and desperate hug, and then she forces herself to walk away. Her head bent down to hide her tears, she scuttles down the path toward the taxi poised on the lane which snakes down the Japanese mountain. She pulls her sweater closer around her and seems to double over, shuddering with a sob, as she nears the car.

My mother has just left me for the first lengthy separation I have ever had from her. She has brought me and my brother here to this Japanese ridge over a day's travel away from Borneo, to attend the missionary boarding school my parents have chosen—a campus with a main school building that looks like a Swiss hotel and dorms to one side, backed by a Buddhist graveyard and scruffy undeveloped land. This is where we will spend the year. I won't see her now until Christmas. I am two months past sixteen.

As my mother walks away—looking so small and hunched, her greying hair blown by the breeze—my chest starts to heave. My belly feels vast and more hollow and emptier than it has ever felt, like a vacuity that could never, ever again be filled. The departure of my mother, who heals so many people's hope, is to lose half my heart. My chest heaves more wretchedly and my eyes begin to spill. I want to cry out, "Mom, come back!"

She left some daisies on the desk in my dormitory room. She writes to me every day. These missives help to fill my belly and my heart, but still there is the hollow. The hollow, the womb only my mother's body can fill.

I will yearn for her forever.

# PERSEPHONE

*He snatched her up all unwilling and carried her off*
*In his chariot of gold, the girl shrieking and in a shrill voice crying out*
*— Homeric Hymn to Demeter*

I am lying on my twin bed in my room at boarding school in Japan.

The first semester here has been surprisingly affirming. I seem to have happened upon a new and happier persona. An unexpected pleasure, due to the fact that my brother and I are stranded together far, far across the world from our parents, has been that we have grown close while at Canadian Academy. We are the only students from a place as far away as Borneo and the only two people on the planet who share our particular version of a country-hopping childhood. It is to be the beginning of a supportive alliance between my brother and me that will deepen over the next decade as we begin to forge our adult lives. Another boon at C.A. is that I have easily made new friends with the daughters of missionaries—the other girls in my dormitory—and I have a tentative but growing and exhilarating awareness that some of the boys give me a second look. It is as though something is budding in me. Sometimes after class I walk up into the graveyard behind the campus to collect wildflowers, feeling strangely blithe and at home in this oddly familiar new realm.

But now, my head is shrieking with headache, my stomach is roiling, and I am so hot and cold I feel as if my body and the whole world are merged in one infinite, swirling and steaming-icy, tropical-Arctic storm. I am limp as a noodle and can feel weeping rising in my chest but I am too weak to make a sound.

The school sends me in a taxi to a strange missionary doctor in an eerie, moss-covered, walled house. I can barely walk; the taxi man helps me in the door.

The doctor examines me, pulling up my clothes here and there as I slump on his table. He sends me home with a packet of pills in my hand.

I swallow some pills and collapse on my bed.

In the morning I am someone nobody knows.

I am woozy and shaky but I force myself to get up, push myself to go to classes. My mother has taught me never to miss school. School is the most important thing. I have an American history paper due and I am in a theatrical performance; I must not let anyone down. These bits of me are recognizable. The others are not.

Once the conscientious good girl, I am now a defiant, rampaging, ne'er do well and a vamp and a fairy girl wafting over the face of the earth. Over the next days, through a curtain of blurry vapor, I hear and feel and watch a tough, saucy rebel saunter up to my friends and brag, "I took acid in the graveyard," "I got drunk with Mary," "I skipped class and went to buy pot." All of this issued in a cocky, sneering voice and every word untrue. I go with a friend to the department store in a glittery mall and flagrantly and rudely and messily—I see only with a strange vagueness in this state I am in—smear lipstick on my lips and slash eye shadow on my eyes. Then I bat them at the salesgirl and my stricken friend and flaunt off down the aisle to try on lacy underwear. I buy ten buttery cakes at a French-style bakery and cram them, one after another, in my mouth.

It is as though I have been spirited away into some dark-bright netherworld that exists just next to or beyond or beneath the usual one. I spend all the day's hours watching my not-self doing antic things that are not me in the old Sara's body and with her own voice. This not-me is charged up and vehement and piratical—and also strangely calm, like a sage watching a child perform. It is as if I am the director of a movie and the actress has gone off-script, and, instead of behaving regally at the ball, has ripped off her clothes and is dancing in the dark sea. But while she dances, she is also feverish and almost fainting from weakness but propelled by a strange antic, elated, over-bright fury.

*Deus ex machina.* This is the first revolution in my life.

# DEMETER

*The headband on her hair*
*she tore off with her own immortal hands*
*and threw a dark cloak over her shoulders.*
*She sped off like a bird, soaring over land and sea,*
*looking and looking…*
*— Homeric Hymn to Demeter*

I am my mother and my mother is me.

Decades later I imagine my mother's story of what happens now. The cataract of her words cascade and flurry out of me as though from some ancient realm.

*Frantic. Frantic. I will get there. I will. Sara's sick. She's sick. My beautiful, pure daughter is sick. Sick in the mind. Kobe, Kobe, that's 2800 miles away from Kuching, a quarter of the world. Charlie will drive me to the airport. I will catch the first plane out—the first plane to anywhere from this godforsaken place. Singapore first, then Guam or Hong Kong or Taipei, then Tokyo, then Kobe, by whatever plane. How ever I can get there...*

Rushing to the desk in Singapore, dragging a bag of Sara's clothes—I couldn't think what else to bring. Charlie has called ahead. An Air Force pilot says he can take me to the Philippines. It's a cargo plane, but has some seats. I can go to Tokyo from there. It's good it's American, a comfort, experienced pilots, war pilots. Just put me in the hold, I say to them. I ride, bumping, bumping through the air. I feel sick but it is my daughter who is sick, sick in the mind. Thinking wrong. Crazy, crazy. How could this happen to my Sara? My Sara, my Sara. I will get there. I will get there, if this turbulence doesn't bring us down as we traverse this god-forsaken empty world. It can't bring us down. I will get there, I will...to my Sara.

Oh my God, I will die if...Oh, I never, ever should have left her at that school. But it seemed okay, it seemed fine. Oh God, I'm such a terrible mother. How could we have put that hardship post over the kids—though the kids said they wanted boarding school. But they didn't know. The truth is, we've simply sacrificed too much. I will kill myself if she...If we get her back, I will never, ever let her go...

Two more planes, hitchhiking on planes—whisking through hollow airs, and the bullet train—speeding through a barren landscape, and Charlie's colleague, what's his name, meets me at the train and takes me in a taxi to the teacher's house where I find her, my Sara. My daughter is lying on a futon on the tatami floor of a tiny apartment the size of a mouse's hole. When she sees me, she sits up. She is alive! She says, "Mom, what are you doing here?" so she can still speak! What joy! For a moment my body is relief and joy, but no. She has said, "Mom, what are you doing here?" instead of rushing over to hug. And her voice was different—surly, obstreperous. She looks different. Deranged, odd, hair tangled, with a strange smile on her face. Not herself. Mussed and dirty, smelling of earth, as though she's been sleeping in an animal's hole. Oh my God, not my Sara at all. That strange look, that mussed hair, that hellish smile, and she doesn't know why I'm here. The teachers say she is saying strange things, doing strange things, lying, not the Sara, the good student they've all known since she began in the fall. Something is wrong, something psychological. She's had a breakdown.

*What should I do? What should I do? On my god, what should I do? The embassy has gotten me a hotel room, a room in a modern, high rising hotel downtown, in modern- too modern Kobe, rebuilt from rubble after the war. I will go there and call Charlie. I go, I call, I call...Long distance, it takes too long. I am having to wait too long, panicking, panicking. She will die. She will die. Our daughter is damaged. On my god, our precious daughter is so sick. She doesn't know where she is. She is brazen, she lies, she parades herself around, she is strange, so strange, not our girl at all. The girl we knew is gone, gone, maybe forever. Oh my God, Charlie, we have to have help. We have to get help. Now. Now.*

*On the bullet train to Tokyo, to the Air Force hospital in Tachikawa, Charlie is with us now—thank God, I watch Sara. My daughter with her lovely long hair, with her skinny body, eating mikans, eating tangerines. Charlie jumped off the train at a station to get her a nylon string bag of them. Orange globes my daughter is eating, sliver by sliver. Nourishing her maybe, a filament of hope, segments of the sun.... I've put on my black glasses to conceal my tears from her. They keep bubbling. I can't help it. And my chest keeps heaving, my belly keeps roiling, I keep needing to run to the bathroom, but I try to keep all this from her, Sara who doesn't know what is going on and keeps saying, in a new, rough, surly voice that is not her voice at all, "What's wrong? Why are you here? I'm fine. I don't need to go to a hospital."*

*At the hospital— Sara puts her feet on the table in the consulting room, so rude, so not the daughter I know at all—the doctors say they will take care of her, but the doctors are young. What do they know? How can they know enough to save my precious daughter, my cherished sweet daughter? They don't know her. I am her mother. I am the one who knows her. How will they know when Sara is herself again?*

*They take Sara away—into a ward with a long grey-green hallway—and put her in a room with a scallywag girl with matted hair who says she is leaving and was just in overnight for drugs. But Sara is not. Sara has something badly wrong with her. Not drugs, they don't think, but the doctors say they will find out what's wrong. That is what they say. But I can't leave her here in this ward full of soldiers, this place full of young fighters back from Vietnam, from battle. Who knows what they have been through, what diseases of the mind they carry. How can that be good for her, for my precious daughter, for the daughter I gave birth to, pushed out of my own body, here in Japan, sixteen years ago? I am going to die.*

*... They have done it! The doctors have done it. It took two days, and she looks weak and frail, like an emptied-out bottle, like a skinny animal from a drought, but our daughter is back. My Sara is back. She's back. But what does it all mean? I don't understand. A fugue, the flue, a headache. They don't know quite what caused it, this temporary psychosis that took over my daughter's mind. They don't know and will keep her a couple of weeks to sort it out. Maybe too much stress, maybe she was working too hard at school. She was a good student, yes, but maybe she was too far from home. Dr. Cohen says that yes, she was brave, that she liked school, but maybe it was too much. Maybe she was too brave. Maybe she wasn't ready. Maybe she missed her parents. You say you are close, they say maybe she missed her mother. Oh my God, maybe Sara missed me. Me. Maybe she missed me, her mother. Oh, why did I do this to my own daughter? I will never leave her again. I will stay and I will hold my daughter to my body and I will keep her safe forever, forever near me, hold her to my breasts...*

# HYSTERIA

*There are times when fear is good.*
*It must keep its watchful place*
*At the heart's controls. There is*
*Advantage*
*In the wisdom won from pain.*
*— Aeschylus*
    *The Eumenides*

"How are you doing today?" Dr. Cohen says.

Faced, in his Tachikawa Air Force Base office, by a sixteen-year-old girl, with long chestnut hair and love beads, and a baffling psychosis, the white-coated, concerned doctor swiftly installed me in Ward 3 of the hospital. There, via twin infusions of kill-your-heart stories of war-shocked soldiers from the Vietnamese battlefields—and massive medicinal cocktails of stelazine and artane, the young Dr. Cohen retrieves me from my fugue, shoves the ground back under my flying feet and forces me to land. Following this deft move, he begins to try to fathom what precipitated my circus flip from conscientious, agreeable teenager to deranged and reckless outlaw...and proceeds to transform my whole view of the world.

We are sitting in a small room off the main hall of the psychiatric ward. This room, like every other, is painted a dull, faded grey-green. It smells faintly of medication and disinfectant. I can see, out the small window, low-cut squares of lawn between the low buildings of the vacant-seeming base.

Dr. Cohen, in regulation khakis beneath his white coat, has blond, military-short hair. His face has a friendly look.

"Are you feeling a little better?" he says.

My mind is fogged and confused, and to be in this strange hospital far from school and far from home in Borneo feels all wrong. There's a roiling surliness in me; I just want to go back to somewhere I know. Simultaneously, though, I feel helpless and weak. I don't know what's going on or how to get things back on track. Something strange and unfathomable has happened.

"How do you feel about being on the ward?" he asks, as if he knows what I'm thinking.

"It's awful," I say.

"It's really tough to be torn out of your school, and to suddenly be in Tachi, in this strange hospital, I bet."

His tone is kind; my testiness ebbs.

"When you got here, it didn't seem like you were really yourself. Today you seem like you're doing a lot better. We gave you some medicine and it seems like it's helping. I'm glad you're back. Your parents and I were really worried about you."

I listen.

He goes on, "Your and my job now is to figure out what happened so that we can work to make sure it doesn't happen again."

"When can I go back to school?" I ask.

"I promise to get you back as soon as we can." His eyes look straight into mine. He seems like he can be trusted.

"Why don't you tell me something about how school's been going and what things were like in the week or so before you came here. That may help us get started on this job of figuring things out."

He asks about my friends, and teachers, and boyfriends, and my boarding school workload, and my family's world-traversing, and my past schools, and past friends, and loneliness, and worries, and sadness, and eating, and headaches, and my brother. He listens closely to everything I say.

And then he says, "How was to it leave your parents and go off to boarding school in a country far away? You are just sixteen, and you're a pretty close family, I've heard."

"Oh, it was fine," I say, wanting to show him that nothing fazes me.

He seems interested in my reply. "It seems like you've had quite a few changes lately. Leaving the States, moving to Borneo, coming to Japan…Changes can be tough even if you're pretty good at being on your own."

When he says, "We'll talk again tomorrow," I feel contented.

The next day, Dr. Cohen asks, "I've been wondering. What have you been feeling lately—back at school and here at Tachi?"

*Feeling?* This is a new word, a new question for me. I'm

confused. What does he mean? Strong people like us foreign service kids don't have feelings. Emotions are to be ignored, disposed of, rushed away—so as to be strong, so as to soldier on, so as to go it alone. We can go anywhere, do anything, and be utterly fine. You can do anything if you put your mind to it. Feelings are irrelevant. They are to be smothered, crushed under foot. But when he asks the questions, something deep down in me stirs. It's like a little animal crouched in the earth is roused and twitching, its ears perked, peeking out, but also scrunching down to hide and ready to dash away.

"I don't know. Okay," I fumble.

His head is cocked. He seems so interested. And like he thinks maybe I have something else to say.

"I guess I've been feeling a little weird," I venture.

Then Dr. Cohen says something even more disconcerting.

"I've also been wondering about your feelings about your mother. Have you missed her a lot while you've been at school?"

His question is a shocking jolt—so wrong. Missed my mother? No, I'm self-reliant and strong. I've been doing fine.

"No. Not really. I'm pretty independent," I say.

Then, watching his face, I add. "Only once in a while, maybe."

He looks at me kindly.

"It would be pretty common for even an independent teenager to miss her mother."

He lets his comment just sit silently in the air for a moment. As it stays there, stationed like the moon, I feel a tide rising inside me.

"You know, any feeling you have is fine," Dr. Cohen says.

I feel sadness starting to surge up, tears starting to brim. When I look at his soft eyes, I almost can't fight them back.

I take a second and manage to suck them down. "Well, I think it's better to ignore feelings," I say. "It's better to be strong, not let them control you. Just ignore them and go on with what you're doing."

"You know feelings aren't bad things," Dr. Cohen says gently. "They just *are*. Both the easy ones and the hard ones. And they aren't wrong. They're just part of being human. Actually, I think, feelings are to be cherished—they tell us what's important to us."

"But don't we have to control them?" I say.

"My sense is that we can't really control *having* feelings. They just come. And trying to pretend they aren't there or trying to ignore them usually doesn't work too well. Often if we try to repress them or ignore them, they burst out with extra force and in strange places."

"That's why feelings *should* be controlled, isn't it?" I say.

The next thing I say, I say half terrified, my chest pounding, as if I'm handling a bomb about to detonate. "The thing is, if you don't control them, you might be hysterical," I say. "My mother sometimes gets hysterical. It's awful," I say.

I think of the times my mother sometimes gets very upset with my father about something to do with his work and her voice gets shrieky and I can tell she wants to push him until she extracts something from him—I don't know what. Her shrieking voice shoves and shoves and my whole body cringes and I want to yell at her to stop. And my father, patting her in a way that is half kind and half treating her like a baby, says, "Now Lois, calm down." And my mother says, "Don't you dare patronize me, Charlie Taber!" And he says, "Now Lois, it'll be alright. Don't get hysterical."

Now I've said it. Said the awful word. My chest is still pounding. I feel like bawling. I've said the bad thing about my family, the bad thing about my mother, admitted the thing in the world I most, most, most don't want to ever, ever be.

And here she is standing before me and inside me, before *us*: *Hysteria*. The she-being I am so afraid of: the storming creature with her wild hair, her red raging eyes, and her grabbing claws…

But Dr. Cohen isn't fazed by her at all. He just goes on.

"Sometimes feelings are really, really difficult," he says. "Sometimes they take us down to deep, dark places. Sometimes they can make anyone, all of us, including mothers, feel wild and not know how to handle them, and burst out, and lose control. But what I've learned in psychiatry is that the best way to handle feelings is to recognize them and name them, realize *I'm feeling very sad right now*, or *I'm feeling anxious*, or *I'm really pissed off*.

"It can be really hard, but if we accept that they are there and call them by their names, it actually gives us more control than if we pretend they aren't there brewing inside us. If we let ourselves feel them rather than fight them, that calms them down, and we can *decide* what to do with them, rather than have them run the show. Rather than their erupting in hysteria."

It is like Dr. Cohen knows everything.

I burst into tears. I suddenly miss my mother and my father and school and my friends and my other countries, and I just cry and cry. And he just sits there, as if this is absolutely good and right and fine.

Dr. Cohen has offered me an answer—to a question I didn't even know I had. In teaching me about feelings, he's shown me a way not to become Hysteria. A way not to become the shrieking female I most fear to be, the version of "woman" that men disdain and label "hysterical." A way not to become my mother. Here it is: Treat a rising feeling as the upset, quaking little girl she is. *Come here, little one. Let me get a look at you. Tell me what is going on inside you. There, there. Let me put my arms around you. It will be okay. We'll see what we can do for you. Don't worry.*

# DEMETER, MY MOTHER

Once again, I imagine, *hear* deep inside, the thoughts rippling through my mother's terrified mind long ago during the days after I returned to school to complete my junior year.

*It is a miracle. Sara is better now, it has been a month, she is back in her classes. She is taking her pills. She is better every day, less tired, even smiling, laughing with her friends. I saw that one day. My daughter is better, smiling, herself, but I will never leave her again. I will never leave this tiny rented apartment down the hill from her school. I will bring my daughter bread and flowers and fruits. I will never again leave my daughter.*

*And forever now—especially in February, the bad month—I will watch her, my heart will jump in my chest, I will watch for signs... signs of my daughter slipping down the well. Sara is no longer down there in the blackness, but I will wait there forever, at vigil, at the well's entrance. I am the mother. No one can stop me. I will curl there in my gown at the top of the well and I will prevent my daughter from falling. At the slightest sign, I will fling my body in front of my daughter's, to stop my daughter from plummeting.*

# PERSIMMONS

*And mother and daughter, seeing each other,*
*rejoiced in their hearts*
*— Homeric Hymn to Demeter*

"Oh, Sara," my mother says to me after school. "Come with me, Sweetie. Let's go see the new persimmons at the vegetable stall! Tonight, let's bake a persimmon pudding like Grandma used to make!"

"Cool, Mom!" I say. "Yes, let's!"

We are living in Tokyo now. Andy is in his sophomore year and I am in my senior year at the American School in Japan. My father has requested a transfer here so I can continue to see Dr. Cohen, the psychiatrist who's saved my mind and hence my mother's too.

The country of my birth is no longer that post-war downtrodden huddle but now, sixteen years later, a hive of busy people hurrying every which way through labyrinths of shiny high rises. Men with briefcases in well-cut suits stride to noodle houses, young women in smart uniforms greet department store shoppers hello, middle aged women in kimonos shuffle onto packed trains, and masses of blue jean-clad young people gather in pods, cigarettes dangling from their slender fingers. They could be American hippies but for the rich blackness of their shaggy hair.

With its Shinkansen bullet trains and its glittering malls of French bakeries and Italian shoes, the country could seem simply a fleeter and more spic-and-span transplant from the west. But that is only at first glance. Very soon the Japanese-ness graciously and subtly sidles up.

It is the air—which smells of persimmons and incense, of soy sauce and green tea. And the sounds—behind the screeches of taxis and rumble of trains, the clatter of wood-soled geta sandals and the interrogatory, blurting, breathiness of spoken Japanese. It is the palette too—the tangerines and mauves of the shawls like hues from another, more subtle planet, the transparent white of a shop window lily. And one chopsticked-up bowl of donburi with its sweet soy sauce-y egg and rice, and Japan is claiming its rightful reign and standing before you proud and sharp and distinctive as a cherry tree.

Japan, during this 1971–72 year, will generously wrap her graceful kimonoed arms around my family as we recover. I have healing still to do from my ordeal, but my father will need to recover too. My father's Tokyo job is a pleasant one as liaison to the Japanese press, but he will receive a devastating electrical jolt related to his work.

Here in our hallowed, beautiful Japanese-Western house, my mother is trying her best to respect my new way of interacting with the world, of talking about feelings all the time, like they are new toys. Dr. Cohen has mentioned to her about the respectability of feelings too. She doesn't quite understand, but she is trying, and his words seem to have soothed her brow and freshened her eyes. He carries some of my 107 pounds now, and life in Tokyo is the calmest since the early years in The Hague. My mother handles me with kid gloves, just grateful her conscientious daughter is back, glad for moments with me, lest I transform again. And she, herself, by grace or Dr. Cohen, seems to have her own feet more firmly *sur terre*, the artist in her, even, stealing out to make an appearance now and then.

Blithe with our errand now, my mother takes my arm, a basket on the other, and, matching strides, we walk down to the green grocer in his long ikat apron and white gloves and watch as, with an artist's attentions, he twists each of our bright globes in a square of paper.

Persimmons: Japanese symbol of *shibui*, of simple, unobtrusive beauty, of subtlety, humility, restraint.

When I think of my mother's plea for me to join her in the kitchen, mushing, like her mother did, that strange, crack-skinned, soft-meat, brilliant-orange fruit, I am flooded with a sense of shibui, the Japanese word my mother seized that year as though it meant everything. "Ah, shibui," she'd say to me when she spotted an irregular teacup, color of wet grass on an overcast day, in a shop window—or a cascading honeysuckle spray in a room. "Shibui. Simple beauty, Sara," she'd say, as though this were the answer to the world.

My mother was not a beauty, nor was her humble pudding: a sort of muddy-russet, lopsided, quivering soufflé of a thing in an earthenware dish. Yet both were a blend of elegant and rough, subtly sweet and nourishing as earth on the tongue.

# AN IRIS

*Let me not forget that I am the daughter of a woman who bent her head, trembling, between the blades of a cactus, her wrinkled face full of ecstasy over the promise of a flower, a woman who herself never ceased to flower untiringly, during three quarters of a century.*
— Sidonie-Gabrielle Colette
*Sido*

My mother snips an iris over the sink. As she does so, she says, wistful and contented, "Flowers are the salve for a woman's soul."

Here in Japan, my mother buys different blooms every week and can spend an hour or more in the dark slot of a kitchen in our rambling house—the kitchen is made for a cook, not a *madame*—just arranging her wands of purple iris or stems of white lilies or bunches of scarlet chrysanthemums, and humming. She took ikebana when I was a baby in Japan, and now she says it is marvelous to get back to it and to have time for flowers again. For this short time in Japan, she has just a small, part-time job, teaching math at a Catholic girls' school. This last year of my childhood is the only year in my life when this is so—when my mother is not devoting herself to the beleaguered. Perhaps, after my harrowing hospitalization of the past year, she had decided she must be completely available. She knew we would be in Tokyo only nine months, so she had perhaps given herself permission—holding her strict Presbyterian work ethic temporarily at bay—to engage in hobbies, so long as her grading and the household tasks were done, while my brother and I were at school.

When my mother arranges flowers in the galley kitchen, her whole body changes. As when she is around cows or birds, when my mother is with flowers, she becomes tranquil and lapping as the tropical sea; it's as though her hands are inspired and shifting on their own. Her mind isn't in control, but rather, some Transcendentalist spirit is guiding her fingers, in the way you hear a painter or writer is moved, by instinct, as to where to brush on the paint or which words to pen.

Perhaps she should not have regarded flower arranging as a hobby but as a necessity. What would her life, then, have been?

# BLACK MARK

My mother is talking to Aunt Marge on the phone in the shadowy back hallway lined with dark, ancient mahogany. The call has to travel on cables across the bottom of the Pacific and traverse the American continent to Florida, so this means it's something important. Her voice, as I eavesdrop from the dining room, thickens and clots with tears.

"Oh my God, Margie, Charlie was right all along. That son of a gun, indeed, was undermining Charlie at every turn, blocking every promotion! Why the hell didn't it all come out earlier? Why didn't Charlie open his mouth? 'Oh no,' he said, 'it wouldn't do any good,' but Marge, it's been fifteen years wasted!"

As events have unrolled, my father has just learned that his frustrations about career advancement have not been imaginary—that, in fact, his boss, Buck from back in Taipei, black-marked his file with words to the effect of "This officer should advance no further." Buck had recently come under scrutiny and reprimand for mistreatment of a number of his staff, but the cost to my father has been incalculable: years of service undermined.

"Oh, I know, it's not all a waste," my mother is saying into the receiver. "I know, Margie...But Charlie's never been assertive enough...You've got to be strong in this world. It's full of lard-bottom son-of-a-guns...I can't believe how nice I've been to Pamela all these years while her husband was doing Charlie in. And I gave up a good career for this to happen...

"Yes, of course, I've been able to find ways to be useful, but Margie, another thing is: We can't let the children know about all this...

"And what do we do now? With Sara about to go to college, how can he quit? If he needs to, so be it, but what on earth will we do? Lord knows, I've sacrificed for him a thousand times, and I can support us...But really, by God, he's just got to stick with it after all we've put in. He can't give up the pension now."

My father's anger about his ill-treatment, though contained, will take up residence and smolder and kick within him, and double my mother's burden for all the years ahead. Her task now will be both to carry the rage he refuses to free, and to simultaneously provide an air of calm—for both her husband and herself. It is a granite truth that a woman's life and plight are inextricably entwined with her husband's.

My mother's voice thickens now, clotting with tears. "Oh, Margie, I think back to when we started all this. We were so optimistic, so proud, so sure. We thought—I thought—we could whip the world. Now I feel like the runt of the litter scrabbling for a teat."

# THE MAGIC CARPET

I am sitting at the dining room table in Tokyo. This is a small room, just big enough for a rectangular table that seats eight. Shoji doors separate it from the big Japanese-style tatami-matted living room on one long side. On the other side of the opposite wall is the western style living room. The opening on one short end leads to the back hall which separates the family living spaces from the kitchen, the maid's room, and her bathroom. The opposite side of the room looks out on the garden through floor-to-ceiling window walls. I am sitting facing the Japanese room, with the garden to my right. I can look out onto the sculpted trees and the open space of the lawn—a rare sanctuary of open space in this clamorous, crowded city—as I think. I have a pad of paper in front of me, and a typewriter, and a big catalogue of colleges Mom ordered from the States. I am writing my autobiography for my applications to send to schools.

It is when I am engaged in this sort of project that my mother and I are in sync and my mother is at her very best. My mother loved anything to do with school and achievement. She was brimming over with drive and ambition and thrived on forward movement. When I was small, she would seize upon any long-term project I had and urge me to take off with it. Learning, to her, was delicious, a promise in the air. It could transport you to the moon, to the stars and beyond. The task assigned by the teacher was, to her, merely an excuse, just the launching pad. You did what was asked, but you didn't stop there. You used the assignment to set your imagination free and let your diligence rip. You were out to out-do yourself.

I can envision my mother, a smart and impatient little girl back in Henryville, looking at the walls of her one-room schoolhouse, almost bursting with her urge to crash through them and barrel across the pasture—or to flap her wings (surely they were there somewhere on her body) and soar into the air. This love of school and of achievement went hand in hand with her firm belief, "You can do anything if you put your mind to it." The American dream was an article of faith to Lois Taber. I feel sure she was born holding it in her tiny fist. *Always do your best. Your excellent work will stand for you. The world is a meritocracy. Brown-nosers and S.O.B.s might win in the short run, but you will reach the promised land in the end. Hard work can fly you anywhere.*

When I was in third grade, in a Bethesda, Maryland, public school, and doing a book report on Robert Frost, my mother suggested I write out, in my best penmanship, "Whose woods these are…" on poster board and go beyond the assignment to illustrate it too. Having sustained my acquiescence, she hurtled to People's Drug in the rusty Rambler for a fresh sheet of poster board and new Magic Markers. She knew just the scent of the materials would set me off. We shared genes for compulsivity.

In Holland in the fourth grade, when I was assigned Argentina for our class's study of South America, she took me all over The Hague to friends' bookshelves so I could look up the main products of Argentina in their reference books. One had *Encyclopedia Britannica*, another the *Book of Knowledge*, another a great illustrated atlas. At home, we had a wonder, the *World Book*, but that single reference wasn't enough to do a really good job. Between the employees of the embassy, toting their books from post to post, one could compile sufficient references for a school report. The library at the American School of The Hague was a marvel-containing crow's nest at the top of the converted Victorian house, rich in fiction but not replete in reference sources.

When I was in the sixth grade my mother waxed larger: "Oh, you have to find out about the Iroquois? Ooh, Sara, why don't you write to the Government Printing Office? They have all sort of wonderful information they send out for free. They're sure to have something on the Iroquois." She brought down the typewriter. I pecked out a letter to Washington, and then—this was another of the wonders of my childhood—I waited, with eager anticipation, for the packet from the diplomatic pouch. Sure enough, after a couple of weeks, there came the tightly wrapped package marked "Miss Sara Mansfield Taber, A.P.O." I am certain I was one of the Government Printing Office's main correspondents. Once I got the hang of this system, this way of obtaining information, I was off and running. In high school in Japan, doing a paper on the weather for biology class? A paper for English on Thoreau? A paper for history class on John Brown? The G.P.O. was my go-to Mecca, the internet of my time.

Because of her own eager mind, my mother was brilliant at urging on my own inclination to learn, aiding and abetting a seize-and-fly attitude toward learning. While in some arenas my mother was constricting, in this one my mother taught me not even the sky was a limit. And so, because of all this, when it was time for me to apply to colleges, she had immediately ordered the big catalogue and sat down with me on the western-style couch in the western-style living room to help me start dreaming about my life's possibilities.

"Oh look, Sara, you could go to this one in Ohio! They have a great English department, or this school in Minnesota. That's where your counselor at Sidwell said you should apply. Or look, you could go to this Colorado school. They study only one thing at a time there! You might love that. Or, look, you could go to this fine liberal arts school in Maine. They've just started taking girls...Or, of course, Wash U is a great school." She says this last wistfully, knowing I'd never set foot at her alma mater.

But my mother's excitement is catching. Her dreaming blends into mine. I am ready to fly and she to fly vicariously, and we are both romping, bounding through the air from cloud to cloud.

As a girl, my mother knew, if she was to live anywhere but Henryville for the rest of her life, or to have the grand career of helping the world she dreamt of, she'd have to work hard and do well in school, and get a scholarship to college, and she did just that. She was valedictorian of her high school class and won the Shields High School Latin Prize, and she was awarded a scholarship to Purdue and then to Washington University in St. Louis. Upon her father's advice, which she now knew to be faulty, she had restrained her ambition (which would surge up with a vengeance and dog her throughout her life) and given up her own beloved dream of being a doctor. As for me, she will make dead sure that I have the opportunity to pursue my heart's desire.

I look out at Japan and dream of doing great things. I dream of America. I dream my mother's dreams. We'll fly together. I'll be a poet. I'll translate at the U.N. I'll become a Japanologist. I'll be an English professor, a Buddhism scholar. I'll make you proud. We are birds in concert in a pastel sky with blending dreams. You'll fly on my carpet with me, Mom.

Sometimes it seemed like that was all of it. My mother and I were sailing together on an oriental tapestry and what I wanted and what my mother wanted were identical, and both of us were fighting with all our might and for our lives, in our own ways, to get it for me—my mother through instructions and sermons about hard work and willpower, and me, myself, through resolutions and diligence. And yet, between the two of us, it was also like one long, losing battle—a battle against nature—this ferocious and over-weening will for me to be happy and fulfilled and reach my potential. And the quest to assure me a happiness never-ending, unveering, and unflappable—in order to assure my mother's never-ending happiness—was so intense and so urgent, since that ultimate happiness and achievement had not yet arrived, that it seemed like the urgency would build and build until, one day, we would no longer able to look into each other's faces for the anguish and shame and disappointment and imperfection of ourselves and each other.

And because of this, sometimes it seemed that I would need to periodically escape into a dark, deep cavern far, far away and hidden from my mother, in order to deny her happiness, in order to grant the happiness we both wanted for me—to her and to me.

# GREEN PEPPER

It is as if she knows the end is near. My mother takes me everywhere with her, as if I am a precious thing: a brand-new baby girl she's just discovered on her doorstep, a fledgling chick that needs all the worms and insects she can bring it to flesh it up, for it will soon fly away. Dr. Cohen has recently told her she must learn to let me go. She came home from that interview and immediately shared with me what he said. "It's hard, Sara," she said. Her lip quivered a little. I glimpsed her vulnerability, her bravery on my behalf, for the first time. It was almost as if she was asking me to hold her to it.

So strange. The tables have turned. Poised to fly, I am the one who now holds the cards. A longing hope in her eyes, my mother says on Saturday, "Let's go to the teahouse I told you about," and we take a rattling train to an ancient, tucked-away thatched hut, and sip green tea from lopsided rustic cups—a twosome for an hour immersed in *wabi-sabi*, the Japanese aesthetic that expresses, in architecture, gardens, art, and pottery, the transience of all things. For that is where we are: suspended in an evanescent world that will soon vanish. It seems like the transitoriness of life is everywhere suddenly: exhibits of tarnished spoons in shop windows, ikebana arrangements of lilies just at the cusp of wilting, coffee ice creams she buys me for a treat—"Would you like a cone, Dear Heart?"—already melting when she places them in my hands.

It is something, a wistfulness her body seems to know, and she acts out of her belly more than from something having to do with words. To say, "I know, Sara, you will be leaving me" would be too much to sign onto. If acknowledged, the emotion would cause us to break. So, it is "Sara, you must come with me to hear the monks chanting in the temple down the street. It won't take long," or "I saw a shop with some funny hand-dyed tops I think you might like. Do you want to go this afternoon?" Anything shared. Any time.

But most of all, it is the green peppers she makes for me to take to school. I open my lunch bag out on the school terrace and have to lift my eyes to the sky to stop myself from welling up. In my lap, out of the bag, appears a hand-work of color and imprecise beauty: a green pepper cup filled with pink tuna and green relish and yellow corn, with its little hat on top. "Eat this," the pepper seems to say, "and you will be forever safe, and you and I will be forever." "Eat me: I am love."

# BOOK TWO

7

# BUT OUGHT A DAUGHTER TO WORK FOR HER MOTHER?

"Go get Mr. Turner," my mother says. "Get the foot pieces for Mr. Johnson's wheelchair from his room." "Go ask the nurse for a sponge."

I am 19 now, this the summer between my freshman and sophomore years of college, and I am working as my mother's physical therapy aide in Washington area nursing homes. After Japan I spent my freshman year at Antioch College. An avid antiwarrior, I had wanted a radical college and had received it. The students were on strike my third semester and classes were held by professors in churches and homes. Able to rise above my idealism enough to see that having my parents pay for this didn't make sense, I would be transferring to Carleton College, a more traditional liberal arts college, in the fall.

Washington had become chastened in just the two years since we'd left for Borneo. Though President Nixon was riding high—the ping pong players had just returned from China—and was still feigning a bad John Wayne, the Southeast Asian war had become a bedraggled albatross flopping around the country's neck. American citizens were getting tired and the revolutionary energy of two years earlier had sputtered into a resigned slang. *Dream on. Bummer. Let it all hang out. No way, Jose.*

"Few things in life work as well as a Volkswagen," said the ad, and this might have been true, in terms of the cars of 1972, but on every highway, there was a broken-down V.W. bug with an owner peering under its chassis. Though the oaks again blaze cinnamon-red and curry-yellow, this was not an ebullient time for the country or the Taber family.

My mother had now moved 26 times. In this instance the

move was into a familiar house—the cottage on Thornapple Street. It was a residential come-down after the breezy *Out of Africa* Kuching manse and the elegant, mahogany-trimmed Japanese abode, but my mother didn't care a fig for such things. What was important, as always, was getting a job—which she had done—providing physical therapy to veterans and other nursing home dwellers. Her patients expressed their appreciation for her with gifts of Hershey bars and Chapstick. My father, on the other hand, was back at the China desk with the man who had smeared him. He was a figure of grim resolution—*I will not be cowed by that unprincipled man*—and held his head high, but this was not happiness. My mother looked at her husband shaking her head, and grilled him steak to keep his iron up. There was one ironic glimmer of hope though: All was not lost (or was it?), for my father was to go to Saigon within the year.

My mother and I are working at three different nursing homes. One is military-run, a clean, erect sort of place with nurses of ramrod postures who fire orders to patients like bullets. Another, located way out in the sprawling Maryland suburbs, slams us with urine reek as we walk in the door. Brick and low-slung, it features shabby furniture and mess everywhere. Knocked-over pill bottles on nurses' stations, wet, grey rags on the floor, patients' clothing left about, the patients themselves strewn every which way in their wheelchairs like so much debris. The nurse's aides seem slovenly and sluggish like the place itself. There is a patient named Mrs. Stern with white Einstein hair who yells, "Shit on you" when people walk by and swings her arms out to hit them. My mother gaily pats her arm and greets her sprightly with, "Good morning. How are you today, Mrs. Stern?" Such courtesy stuns her momentarily into silence. I scuttle around her for fear she'll hit me with her bony hands, and hurry after my mother, hoping if I look straight ahead, I won't have to take in the half-dressed old men and old women yelling for help that doesn't come. The third home is Quaker and seems benevolent and positive—clean and Spartan like the army one, but more relaxed, with a brighter spirit. The receptionist wears a smile and the staff we meet in the hall hug my mother hello.

I hate the conservative clothes I have to wear—instead of my jeans, blouses with collars, skirts that are almost knee-length—and having to pin up my long hair. I pass my eight hours fetching patients in wheelchairs or who use walkers from their rooms, and when I get them to the therapy room, I start them on whatever treatment my mother has prescribed. I hand them little barbells to lift and lower, I draw the whirlpool bath and help them put their swollen legs in it, I lay the soaked heating pads on their shoulders, or drill them on their leg lifts. There are always three or four patients in the room at once, and my mother moves back and forth between them, saying things like, "Mr. Martin, how's that gorgeous little granddaughter of yours?" or "Come on, Mrs. Goldstein, you can do better than that. Lift that leg higher." All the people seem to like my mother even though she badgers them and cajoles and goads them and makes them rouse themselves even if they look grim or their cheeks quiver like they are about to cry.

All day long, I scurry to do my mother's bidding, trying to be my most diplomatic, kind, and helpful good girl-little ambassador self with the patients. I am half in love with the young paraplegic CIA officer we work with at the Quaker home, but having to follow my mother's orders for eight hours straight and be the obedient, old-fashioned daughter my mother has always wanted feels like too much togetherness and demands all the patience I muster.

In spite of my inner surliness, I can't help but admire my mother. She battles doctors and insurance companies to assure her patients the care they need; she is expert at healing people's bodies. Patients arrive aching and unhappy and they leave feeling limbered up and heartened by her conversation and massages and drill sergeant exercise routines. The work is perfect for her. She can help the world by ordering people about and making them do things for their own good.

Watching my mother alternately instruct doctors, put them in their places, and argue with them on behalf of her patients' needs and rights, I witness how a woman can prevail over arrogant men. I note how critical it is for women to assert their knowledge. I will never be as effective at this as my mother, but she is planting me in a green world where women possess rights and wisdom.

Even with all this, I leave the nursing homes in a tumult. On the one hand, I've done my duty. I've earned some money for college and assisted my mother in her indisputably noble work, and helped, and even enjoyed helping, some kind old people, but I resent having to spend my days serving my mother—and to complicate things even further, I feel terribly guilty about that resentment. The truth is, I feel like I am living my mother's life, one that ill suits me.

My mother leaves work chirping with satisfaction. "Oh, Sara, what a productive day we've had." My mother receives joy from helping people heal their bodies, and I sense that she experiences a deep happiness, or is it, rather, a thrill of triumph from getting me to work alongside her? I suspect that I am finally acting correctly the supporting role in *The Book of Lois Taber*. More probably and more generously, my mother sees herself as passing on to me a useful skill for the world, one that could get me through. Even more generously, perhaps she just loves having her own beloved daughter day-long at her side.

Whichever it was, or whatever mix of altruism and self-satisfaction or love my mother derived, by the time we arrive home from work at the end of the day, and I step out of the car on Thornapple Street into the damp 90-degree heat, I'm so pent up and confined I feel like I could explode. I still sense a strong

206

magnetic pull from my mother's body—to stay home and revel with her in a day well spent, in order to keep pleasing her and remain her ideal daughter—but my stomach clenches, the skin of my face is taut, my clothes itch, I am sweaty, and I can still smell urine, as though it is on my own body. I feel so suffocated I want to race, screeching, straight down the street and away from my mother and across the world as fast as I can.

How does a daughter begin?

# THERE ARE MOTHERS
# AND MOTHERS

My new Carleton friend Em, whose mother lives down the street from the college, one day makes a comment that draws my attention to one of my mother's remarkable qualities.

My parents were now in Saigon—they'd moved there this fall of 1973 as soon as I left to start at Carleton, a college in Minnesota. I'd immediately felt completely comfortable at my new school, with its rigorous classes and close student-professor relationships. If over the summer in Washington I'd longed to be a world away from her, now that my mother *was* almost 9,000 miles across the sea, I missed her and felt warmly connected to her. She wrote to me nearly daily and I was buoyed by her vivid descriptions of Saigon life, delicious meals made by their Chinese cook, and her avid encouragement of my scholastic pursuits. I didn't really think about what other things she might be experiencing in that war-shattered place. I wrote back to her long rapturous letters about the new friends I'd made and about the classes I was taking in such subjects as French, Greek drama, and Japanese history. Now and then I received a package from her—a beautiful weaving made by the Montagnards or a new blouse sent in response to my passing mention of a wish for one. I took the packages to my dorm room and opened them in private and, beholding the contents whatever they were, my whole body would fill for a few minutes with a wistful yearning to touch my mother and see her face.

Em is talking about her need for curtains in her dorm room. "My mom said she'd make me some. I doubt she'll get to it, though...

"But, Sara," Em says, knowing all my tumultuous feelings about my mother, "your mom would have them made and sent to you by the end of the week." My mother is in Vietnam, half the world away and yet, what Em says is true. She'd find a way to make the curtains and have them to me, by embassy pouch if need be, so that I wouldn't suffer curtain-less for a day longer than necessary.

There are mothers, it seems, who are mild, and mothers who are intense, mothers who are water and mothers who are fire. There are families that are close and tight-woven like those childhood potholders, in which the parents are involved in their children's every decision—and there are families that don't know what is going on with each other. They are like fishing nets; a lot passes through. Em's mother was the mild kind. She had a water mother and a fishing net family.

When Em points out this truth about my mother and the curtains, I stumble into the bathroom and burst into tears.

The piercing exquisiteness of longing and joy, pain and pleasure so strangely the same...

# THE DUC HOTEL

I arrive in Vietnam, my parents' new post, for the summer between my sophomore and junior years of college literally and figuratively soaring. I've just traveled halfway around the world on my own. I've stopped off to work at Japanese dairy farms on the way, and had an overnight in a glittery Hong Kong high-rise hotel by myself en route. I feel independent and indomitable, as if I could land anywhere, anytime, and saunter on, unflappable. I step off the plane at Tan Son Nhut airport, feeling regal as a princess and strong as a marine.

Once we've deposited my suitcases inside the front door, and are relaxing, sipping Fantas served by the maid, my mother says, "The house only has two bedrooms, so we thought, since you're older, that you might like to stay at the Duc. That's the embassy hotel. You'll have your own room and room service. It'll be fun."

My mother thinks she's making me happy. She knows I want my independence—Dr. Cohen told her to expect this—and so she thinks I might enjoy having my own realm, apart from my brother and apart from her and my father.

But she is so wrong. I might like to be independent, yes, but some of the pleasure of expressing independence is derived from declaring independence *against* something—and wanting to be independent doesn't mean I want to be disconnected or alone or apart from my family. Rather than leaping at the chance for my own private space, I consider that my mother doesn't really want me there. Maybe it is my mother who wants independence—from me, I surmise. Or maybe she just wants my father and brother to herself. Either way, I am chagrined and hurt—and chagrined to be hurt. Mothering is such a trial-and-error affair, an endless tidal dance of embracing and withdrawing. It is sometimes impossible for a mother to get the calibrations right.

My mother soon reads my sad face and in a few days erects a rice paper screen in my brother's bedroom so we can each have a space, and I recover my buoyancy as I walk the scooter-

and people-choked streets smelling of rice and fish sauce on my way to work. Life assumes a pleasant routine. All four of us are working for the embassy. I have been given the job of revising the manual for the embassy personnel who will within eight months have fled the country, and my brother is working in the Mission Warden, the Embassy security office, sorting and counting weapons. In the mornings, Andy and I strike out into the heat for the embassy with our father while my mother bustles off into unknown precincts across the city to help all variety of people in need.

# MY MOTHER, THE LION-HEARTED

I trudge home from work, my hair sticking to my hot face. Heat sags like a wet rag over the once-lovely city, its grand avenues, graceful plantings, and brave residents crumbled and pockmarked by decades of war. The air stinks of diesel and rotting fruit and sweat. At the sandbag-piled street corners, soldiers slouch, guns slung slack over their shoulders. Other men on stumped legs crutch through the market stalls to buy cigarettes. The bluebird and canary trousers of beautiful hard-faced women flap as they hurry to purchase rice and baguettes. To my side—and all day long and all the night—motorbikes racket and cars screech while in the distance, at intervals, mortars thump. The city seems worn out. No one along the narrow sidewalks even bothers to watch as convoys of tanks and jeeps part the traffic, engines gunning, horns blaring.

My parents, who landed in the middle of 1973, will be here in Vietnam until the U.S. helicopters of 1975 depart over the South China Sea.

Upon her arrival in Saigon, my mother immediately went into full-throttle, take-on-the-world's-problems mode, quickly assuming the position of embassy social service coordinator as well as taking a job teaching math to the students at Saigon's tiny makeshift American school. My father's assignment in Saigon was with the CIA propaganda force. Specifically, his job was to run a "black" radio station with programing aimed to dishearten the enemy. Our country was still on its ill-fated mission to overthrow the Communist North pursuant to the Domino Theory—a last ditch and failing effort at this point.

At first my parents' life in Saigon looked to me to be hunky-dory. They were reaping the unmatchable intimacies of hardship posts, and seemed bonded by the strictures and demands inherent to life in a war zone. They were warm and cherishing of each other, and embraced each other frequently, looking with love into each other's eyes. On weekends they ate French food and swapped stories with their new fast friends in bistros left by the last un-conquerors.

As the summer progresses, though, I will see another side to my father's work and to his state of mind. Especially at the Embassy pool, where our whole family gathers on weekends and after work along with my father's colleagues, I pick up the mixed feelings my father has about his work and the U.S. Vietnamese mission. On the one hand, my father admires the dedication of his Vietnamese colleagues—actors, newscasters, propaganda writers working on the radio programming—but the cynicism of all the Agency men as they sit around the gleaming turquoise pool hidden from the racket of the torn-up city is blatant and steaming. While the Ambassador is making big pronouncements that the South will still win the war, the CIA men are tracking the steady southward progress of the Viet Cong and the North Vietnamese. In their swim trunks, they drink beer and take dips in the pool and carry on like stalwart American true believers, while joking about how many days they've got left in country. And my father is right in there with them. He has a new tone in his voice—one of bald cynicism about the American mission.

My mother complains sometimes to my father about the nastiness of the men—she insists that our country was trying to do good. I'm sure my parents talked incessantly about the military situation, and my mother must have had to support my father mightily as he coped with a deteriorating and increasingly baffling and outraging work environment, but I was not party to these conversations. What I saw was a woman bent on helping as many people as she possibly could before all hell broke loose.

Sweating through my batik dress, I pass through the gate in the concrete wall, step across the courtyard and into the villa where we are living. It is pure relief to stand for a moment in the entrance hall with its beautiful black and white tiled floor and soaring ceilings, just feeling the cool air conditioning swish over me. Then I hear the women and the babies and I smile.

In the living room, as on many other days, five or six American women from the embassy are sitting or standing, all of them bouncing babies on their laps or jiggling them in their arms. My mother looks up, "Oh, Sara, there you are!" She looks as happy as I've ever seen her. She holds a beautiful little girl against her bosom and my mother's face is like a spring bouquet. It is as if she holds a bundle of forsythia, daffodils, tulips of such quantity and abundance the blooms are spilling free. Her eyes spark with delight, her body radiates joy.

"Come! Hold little Anh!" As she places the baby in my arms her eyes shine into mine like those of a loving angel offering me the greatest of gifts.

I take the little girl, the child of a Vietnamese mother and black American father, and, for a few moments, nestling her against my breasts as my mother does, I *am*, for a few minutes, *my mother*. I feel billowing within in me a love for all the babies of the world.

Little Anh is one of the orphans my mother and the other embassy women are preparing for their flights across oceans to new parents and new worlds.

My mother, like many other of the embassy wives—almost all the embassy employees are men in 1974 so the term "trailing spouses" has not yet been coined—has committed herself to helping the children orphaned by the war in which our country has played such a determinative and destructive role. It is as though the women are the corrective to what the men are doing. They are the homemade, improvised Indiana poultices and salves to the men's highly technological bombing campaigns. It seems as if there are two types of patriotism in operation: one that takes the American point of view and one that takes the Vietnamese; one that believes America can do no wrong and one that admits mistakes and tries to recompense its harms. The women are doves cooing as the hawks charge and plummet through the air.

Of special concern to the women are the orphaned mixed-race children begotten by American servicemen and Vietnamese women. These children are viewed with prejudice by the Vietnamese. Their lives were they to grow up as orphans in Vietnam would be doubly hard. The women feel a particular and heightened sense of obligation to get these children out of the country as expeditiously as possible. Anh, one of these children, is special to my mother as she would be adopted by friends of our family. In fact, the adoptive parents are the teachers who took me in when I was in crisis at boarding school in Japan. They saved her daughter; she would save a daughter for them.

Saigon is weary and our country on the verge of defeat now in the summer of 1974, but my mother is pure heart and vigor and drive. This city of clamor and reek and begging sadness is the post to which her government has assigned her, and she has armed herself to conquer the enemy—her enemy. Baby-tending is just one thing she does as the coordinator of the embassy social services group. If she is part contented cow offering her rich and plentiful milk to all the hungry babies she can find, every day now she is also a hurtling force, whipping around obstacles in the cluttered roads, racing to rescue an abandoned child, crossing town to fetch ointment, hustling to a meeting about a twelve-year-old prostitute with an undefined sickness. She flies up to Can Tho to bring three injured orphans to Saigon for treatment. She collects the onion skins and mango peel garbage from the Embassy villas to feed orphanage pigs. She checks out an East European orphanage director. She teaches exhausted nurses at the hospital, where patients sleep under each other's beds, how to exercise the limbs of amputees and those with napalm burns. She serves tea to the young Canadian woman who runs houses for street girls. She hands a Catholic sister and a Buddhist nun fistfuls of dollars for rice for homeless widows.

I feel a surge of pride as I watch her these days charging around Saigon in her old tan skirt and the British sandals, now worn and cracking, that she bought as a rare indulgence on my parents' first CIA tour in Hong Kong. She is living her beliefs. *Muster your courage. Keep going. Any difficulty may be tackled. Even the most onerous opponent may be vanquished through determination.*

Over the years, I have watched my mother exercise the legs of Chinese tots with polio, spoon-feed disabled veterans, arrange masturbation services for paraplegic men, massage the disease-gnarled, toe-less feet of people afflicted with leprosy, all with equanimity and optimistic cheer. To Lois Taber, helping others is what you do with life. I remember how, when we left Holland, the women at the embassy gave my mother a silver plate engraved with the words, "Every post should have a Lois Taber."

Two years from now, in my first job as a social worker I will be assigned casework with a teenage mother named Leona whose named suited her perfectly. Her husband had dumped her with a couple of preschoolers, she had a two-bit job as a waitress and could barely keep macaroni in the bowls, but her defense of her children was ferocious. My mother at this time of her life, too, is leonine. I like this picture of my mother best. The way she held herself, gold-furred and shining. This is the emblem of Lois before the tumult: the lioness of Saigon.

A deep and abiding pleasure fills me as, across the airy, vaulted room, my mother chatters with the other women, absorbed in her life, bouncing little Anh on her knee. She is separate from me, and happy, and this gives me a deep and freeing pleasure. We are each independent beings and each whole. I feel as though I am a young lioness gaining her stride.

My mother, in Saigon, it might be said—especially in light of what is soon to come—is at the apex of her life. She is truly flourishing in this beleaguered country. She has a boy and a girl almost grown. She has a kind and elegant husband. She has achieved the American woman's primary feat—produced a lovely family. Though her husband hasn't risen in the spy service as far as she'd have liked, it is due to his nobility—her outrage about his having been wronged she holds at bay, his job is secure and offers good retirement benefits. She has lived in countries all over the world. She has ranged as far from Henryville as a girl deserves to dream of. She is doing the good works that make her feel worthwhile, and she's living a solidly middle-class life. Her children are getting degrees from good colleges. She feels very lucky. She can go to a cocktail party and hold her own with the fanciest of them. What can go wrong?

Things can. A woman can break. Even an industrial strength Indiana worker girl.

It is so infinite, this endeavor to discern why and how things unfold as they do: where a person thrives and where she breaks, and how this comes to pass. What occurs seems, in the end, almost inexorable. As though a life has its own agenda apart from the one living it.

I've scrabbled and floundered endlessly, trying to identify the prime mover behind the upcoming turns in my mother. Along the way I chanced into a description of human experience in Greek mythology that offered me some consolation. Therein, the destiny—including the life thread, portions of happiness and misfortune, and the final moment of doom—of every human being was preordained and controlled by the Moirai. The Moirai were sometimes represented as three Fates—Clotho-the-Spinner, Lachesis-the-Allotter, and Atropos-the-Unturnable—who were seen to have the person in hand.

The notion of destiny has helped me to a story of what so often has seemed inexplicable. Another line of thinking I've happened on is that, in addition to a powerful, determining external force, each life has its own trajectory vesseled within it, each contains its private weather. Some people seem to lope along in tranquil flatlands while others, like my mother, trek the extremes—the mountains, the poles. These last have certain tendencies—needs for control, quick-lit minds and emotions—that render their relations electric: conflictual and demanding perhaps, but passionately affectionate and warm. This sort of up-down flashing life feels correct to them. They can negotiate the pressure changes.

And then, somehow, for some of these, due to murky forces—some dazzling interplay of psyche, chemistry, and event, perhaps—the pace speeds and a new rhythm gets going.

They suddenly shift movements, like a symphony from capriccioso to crescendo.

At these mystifying instants, the measure on the Beaufort scale ticks from every day's light breeze to strong gale. The sea draws back from the continent, gathering force. The fighter jet opens its hatch, lets loose its bomb. The drumbeat starts up. The arteries begin to fill. The chemicals in the Bunsen burner start to bubble their toxic interplay.

**8**

8

# THE FLAPPING OF WINGS

I travel back to Minnesota at the end of the summer, chastened by the tragedy in the Saigon air and by the injured people hobbling down the sidewalks, but also uplifted from the infusion of my mother's confidence and high spirits. I've soaked in her sense that a woman can make a difference. A woman, through love and care and her own native strength and willpower, can take on, confront, counteract, defy, and triumph over the destructive forces in the world. And four decades on, I know even more how much she passed on to me: the capacity to face the very hardest things, to refuse their force, and thrust past them.

My junior year at college, from my side of the Pacific, starts smoothly. My mother writes to me tales about the babies, especially baby Anh. "The Embassy women are getting nutritious food to the orphanage and she's gained three pounds!"

I am sitting on the couch in a friend's borrowed house in Washington. My mother has recently flown from Saigon to deliver three tiny orphans to their new families and I've flown to meet her here in Washington for a brief visit. She's described with delight the sight of the American parents bursting into tears as she passed their new babies into their arms. But there is something else in her. She now does something that sears itself into my memory:

She is talking on the telephone in the borrowed living room and I listen to her speak into the receiver. "Why weren't you in West Virginia? That was our agreement. It was your job to be there." Her voice has the scolding, imperious tone that makes me cringe whenever I hear it. Having been its target in the past, I smart for the person at the other end of the line.

There is a long silence as my mother listens to the person's answer.

At the end of the call, she says, "Yes, I'm very sorry, but still, you should have been at the farm. That was our agreement." She doesn't sound sorry at all. Her voice remains stern and punitive, and, though I don't know precisely what is going on, I hear the frightening wing-flaps that herald one of my mother's take-offs, and a heavy stone of dread drops in my belly.

While my parents were in Vietnam my family still owned an old, broken down farm in West Virginia near Berkeley Springs—a weekend getaway for my parents who loved the country. We'd enjoyed going there when I was in high school to walk in the meadow and plant vegetables and fix up the one-story house with four rooms that had "grown like topsy," as my mother said, while some previous owner had tried to eke out a living. There were a couple of outbuildings with rusting farm equipment and tools to sort through, and hikes around the nearby pond. The main problem with the place wasn't the rustic simplicity and mosquitoes which were its hallmarks, but the fact that the neighbors stole anything my parents installed or left there: the new stove, the water pump, the tools. We actually saw our stove in the kitchen of the neighbors when we dropped by at the end of one weekend visit. My father laughed afterward while my mother stomped around. The neighbors were an old-time West Virginia family. I remember when we stopped in their living room seemed very shabby. The stuffing of the chairs was poking out in clumps and everything was an ugly brown. Our house down the dirt road was also shabbily furnished, but our shabbiness was, in fact, a kind of luxury, a lark, while this was the shabbiness of poverty.

To stand in the living room of this West Virginia couple was to peer into a different world, into a different type of mind. The husband was lanky and had almost no teeth. The one conversational remark I recall with accuracy came from the wife, who wore faded, shapeless housedresses and a peaked look of strain and bruising around her eyes. She explained to us, seated in one of the sloping, mouse-eaten chairs, "I'm not doing so well. The doctor says my bowel is wrapped around my ovary." I remember being struck that my family was strangely at the mercy of this couple—my parents had to be solicitous toward them lest they do more harm. Furthermore, the couple was, in a strange and ironic way, our protection against worse thievery and vandalism in that wooly neck of the woods. Interactions with the duo shed a new light on my parents: educated, sophisticated people, yet powerless against the actions of a pair with a completely different worldview, people, in fact, with a profound ignorance but uncanny canniness.

The consequence of this situation was that, when my parents were assigned to Vietnam, they hired a young, recently married Bethesda couple to house-sit while they were abroad.

It was the husband of this house-sitting couple to whom my mother was talking. What had elicited my mother's punitive tone was this: The young couple had had a baby while my parents were in Saigon and the wife, the husband explained, had found the isolation of the farm terribly hard, so they had come back to Bethesda for a while. The wife's family was in suburban Washington, and she could get some help with the baby on visits there. Any person, almost certainly, would feel desperate if stuck with a little baby out in that scrubby countryside with just the pump-stealing family down the road for company. My mother should have known this sort of loneliness better than anyone. When I was born, after all, she had plunged into a deep depression, partly because she was isolated, far from anywhere she'd ever known. But sometimes hardship can turn a person hard toward others who've shared the same brand of trouble, and my mother could be competitive about hardship. She might have thought to herself, "You don't have a clue what isolation and depression are."

What had transpired was this: At the end of their respite in Washington, when the Bethesda couple and their infant had set out to return to West Virginia in their Volkswagen bug, they had been merging from River Road onto the Beltway and had smashed into, or been smashed by, another car. The wife had been killed. The baby was in the ICU. My mother was speaking with the husband, who had been at the hospital for days. He had some injuries, but would recover. While my mother was speaking to him, he was holding vigil, to see if his baby daughter was going to survive.

"Mom, how *could* you?" I ask, having picked up the gist, when she gets off the phone.

"There's no excuse," she says. "We were paying them to be at the farm during the week and it was the middle of the week."

I am dismayed. Filled with cold stone, my gorge rising. How could my mother do this? Say these things?

For years I groped for answers:

Maybe my mother simply lacked all empathy for the house-sitting couple.

Maybe—trying to cast my mother's behavior with more hope—she was so saturated with empathy and sorrow by this time in her life, all sense had fled. This seemed possibly somewhat true, but didn't satisfy...

Perhaps in my mother's mind, if the couple had only been at the farm as they should have been, the whole thing wouldn't have happened. In her eyes, catastrophes were always, in some way, the fault of the victim—and the behavior that wrought the disaster could be rectified through scolding and punishment. After all, she'd been taught this by her mother as a little girl back at the forestry. This notion rang a little closer to true.

Taking the last construal further, this castigating outlook might have been my mother's strange way of explaining the sad or inexplicable, and maybe of asserting power over catastrophe. If you live in a swirling world where arbitrary and harmful mishaps occur, and you are a determined someone like my mother, maybe it is easier to assume people always have control over what happens to them—to believe people made a mistake when bad things happen—rather than acknowledge the possibility of rotten luck or arbitrariness in life. The latter would be tantamount to seeing oneself as a victim, to waving the white flag of defeat. This would have been insupportable to my mother. Surely one could control the world if one were responsible and good enough, if one had enough integrity.

But I couldn't escape it. There was also that something else about my mother—that something more: the mad, punitive, tyrannical woman who would suddenly take over my mother's body when disasters befell or nearly befell people. While most often my mother was the first to rush to the rescue when people were hurt and would aid them with calm efficiency, once in a while, she became an electric bolt and lashed out at the injured. I don't know how often this occurred. I'm sure I've blocked some incidents out and don't know of others. Perhaps there really was a loose connection in her brain. Perhaps a chaotic fury would simply suddenly rise up in her. The Fates would seize her.

Another possibility: maybe my mother had seen so much bodily harm in Saigon by this time that a Beltway accident seemed minor in comparison. I could only, ever, guess at my mother's internal workings.

Or maybe there was something, some piece, I didn't know.

In any case, for me, the daughter, hearing the impinging harshness of my mother's voice in response to tragedy was itself frightening, a kind of tossing into an arbitrary world. Maybe, with your defenses, in trying to keep the world righted, you always create what you fear. My mother kept the world straight and clean for herself while making it very dirty for her daughter. From all of this, I was left with an indelible image: of a Volkswagen crushed at the side of a Beltway on-ramp, with dark-hearted, winged spirits swirling around the accident scene. And I was also left with a lump of fear in my gut: make one false move and you will be crushed—and then immediately afterward you will be knifed, too. My mother could climb on. Sometimes, out of the blue and arbitrarily, she seemed to go for blood.

Aside from adding to an ever-accumulating fear of my mother's capacity for sudden wrath, and of the peril of imperfection, I came away from this overheard phone conversation with a Beltway phobia I'd struggle with for years.

This strange streak of wild blaming out of the blue was an omen.

## "I THOUGHT I WOULD DIE"

These, I imagine, were my mother's thoughts in the spring of 1975:

*I thought I would die. I thought I would die. Saigon almost finished me.*

## THE EXODUS

It is during the third quarter of my junior year that I receive a call from Saigon.

I'd arranged to spend the winter term of my junior year in Minneapolis, away from the college, doing an independent study on death and dying. I was swept up in the notion that Americans denied the reality of death and had seized an opportunity to study with a theologian who admired and taught the work of Elisabeth Kubler Ross. Though I'd been protected from most Vietnamese realities, I suspect that the wounded men I'd seen on the streets and the scarred look in the eyes of the women hustling along on the sidewalks played a part in this choice. I'd thrown myself into my reading and the tutorials with my mentor with my usual compulsiveness—that capacity for devotion passed down on the maternal line.

In spite of the fact that I knew, from brief exposures to the news, that matters were coming to a head in Saigon, my father had been so reassuring in his letters and on a brief visit to me at college—while acknowledging that the American presence in Vietnam was going to end, he said it would still be a long time—that I thought little of what might be unfolding there on the ground. My parents were almost too good at offering me independence as well as protection and freedom from worry.

I am back on campus for spring quarter and one of my dorm mates calls out, "Hey, Sara, you have a phone call. I think it's from far away." I go out to the phone perched on the wall of the dormitory's long hallway. There is no privacy; anyone can overhear the conversation. It is my father on the end of the line.

I am blithe, assuming he's just calling for a luxurious rare check on me.

"Your mother is being evacuated to Taipei," my father says. "I've been deemed essential so I'm staying on. But don't worry. The embassy has everything under control. We'll both be fine. We'll both be home soon..."

It takes a moment for this to register. I stutter, "You mean we're getting out?"

My mother gets on the phone now and says, "Don't worry, Sweetie. We'll be fine. This too shall pass..." Her voice is higher than usual and I sense a tiny tremor, but the forced bravery in her voice makes me overlook this. She's a spy's wife, an expert at obfuscation.

I get off the phone, finally having absorbed the basic message, filled with adrenaline and even a sense of thrill. I tell my friends, "You won't believe this. My mom is being evacuated from Vietnam! The war is finally ending!"

I am so caught up in the drama of it that I don't even have

the sense to be much concerned about my parents' lives—a concern that would make sense if I thought a little harder. Wisps of fear do briefly pass though me that night as I lie on my bed in the dark with my eyes open, but both of my parents, practiced through the years, are skilled at conveying a sense of confidence that they have everything in hand, that everything will be okay. Threats can be thwarted.

It is only when my parents arrive back on American soil a month or so later that I'll hear the full story of what transpired for each of them. Or almost the full story.

It was about three weeks before the famed exodus of the helicopters from the U.S. embassy roof that my mother, with other American dependents, was evacuated to Taipei.

I gripped that same phone in the dormitory hall a couple of days after she was evacuated, as my mother told me over the crackly line from Taipei, "When your father took me to the airport and made me get on that plane without him and leave him there, I thought I would die." She immediately covered up her worry, again, by saying the Embassy had a plan for him. But, of course, stranded there in Taipei, though she didn't tell me this, she was terrified. Who knew how the end would come and how the remaining Americans would get out of the country. What would happen to her dear Charlie?

Back in Saigon at this time, while everyone in the American mission knew the exodus was just days away, and despite the ongoing evacuation of dependents, the ambassador was still operating under an illusion that the situation might be saved— and making proclamations to this effect. When, on April 29th, the airport was bombed by the North Vietnamese, Ambassador Martin finally agreed to begin "Operation Frequent Wind," the evacuation of all U.S. personnel in the country. Plans had not been made, however, for the evacuation of my father and his crew of Vietnamese CIA employees.

The whole of "House Seven," the pseudonym for the clandestine radio station my father ran with two other CIA officers, had, by this time, been moved to Phu Quoc Island off the south border of the country where the ostensible plan was that they would continue beaming propaganda to undermine the enemy. My father, his colleagues, a radio communicator, their Vietnamese employees and all the members of their extended families—a total of 1300 people—had moved to an abandoned American military camp where my father and the others raced to set up adequate housing and a working operation. The plan was that they would continue working until it was no longer possible. If the end came, my father and his colleagues were determined that they would evacuate all the employees who had devoted themselves to their particular arm of the American mission. In contrast to the actions of some American officials of the past, they were determined not to abandon those who had devoted their lives to American goals—and whose lives would be in jeopardy if left behind.

As events transpired during the chaos after Ambassador Martin finally agreed to a U.S. evacuation, there was no plan for the evacuation of the House Seven group, either the Americans or the Vietnamese. When the communicator finally got through to the embassy on April 30th, he was told "Get out any way you can." My father and the others were, in fact, abandoned in Vietnam when the helicopters took off from the embassy roof.

By swift thinking and mad scrambling, my father and his colleagues managed the exodus of the entire House Seven crew, by contacting an American freighter. Ironically, they departed Vietnam under South Vietnamese gunfire. The Vietnamese being left behind were no longer pleased with their American allies.

The freighter was loaded like a pilgrim ship with people crammed together sleeping on deck, and giant pots of food cooked by the sailors. It was not comfortable quarters, and two babies were born on board, but everyone survived the five-day journey to Guam, where the Vietnamese employees and their families were housed until they were resettled safely in the U.S. As soon as the House Seven crew was allotted quarters, my exhausted father made his way to Taipei.

My mother, meanwhile, had had little idea of what was transpiring. The communiqués from my father had been terse, sparse, few and far between. All she knew for a long while was that my father had been left in a country taken over by the enemy. She had trudged along in a clanging, bustling Taipei—no longer recognizable as the bedraggled city of thirteen years before—heartsick and wrung, worries running amok, with no way to save anyone. She smoked a pack a day—she'd resumed the given-up habit when she got to Saigon—she bought bottles of wine, she talked to the two other women evacuees billeted in the little house with her, killing time until the evening when the men might possibly call—if, that is, they were okay.

"I was so worried about your father in Taipei," my mother said in May, at the end of the great American debacle, "the only thing I could eat was mashed potatoes." My mother could have lived in a hole along the Ho Chi Minh Trail, but, in her mind, my father was not spun of the same stuff. She was burlap. He was silk. He had shown himself made of pretty sturdy silk, as it turned out. Her relief when she finally held him in her arms again was beyond expression.

My father's odyssey—the arduous efforts to house everyone on Phu Quoc, to get everyone fed, to obtain medical care for those who needed it, and then to locate and hail an American ship and convince its captain to take 1,300 people on board—became *the story* my mother told about Vietnam. My modest father was not one for self-aggrandizement, but his experience on Phu Quoc, and the trauma leading up to his departure from Saigon, stayed in his bones, and was one aspect of his career of which he was unambivalently proud. He wrote a book about it toward the end of his life. The greater CIA, too, heralded the House Seven exodus as one of the noble outcomes of the ill-fated war. My father eventually received a medal—which he could never talk about in public—for his role in the successful evacuation.

What was not mentioned was what my mother had experienced around the time of her own evacuation from Saigon. The men, as usual, rather than their devoted wives, received all the credit. The women, the services they provided and sacrifices they made, and the terrors they, in particular, experienced, were not even noticed, much less acknowledged. It was as though they were minused out.

My mother was still trembling when I finally saw her in person in late May. I assumed the tremor was a residue of the terror about my father's safety. I was so happy to see my mother and to have her back. I didn't know "back" can be a misnomer, that "return" can be misdirection.

Stateside, my mother soon transformed their harrowing experience into an entertaining story. This was one of my mother's ingenious adaptations to the stresses of her unusual life: she could translate any mishap into comedy. Funny misery stories were one of my family's specialties. She told hilarious tales about lice and worms and near-misses all the time. The story of my father's escape from Phu Quoc became a merry tale my mother told at dinner parties. After recounting my father's chancy odyssey, she'd say of her anxious waiting, "All I could eat was mashed potatoes," making a funny face, and everyone would laugh.

# DOGS

*Grief on grief accumulates.*
– Euripides
  *Trojan Women*

"Hey Mom, are you going to get a dog? Why don't we go look at some puppies?"

I assume this idea will make my mother giddy like the thought of dogs always has in the past. Williamsburg, Virginia, seems like the perfect place for a dog.

All is green in my parents' new landing place. Green and fecund and pungent with swampy trees and low-hanging moss. The air smells of wax and honey. It smells of humus and bayberry and pines. Deer munch grass at dusk, aluminum rowboats clunk in ponds. Young men in khakis run in the woods, shooting deer and hiding from each other in mounds of leaves. Men, my father's men, hurry through the nearby town in small posses, laying clues, practicing their stealing and listening.

My parents are now living in an old brick farmhouse at "The Farm," a nickname for Camp Perry, the spy training base near colonial Williamsburg where my father has been "put out to pasture," as he wryly puts it. The creaky, roomy, slightly ramshackle farmhouse my parents are allotted is set alone, a friendly-looking homestead in a large lawn, backed by forest through which you can see no other houses.

My parents arrived home from Vietnam frayed and shaken, and Camp Perry—despite its grey mission—seemed an ideal salve. The perfect place for my parents to heal—from whatever they'd seen in Saigon. If it was possible to heal from such things as they had seen. Williamsburg was the south, life was slow, the house was roomy, and both of them had satisfying work, not so pressured as in Washington. My father was learning to make training films with the new camcorders and putting recent recruits through their paces, having them practice using aliases, wearing wigs, laying trails, planting clues, reconnoitering dead drop spots. While not so interesting as work abroad, this training job was not fraught with large moral questions. My father's conscience was enjoying a welcome rest, which was also a respite for my mother. While tourists watched candles being dipped and muskets shot in the make-believe village of colonial America, my father and his crew made believe they were stalking Russians or Chinese or Latin American communists behind the silversmith or in the printer's shop where sealing wax and fake parchments of the Declaration of Independence were sold. Maybe all the world is make believe.

While my father and his students joshed, engaged in fakery, and blundered, my mother, meanwhile, was a white-tailed deer confidently stealing carrots from Virginia gardens. She was satisfied and plump with mess hall breakfasts of scrapple and sausages and with lip-smacking work. Having put herself on her usual demanding diet of helping and teaching, she was trilling, "I am of use!" This time she was providing physical therapy to Eastern State Hospital's institutionalized children with autism, encouraging them to sing instead of curl like fists, to swing instead of bang their heads, to look at her sideways and flash brief grins as she gently moved their tender legs. To fulfill that other inner urge in her—she had gotten herself a job at a Catholic girls' academy where, Unitarian that she was, she led her classes in prayers that requested her plaid-skirted charges to be good human beings by obeying the golden rule. She told them about Taiwanese orphans and people with leprosy in far away Borneo. "Do unto others," she always said, "Think of your fellow man. Amen." The nuns loved Mrs. Taber and she loved all those eager girls in their plaid uniforms.

Afternoons and evenings after work, my parents tended the luxuriant garden my mother had planted, and my mother counted her Unitarian blessings. Her children were safe, her husband worked a mere stroll away, she had good work, life's pace was slowed and productive.

A dog, it seems to me, visiting them from college, would be the perfect final touch to my parents' new life. "When you come home from work, unlike anyone else in the house, dogs are always happy to see you," my mother has always said.

All dog owners say this about their dogs, but if ever my mother was feeling low, just the sight of a dog on the street could perk her up. She'd be chanting to me, "Oh, Sara, you should have seen the Labrador puppy I saw today. It had a stuffed zebra in its mouth. Cutest thing you've ever seen!" It is striking how the low-spirited who are endowed with the right genes can be filled to the nodules at the ends of their noses and to the tips of their tails with a cooing contentment, in which everything else, the whole world, is forgotten—at the sight of a dog. It is a gift, this glee in puppies.

Also, for my mother, the key to happiness was another being to look after.

My mother had had four dogs over the years. Her first canine companion was a regal, pedigreed Dutch Labrador retriever. In Borneo she'd come by an orphaned terrier-like mongrel named Buchoi for "Spot." In Tokyo she bought me a self-possessed Corgi, but since I was off to college, this short-legged force attached primarily to her, and in Saigon she acquired the strangest member of the animal kingdom I had ever seen.

The fact that my mother could take the creature she found in Vietnam into her heart indicates the extent of her generosity, or the indiscriminacy or the depth of the hunger of her dog-love. For this was a dog that looked like a rat. A gaunt Alice in Wonderland creature that resembled a miniature deer, shrunk down 100 times; you could hold the little being in two palms. Moreover, it was bald, and a leaper. It sprang from tiled floor to sofa, to armchair, light as air, as if winged—a mix of Mexican jumping bean, circus performer, and canine aeronaut.

My mother had had to give up each of her dogs due to cross-ocean moves, and each of these canine handovers tore my mother's insides. She wept harder with each loss. When my father left Saigon with his crew to Phu Quoc Island—my mother had by that time already been sent to Taiwan—they spoke during a rare phone call about what my father should do with little Jenny. My mother agreed that they might as well give her to the guard. Both of them knew there was a good chance that he, or someone else, would eat her.

I assume now that my idea of a dog will make my mother's eyes light up like a little girl's, but instead they flash dark. For a vanishing instant, she looks stricken. Her voice is tight, commanding, fierce, and final.

"I am never getting another dog again."

A steel object strikes my insides from the force of my mother's intense vehemence, but she immediately turns away and tells me to wash the lettuce for the salad and I hurry to rinse the romaine.

In theory, I might have taken close note of my mother's absoluteness, as a caring daughter, and wondered what caused it. Or, as a young woman striving to establish her own life, should I have been expected to be that tuned into my mother?

# GOOD FAIRY

My college boyfriend is enchanted.

When he arrives at the storybook Camp Perry house, already entranced by having been closely questioned by the guard at the base entrance in what seems to him very espionage-ish way, my mother is waiting for him like a fairy godmother in an apron.

We enter through the back door into the kitchen where my mother has waiting a couple of quiches fresh out of the oven, a colorful salad tossed from all the vegetables she's grown in her huge garden out back, and a chocolate pie. She's gone all out. She took a dislike to my previous boyfriend but what she's heard about this one makes her disposed to like him, and it turns out she does.

To my New Englander chum, from a big family where there is never quite enough food on the table, just to look at the bounty laid out on my mother's kitchen counters is miraculous. Perhaps Indiana and New England farmers have different views of provision.

To Peter, my mother seemed the most gracious, welcoming and generous hostess he'd ever encountered. That first meal, taken leisurely on the porch, was just the beginning of the treats my mother had in store. There was a trip to a colonial tavern for brunch, a ride in a clanking old Camp Perry rowboat, a visit to Jamestown. There were walks in the woods, a visit to the glen where fawns gamboled at dusk, and fabulous meal after fabulous meal. A Chinese hot pot, a boeuf bourguignon, a Malaysian curry. My mother had discovered *The Spice Cookbook*, and she'd run with it.

My mother's generosity did not stop at food and outings. The other ingredient that nourished Peter that first visit was my mother's attentiveness—what I sometimes experienced as the third degree. As we sat around the long table on the porch overlooking the bucolic scene, she sprinkled him with questions, her eyes sparkling with interest. What was his favorite subject in college? Where did he want to live? Where did he see himself in ten years? What sort of job was he hoping for? Wildlife biology? Oh, she had some ideas about that. What about trying this—or that? She knew someone...She had a friend...Oh, how exciting! He could go to England and look at hedgehogs, or to Greece for the voles...He'd never had this kind of attention before. Again, five children is different on a pair of parents than two. With just two, a parent has energy left over—for others' children...It was delicious to him. He lapped up all my mother plied him with.

I don't know where my mother got it from—this avid affiliative instinct—whether, as the ninth child she'd had to cultivate charm and flattery to get anywhere in her family, or whether she'd been a quick study in protocol at the Foreign Service Institute, or whether she was born gregarious—but she took a keen interest in the lives and well-being of everyone she met. Perhaps she engaged in this attention out of courtesy in part, but it was also utterly sincere. She loved people. She could sense people's troubles and had a compulsion to solve them. Even when she was desolate, she could summon up this interest in other human beings. It was like a ready pocket handkerchief for soothing her woes. Furthermore, she just adored hearing about people's lives. Young people especially interested her, and she loved to draw out their dreams. She seemed to live vicariously through each and every one of them, imagining the best that could come of who they were, the bliss and boon their lives could offer them. She had an unstoppable imagination when it came to people's potential and promise, perhaps because she was so driven herself. This ambition of hers was a gift to all my friends, few of whose parents matched my mother in interest in talking to young people, though it was ultimately a curse to herself. She was so ambitious I'm not sure she could ever be fulfilled.

My mother seemed to me in fine fettle at Camp Perry. What was causing my mother to flourish there despite what she'd been through, I think—a happiness my boyfriend picked up and feasted on along with her attentive interest in him and her actual culinary feasts—was the garden. Having a big, flat piece of ground to dig up and poke seeds into, soil to sink her hands into, I suspect, transported her straight back to her childhood in Indiana. A part of her, despite all the glamorous travels, the clandestine thrills of spying, the privileges associated with embassy life, felt she'd finally come home, returned to her cow-loving Guernsey self. Peering through the porthole back at that Camp Perry era, she appears to me more at home there, perhaps, than at any other time of her life. Virginia had "good black dirt," as she relished saying, and grasping those plump, firm tomatoes and smooth, perky cucumbers and crisp, crunchy beans just made her insides light up.

My parents' Camp Perry era seemed a time out of time, a magic limbo. Certain places *can* heal, perhaps. But the fact is, now and for the next decade I am not living near my mother. I only see her in glimpses, on treasured, brief visits home, when both of us are caught up in the pure pleasure of being reunited. I really don't know what's going on inside her. And hurts can go underground. A dragon can retreat to its den. Once in a while, though, out of a stream of mostly pleasant interactions would shoot a wayward one, fierce and angry, and inexplicable, like a sign of something roiling.

# CALIFORNIA

I am setting out for California today with my brother and Peter. We are leaving from Williamsburg, in two cars. The two men are headed for college at U.C.-Santa Cruz and I am bent for graduate school at the University of Washington. Peter and I are driving my Karmann Ghia and Andy is driving his Rabbit. We are 23, 22, and 21. We are fizzed up with our adventure. We're beating it for freedom, topped up with American "Go west, young man!" spirit.

We are moving in and out of the kitchen lugging duffel bags and backpacks and gathering food for the road.

"Don't drive over 50," my mother says, as we slap together peanut butter sandwiches.

"Don't you dare forget your traveler's checks anywhere," she says as we pile apples into a paper bag. "If anyone finds them, the money's gone."

"Don't camp next to any scruffy-looking people. You never know what they might do," she says as we begin hauling our Indian bags and knapsacks and battered suitcases to the cars.

"Don't look at the scenery when you're driving on those mountain roads. You could go off a cliff," she says, as I hurry back into the house for a last pit stop.

"Don't let Sara go into a gas station by herself," she says, as we mash our last duffel bag into the back of the Ghia. "You never know who could be in those gas station bathrooms."

"Stay within sight of each other at all times," she says, as we hug her and my father and get into the two cars.

"And don't let yourselves run out of gas," she says as we lean out the windows, waving as we set off.

"Mom, we'll be fine," I say, just before we pull away, but the truth is, I am frothed up with my mother's anxious carbonation, quaking by now with worry about all the terrors and dangers we're destined to encounter during the six days ahead.

Peter says, as we pass through the guard post into the real world, "Do you think we should just check into the hospital now?"

Two miles down the road, before we even get to the highway, the gas cap on my brother's car flies off into the roadside scrub. We stop the cars and hunt all around the trees and bushes, but we can't find it anywhere. Andy stuffs a brown paper bag into the gas hole and we head for the highway.

It takes me until Ohio before I begin to calm into the groove of the drive and begin to suspect that we might live through it.

# A DAUGHTER'S HAIR

On a visit to my mother from Seattle, where I am now, completing my social work training, my mother says, the minute I come in the door, "Sara, what have you done to your hair?"

This is the same question I receive upon every arrival. My mother is like clockwork. Within a few minutes of my return to her life—from California, from Patagonia, from Washington state, she predictably says:

"Oh, Sara, you've got to get a haircut."

"You look all ragged. We've got to do something about your hair."

Or: "I'll pay for you to get a haircut tomorrow."

I always bristle. I can hear her thoughts ranting in my own head:

*Look at her. Look at her. That hair. That hair. She's got to get it cut. She'd look so much better without those bangs. Why did she ever have those cut? She looks cheap now. She used to be elegant when she had it cut my way, back in Holland. She needs it shaped around her face, and a part on the side to give her face some girth. And look at those jeans. She always buys her clothes too big. Will she ever learn to buy the right size? She'd look good in some grey flannel slacks. I always offer to get her some from Talbot's but she'd rather wear those old jeans. Always jeans. She could look so smart. She's so slim like I never was. I've always had this damn gut. But she has the perfect figure...Better than Cary's, even though Barbara always bragged about her daughter's figure. Cary has that big can. I've always had a big can.*

*Now Marge, my darned sister, always had the perfect figure. She was always so long and lanky and thin. Mom loved her best because she had spunk. I never had spunk. I tried, but I was whiney. No matter how fast I ran, I couldn't keep up with Marge and Norma. I always wanted to have Marge's spunk. And Sara should have spunk. She never has had it...*

*Sara was always so sensitive, getting her feelings hurt all the time every which way. I was always tough. I had to be, with Mom worrying about the boys off at war. I was the last one, I was just a pest so I had to be scrappy. If I had a wound I had to go in the barn and lick it myself. Charlie is who Sara got it from, all that damned sensitivity. She needs to stand up for herself. People say she is so poised but she wasn't always. God, I remember those times back in Taipei when I'd have to tear her off my skirt just to get her to stand up straight and say hello to the DCM's wife. God, that was awful. That Mrs. Wilson was an awful woman. She had those girls with those permanents who thought they were God's gift and their mother, what a thing she was. Lady Bountiful, prancing around like a duchess while all the Chinese women were taking baths in those buckets in the streets. If only Sara could stand up with dignity to a woman like that. Show her who is smart and who is pretty and what*

240

*is important. Show her what the daughter of an Indiana farm girl is made of. She's not cheap goods. She's real class. She's got all those degrees now and she's got a good job, but that hair. If only she'd get it cut.*

Another perspective on hair. When I am a fledgling social worker a year later, I will take a workshop with Marianne Walters, a therapist who specializes in the mother-daughter relationship. She will propose that mothers focus on their daughters' hair, not to undermine them or to be controlling or out of narcissism, but because they think their daughters beautiful. This shifts my perspective on my mother's comments from a sense of being diminished to a sense of being cared about. I come to see that my mother focuses on my hair because she thinks I am pretty, because she envies me my thick hair, because she likes to look at me, and because she wants me to look my most attractive. She focuses on my hair both for her own vicarious pleasure, and out of a wish for the best for me. And also because, it has to be said, she likes my hair a certain way. There is some tangling here. Is my hair mine or hers?

After the Walters talk, I feel more generous. Perspective-twisting does help. But then again, when my mother and I are at our most truculent, I think, who is Medusa to tell her daughter what to do with her hair?

# THE POWER OF
# WOMEN

*Time and trouble will tame an advanced young woman, but an advanced old woman is unstoppable by any earthly force.*
– Dorothy Sayers

I am sitting on the cliff overlooking the Patuxent River beside my mother and her friend Lily. Lily is a treasured friend from back in the days before I was born, when Lily's husband and my father were both involved in the secret operation near Sagami Bay. They have known each other by now for close to thirty years.

Whenever I have the chance, I like to sidle up to, or eavesdrop on my mother and Lily when they are together because there is an intimacy and exclusivity between them, an intimacy that certainly excludes me—and so is an elixir and an intrigue. It is, of course, that I am young, in my twenties, while they are experienced, grown women and so know things beyond my reach, but it is the special synchrony between them that I sense and long to experience on my skin. They seemed to toss about secrets—if I can just catch them as they dart in the air between them.

Lily was one of those innately elegant women. Her features weren't striking in themselves. She had soft, brown wavy hair that curled around her ears—always studded loosely with the same beautifully bezeled pearls, a comfortable, strong body—she swam in the Patuxent each day, and a surprising loud voice and laugh. She sported no feature immediately obvious—no aquiline nose, sculpted thinness, or dazzling eyes—but somehow she possessed an effortless, compelling attractiveness. It is impossible to name what makes someone attractive or compelling; it just *is*. Part of it was that she was from Alabama, her father was a Methodist preacher, and she had that laughing southern grace. My mother was not a striking beauty either, but she, too, issued a pull—the way lots of late children in big families do. They'd better come up with something or give up—and lots of them devise some kind of unignorable charm. My mother didn't care about adornment—Lily, in contrast, did wear exquisite wool scarves and fine fabrics when she dressed up—but my mother could blot on some lipstick and throw on a dress, and rivet a whole dinner party with a story of going to see a portly Dutch burgher with a penchant for sausages, spinning a simple trip into a tale of belly-clutching hilarity. Somehow, they chimed, this southern preacher's daughter and this Indiana forester's kit—each transported from small American towns to the great game of the world.

Grabbing lunches and coffee over the years—snagging each other between their various tours in Mexico, Uruguay, Holland, Vietnam, and other foreign locales—they talked as though there had never been a hiatus in the conversation. They compared notes on their children—my hypersensitivity, no doubt, her daughter's underwhelming school performance and boy-craziness, my brother's Ds in the subjects that didn't interest him, her oldest son's blindness in one eye. They talked about husbands—hers who spied on Latin America and the Soviet Union, and my father, the China-tracker. They talked about the past—all those babies they'd given birth to and tended in Japan back in the days when that country was a bedraggled place just after the war. And they chewed over their own lives as women—their urge to help people, their drive for fulfillment and to make the world a better place. Lily had a social work degree and had helped lots of people, volunteering in Mexico, and now assisting others through her Methodist church. My mother had worked like a dog everywhere she went, doing physical therapy with anyone she spotted in need wherever she landed.

Lily and my mother had lived full, full lives as women by now. All their children were grown and more-or-less launched. They'd suffered and weathered plenty. Lily had had a double mastectomy way back in the middle of her children's childhoods when the whole procedure was barbaric. One child had struggled with addiction. Another had suffered a life-altering injury. My mother had soldiered through my teenage psychiatric hospitalization, my brother's near-death in a boating accident, my father's unrelenting career tortures. And there was lots more—all manner of mishaps and cock-ups along the way.

But now, perched on that cliff, the sun glowing in their hair, the wide, gleaming river flowing across their vision like life itself, two women in their fifties, they seemed at the summit of their lives.

One thing I remember crisply from that day when I was

sitting beside them at a little remove, as they chatted on the grass overlooking the river. My mother remarked to Lily, as if it were a simple, established truth, "We are now at an age when we know we can do *anything*."

# FREEDOM

*"Beauty" my mother would call me, and "Jewel of pure gold"; then she would let me go, watching her creation—her master-piece, as she said—grow smaller as I ran down the slope.*
— Sidonie-Gabrielle Colette
  *Sido*

We are at Dulles Airport. I am midway through my graduate training in social work, taking a leave to study whales with Peter, departing for Patagonia for a year and a half. My stomach is a vast emptiness with moths flying around hitting its walls. Leaving my mother, I well up. Every separation since that first one in Japan six years ago hollows my belly and mourns my heart. "Oh, Mom, I can't stand it," I say.

She says, "Oh, you know what I always say, 'I hate it when you come home because you always have to go away again.'" Then, for a moment, her voice quavers as she pulls me to her "Oh, Sweetie, it'll be okay. It'll be okay." Then she puts on her hearty voice and pulls herself up straight like a little girl bracing herself to cross into the woods. "Oh poot, Sara," she says, "It's going to be great."

She gives me another quick, tight hug, and says, "Now you go!" pushing me toward the turnstile.

Instantly then, she turns away without looking at me, and says, "Okay, Charlie, let's go." I know the tears are flowing now, and as she hustles away, hanging onto my father's arm, her head is bent, her other hand up wiping her eyes.

It is thus my mother sets me free. She's always said, "I want my children, at each age, to be as independent as they can possibly be. In case something happens to me, I want them to be able to make it on their own." Against every instinct in her, against every maternal urge to cushion, guard, and protect, she allows me to go greet my life.

As I descend the escalator with my knapsack I am sobbing— and, by the time I reach the bottom, swell with exhilaration.

# TRILLING

*Mother is to whom you hurry when you are troubled.*
— Emily Dickinson

As a twenty-something, I live a lot of places. I call my mother from Washington state, from California, from Argentina—and I will call her from Spain when I am studying Basque farmers for my doctorate. She always wants to hear everything.

I call her from social work school in Seattle. I am living in a basement apartment. It rains all the time. I am very unhappy. In three days, a package arrives: a new blouse, cookies, a note inside that says she loves me, and "Sweetie, you're doing good work. This too shall pass."

I call her from a tiny telephone office in remote Argentina where I am studying whale behavior. It is Christmas. The line is crackly and she tears up. "I want to give you a big hug," she says. "I can't stand it that you're there and we're here."

I call her from California, from my first social work job. I tell her about my crazy clients. I tell her I've got a wrenched shoulder. She tells me to alternate hot pads and cold packs and it will help. "Tell me if you need me to send you some."

My mother cares if my ear itches. Who could ever replace my mother? Who could ever replace a mother?

When I call my mother to tell her I've been accepted at three doctoral programs, her voice cracks with pleasure. "Oh, Sara, you've outdone yourself this time! Just a minute, let me tell Charlie!"

It is like the days in high school when my mother squeezed me tight after I told her I'd made the honor roll. "Oh, Sara, how marvelous! Come have a cookie and a glass of milk!" she'd trilled.

When my mother trills at what I do, my chest rises in a silent trill in tune with hers. Her pleasure and pride multiply mine. At my mother's trilling, I take wing and spin in the sky. Only a mother's pleasure can infect a daughter so.

I am my mother's product, the fresh yellow butter she has churned with her own strong arm. My hard work is hers. She is right to claim it as partly hers, to slather it on her bread. Perhaps this is true for most mothers: the butter she has made of me is much more delicious to her than the butter she has made of herself.

These moments it is as though we are descendants of an ancient female duet. We are a woman in her fifties and a woman in her twenties strolling hand in hand through meadows, sowing seeds together.

# DOORS

My mother calls me from Williamsburg with some big news.

"It's Bonn, for heaven's sake, Sara! I've got to give him this. He's sacrificed so much…"

To be offered a tour in Germany is a wonder, a luxury for a CIA officer. I'm excited for my father who adores Europe, but my stomach clenches at the same time as I think of how my mother must feel.

Several months before, when my father had put in his request for a European post from Camp Perry, my mother had told me, "Your father keeps mulling about leaving the Agency, so just for the heck of it, I'm going to apply for P.T. jobs overseas in *my* kinds of countries." I'd thought to myself, "Yay, Mom! Finally—yes, try for what *you* want!" My father had endorsed her applications too.

Then, just two days before this current call, my mother had phoned me with other news. She was exhilarated. "I never thought the Tom Dooley Foundation would come through! I've been dreaming of working for them in Nepal for years!"

"Mom, that's fabulous!" I said. I'd known of her dream of work in Nepal and I was thrilled for her. It seemed like divine justice. I could see my mother walking those beautiful terraces at the foothills of high mountains, squatting to help impoverished children. She'd said she and my father were talking about whether it made sense for her to take the job but I could tell her hopes were up.

Next my mother is saying, "Charlie says he'll quit now so I can take the Tom Dooley job, but of course he can't. He's just gotten *Bonn*, for God's sake. He deserves something good after all he's done for that place..."

"Oh, Mom, this is awful." I can see in my mind my mother's downcast eyes.

"Charlie says I can try them again in a couple of years," my mother says, "but the Tom Dooley offer won't come again. I know by now how the world works. You don't get offered your dream twice. That door's closed."

I envision in her body the shift I hear in her voice. She is gritting her jaw and looking out into the distance, bravely girding herself for sacrifice again.

# OVARIES

I've been having sharp pain. I am a social work intern now, working at a Palo Alto mental health clinic. My supervisor there sends me to her doctor, and the doctor says I have a mass on my ovary. I am 26. I call my mother, far across the Atlantic, that night. She says, "Oh, Sara! I'll be on the plane tomorrow." Hearing the warmth in her voice makes me choke up but I'm not sure I need her to come. "Wait a minute, Mom," I say. "Shouldn't we find out…" But she is gone. Rescuing is her thing, her thrill, her brilliance. Men may relish fighting for their countries. Some mothers relish sacrifice for their bodies' creations.

My parents were now posted to Bonn, enjoying the European tour with which some lucky operatives were rewarded toward the end of their careers. This time around at the embassy, my father's assignment was to monitor the activities of Russian communists on German soil. The German capital was a sedate, gracious place where drizzle clung to the air, the residents in loden coats strolled arm in arm, and the town square smelled of fresh-baked schwarz-brot.

My mother wrote me long letters about their new life. In the evenings, they took walks along the Rhine, a waterway with the dignified cool of a Shakespearean noble. On week-ends they forayed to half-timbered villages, fantasy castles, and beer-gardens decked with flowers. They joined German friends for volksmarches through stately, ancient forests, greeting passersby, as the Germans did, with the words, "Have you eaten?" Following afternoon tea with chocolatey sacher tortes that made the taste buds sigh, they raised glasses of Krombacher beer and dined heartily, with other spy couples, on roasted boar and rich venison stew.

My mother was providing math tutoring to children at the American school, taking daily German lessons at the *Universität*, and had joined German women for a class in *bauernmalerei*. She was learning to paint folk art flowers and fruits on hangars and breadboards like a nineteenth century German farm woman. Bonn seemed a perfect setting for happiness, and for about a year my parents felt as though they'd been deposited in Candyland.

A day and a half after my phone call, my mother arrived in Santa Cruz, almost halfway around the world again, to the little white half-of-a-cottage I shared with Peter on Hammond Street, breathless, ready to launch into action. She hugged me, saying, "Oh, Sara," again, shoved into our arms gifts of chocolate and German ginger cookies, and then asked what she could make for dinner. My appointment for an ultrasound was not for a few days. In the meantime, during the day, she set to work. While I commuted to my social work job, she borrowed my sewing kit, went to the fabric shop, bought a hunk of remaindered denim and a length of a blue floral quilted stuff, and sewed: a cover for the foam rubber cushion on the bench my boyfriend had made for a couch and a pillowed backrest that she suspended from the wall. She also scrubbed the entire apartment, rearranged the dish storage, and cooked nonstop, making sure she was useful every minute. To her, this was a moral obligation. To make productive use of her time was an absolute, like her other motto, "Cleanliness is next to godliness."

When I got home from work, she fluttered over me, making me sit down while she served me Indian lentils and hearty stew and bountiful salads full of bright California vegetables. She ate a lot of avocados herself: her one indulgence. They weren't easily had in Bonn. As for conversation, her mind returned, always, to my prospects, and to the worst possible scenarios. She had been through The Depression and CIA evacuations. One always had to be prepared to face, and then to tackle, and then to survive the worst. She was an anxiety goddess. She could produce little anxiety bunnies as fast as a rabbit in a field. In all arenas with which she engaged, she was nothing if not productive. Her mind leapt from one anticipated disaster to the next.

"Sara, if it's cancer and they have to take the ovary, or both ovaries, don't worry," my mother yells out, while scrubbing the toilet. "I'll take you back to Bonn and we'll go to the market and eat *kuchen* and it'll be okay." Or while we are driving to get ice cream, she'll comment, as though she's just commenting on the weather, "If you have to have a hysterectomy, don't worry. You can always adopt." I hadn't even thought about the possible fertility issues I might be facing.

Peter, who knows how my mother can stir me up, says at dinner, "Lois, the doctor doesn't even know yet..." But she brushes him off and serves us both more ice cream. She knew how these things went. She was a *mere poule* and Woody Allen all in one.

I fought the anxiety that was growing exponentially now that my mother was with me, tried to focus on my troubled patients at work, and then, at five thirty, drove, spent, over the mountain on high-speed, winding Highway 17, to my mother's bountiful helpings of vegetables and worries.

The morning of the ultrasound, my mother sat beside me in the waiting room, touching my arm, her thumb making almost imperceptible circles on my skin. I was in a torture of retention that would be humorous in a film but wasn't in the moment. I'd had to drink eight glasses of water. Then hold it throughout the 45-minute drive to Stanford Hospital. Now I had to wait another hour in the waiting room, overcome with the need to evacuate. At one point, seeing my face, a nurse came out and said I could release a little if I wished. The brief releasing was as much torture as the holding because one couldn't let go. Finally, I lay on the table, and the curt, slim Chinese doctor ran the ultrasound wand back and forth over my jellied-up, domed and distended abdomen. She slid it back and forth many times. I was counting the seconds. Finally, she said, "Okay, make use of the restroom."

When I returned, the nurse had me dress. I was so relieved

to be putting my clothes on, and to have the whole thing over with, that I didn't even think about the possible bad news to come.

But it wasn't bad news. "It is just a cyst," Doctor Li said. "It will probably dissolve itself in time."

"But," my mother sputtered, for she'd been primed for action, "Are you sure? Shouldn't it be removed?" She preferred drastic measures and throve on adrenaline.

"No, we'll keep a watch on it. In young women, these things usually go away, we find."

On the way back to Santa Cruz, my mother at first seemed deflated. Once back at the ranch, she galvanized herself and again spun into forward motion. She got herself the earliest possible flight back to Germany, saying "Charlie needs me," cleaned up all her sewing supplies, gave the house another once-over, and I dropped her at the San Francisco airport on my way to work the next day.

# CHANGE OF WOMAN

"She'll be okay. Soon she'll be as good as new," my father says, unexpectedly calling from Bonn.

Within a week of my mother's return to Germany from her rescue trip to California, *she* is in the hospital, having a mass removed from her thyroid. It was *she* who had been in urgent need of medical care, not I. (*Who*, I ask, is *who*, in this scenario?) My mother wasn't worth a fig to herself. Babies always came first—she'd never be one to obey the flight attendant and put her oxygen mask on before her baby's.

The surgery that followed drastically altered my mother's life—in more ways than one. The operation successfully removed her thyroid, but the Wiesbaden military surgeon damaged a nerve in her neck—and left my mother with unremitting pain. The medical system of the time—perhaps especially the military one—didn't care much for older women. They were dispensable. Perhaps the surgeon was hasty; perhaps he'd been distracted by a hot date he had set up for after the surgery.

Pain distorts. Furthermore, the replacement hormone my mother took thereafter never seemed to be the right dose. An already anxious, close-to-manic woman was given a stimulant. She was forever after agitated, filled with a frenetic energy. The Synthroid sped her up beyond her usual nonstop rate of productivity, to the point that I am pretty sure she never sat down to relax again.

My mother was 53 by the time of her thyroid surgery. At the same time she was undergoing this drastic flux in her thyroid production, she was in the midst of the change of life. My *mother's* ovaries were the ones of greater concern. I grasp to imagine and understand what caused the now-begun cascade of alterations in my mother. It is possible, perhaps, that a profound dosage change in two hormones at once—both thyroid and estrogen—might be experienced as a two-pronged chemical assault and set a woman into strange and turbulent waters. With hormonal shifts, subtle cognitive changes might occur also, conceivably—ones that can't be detected save for subtle and not so subtle changes in a woman's cast of mind. The composition of a woman's mind, indeed, might possibly literally alter. Add to this new, chronic, grinding pain, and a woman's personality might be forever changed.

It is said that menopause is the point in their lives when women are, in a sense, returned to themselves. With the estrogen flight, their bodies, and thus their very selves, in some senses, are cast off by the world. No longer producers of producers or of cannon fodder, no longer lusted after by men, their biological utility to others is used up. It is imaginable that this changed view from the outside could transform a sensitive woman's inside view on herself and the world. This new invisibility, the rejection a woman might accurately feel, could conceivably cause a woman to take a strange and desperate turn.

What I know is that my mother was never quite the same after she came to see me that time in Santa Cruz. Undauntable though—fighting pain, and, as ever, trying to earn her right to be in the world through unceasing work—my mother became efficiency gone amok. This year, she metamorphosed from one mother into another. Demeter, "giver of splendid gifts," with her tireless sowing, her bottomless love, her beauty and her woes, seemed to have gone under yoke.

My father predicts that my mother will be as good as new. It turns out, this will not be true.

# YOGA IN PLITTERSDORF

On a visit to Bonn, I eat a piece of earthy, nutty, dark German bread and a hunk of cheese for breakfast, watching my mother race around gathering her books for her German class while simultaneously setting up her day's tutoring on the phone. Ever since her neck operation my mother has been unable to sit down or stop doing. My mother is nothing if not fierce though, even in the face of this terrible pain that makes her face crumple and her eyes well if I inquire about how she is feeling. Sometimes when she thinks she's alone, I can see the pain shoot through her, and her face clenches, and it makes me want to weep too. Her theory is that you outrun pain, so she is like a whirlwind.

My mother has now become a spinning top; I keep wondering if she will topple. She is driving my father crazy with the vehemence of her German language study. She is at her books all the time, muttering German phrases to herself while she cooks in their kitchen in Plittersdorf, the American embassy apartment complex at the edge of Bonn. In her fifties she has come by an ability to learn languages she didn't have before. All she does is study—and tutor kids at the American school, and go to German conversation classes, and take German crafts classes, and, and...

Margaret Fuller wrote of women:

*[Men] are astonished at our instincts. They do not see where we get our knowledge, and, while they tramp on in their clumsy way, we wheel & fly, & dart & thither, & seize with ready eye all the weak points, like Saladin in the desert.*

My father begs my mother to slow down, but she can't. My mother always has been, but is even more now, all about accomplishment. On my visits to them from California, she questions me about my career, urging me to get my PhD, though I've recently gotten my master's in social work and have only just started on my clinical practice. After she feels satisfied she's got me sufficiently agitated about my prospects, she takes me to all the Christmas markets and to all the good kuchen places. We eat sacher torte and tea at breakneck speed before my mother's body starts to wriggle on her chair and we rush on.

One morning my mother mentions that she is taking a yoga class. Oh good, I think, maybe that is one activity in which she is forced to slow down and her poor body can rest. In the evening, she has guests for dinner, a gathering of German friends and American embassy people. They're all dignitaries and a little stiff, minding their diplomatic P's and Q's, praising my mother's delicious pot au feu and talking politely about NATO and the youth demonstrations down-town. After dinner, though, my mother, now with a couple of glasses of Riesling in her, proposes everyone do a little yoga. She's taking a class. She'll show them how. Wow, I think. Cool.

There's something about my mother's mix of outrageous Indiana cornpone charm, foreign-service-honed grace, and her innate ability to connect with people that makes all those formally attired Germans and those Brooks Brothers men and Talbots women get up and adjourn in the living room, scattered across the carpet with my mother at their head. My mother has flashes of reckless madness and also flashes of kooky happiness. Her ability to thus enchant people is an uncanny gift. She has everyone in her hands, like a good witch.

"We are poor indeed if we are only sane," wrote D.W. Winnicott.

"Okay," my mother says, "here we go." In her silk batik blouse and slacks, she reaches for the sky. She squats to the carpet. And everyone, in an odd parody of diplomatic politesse, follows. It's the fastest yoga you've ever seen.

## M.C.P.S

"Pop, what do you think of what the president told the Russians this week?" I ask my father, sitting with my parents after dinner.

"He's just another M.C.P.," my mother jumps in. She doesn't give my father a chance to answer. She's fallen in love with the popular feminist acronym for "male chauvinist pig" and tosses it out at every opportunity. She says over and over again, "I'm fed up with boring men. They think they know everything," referring to the men my father and mother interact with all the time at embassy parties. She's getting fed up with male self-centeredness in general, and her voice has a mix of fury and apoplexy in it these days whenever the subject of men arises. She says she's had it with male behavior. She loves the German word for "meathead" or "jackass." "All the men your father works with are a bunch of *dummkopfs*...I've had enough of all those blasted men jockeying for position, brown-nosing, back-stabbing, and strutting around. I've had thirty years of this from the Agency men and it's all a bunch of baloney...Those buffoons don't give women the time of day." I cringe at my mother's sharp vehemence with its bite of anger. I worry she'll blurt out something outrageous when someone outside the family would hear.

In a couple of decades, I'll recall my mother's ranting in Bonn and think my mother had a valid point. Menopause, I'll realize, can have negative effects, yes, but also positive ones. One of the advantages is that it can loosen women's tongues.

No longer inclined to please just for pleasing's sake, they utter the blunt truth. "Damned men," my mother has started to say on a regular basis. "They think everything they do is so important. What do they think about what we women do, for God's sake?"

Why *did* people—all of us, in fact, back then—value what men did over what my mother had done with her life? To choose just one instance: How was what the men did in Vietnam superior to what she had done there? In her calmer moments, my mother would shrug and say, "It was ever thus," but I will think as I reconsider, it was indeed outrageous how little control she or any women had had over what men did in the world.

At this point, in Bonn, I am only 26. I still really believe men are superior. "What do *you* think, Pop?" I attempt again. I am frustrated that my mother always wants to dominate and never lets me talk to my father, and I want my father's considered opinion, not her crazy knee-jerk one.

My father doesn't have time to answer. My mother declares, "The dummkopf men at the helm should be castrated. It would only take one or two."

# PARIS

"The Louvre is too god-damned big," my mother says as we walk down the immense, beauteous halls of the art-filled palace. "I don't know why you had to see the Mona Lisa, Sara. You've seen it before."

"This baguette is stale," my mother says as we sit in a brasserie, waiting for our steak-frites, the smell of French fries wafting. "I told you we should have gone to that other place I saw, but oh no, you had to have a restaurant where you could sit outside."

"You and your god-damned feet," my mother says as we walk out of a shoe store where I've been unsuccessfully trying on boots. The street is clicking with chic French women swinging shopping bags. "It's all shoes, shoes, shoes. You should have just bought those first ones I showed you. I've spent my whole life with you being obsessed about your god-damned feet."

My mother, my father, Peter, my brother, and I are taking a supposed holiday in France and Holland, but this is the opposite of a fun time. My mother can't stand anything I say or do. She is loaded against bêtes noires. She sees them everywhere, mostly in the guise of me.

By the time we reach Scheveningen in Holland, she is so pissy that she is nearly spitting at me. The minute we straggle into the little beach hotel in the dunes, we all go to bed, even though it is seven in the evening, because my mother and I can no longer stand to be in the same vicinity. Peter, Andy, and I dig peanut butter and bread out of our packs and that is dinner.

It happens to be New Year's Eve, and at midnight some kids start setting off fireworks in the street below the pension. I'm exhausted and usually dislike loud noises, but these explosions make me ecstatic.

I wonder now about my mother's spitting dislike of me on that European trip. Was my mother simply in ceaseless pain? Pain can turn anyone toward rancor. How can you be patient with a daughter obsessed with boots when you are barely coping?

But it was something more. On that journey with my mother, I simply could not please her with anything I did or said. She oozed hatred for me. Everything I did looked to her not only selfish but persecutory. The eyes darted dark and the spurts of fury multiplied and picked up their pace on that trip. Our relationship burned, presaging more to come.

Years later I will read Aristotle's *Poetics*. In that slim classic the philosopher puts forth that both literature and life are narratives made up of moments of *recognition*, moments when the truth shines—and moments of *reversal*, of setbacks when events transpire contrary to expectation and the action is thrown in a new direction. This was a moment of reversal.

# TETHERS AND UDDERS

"You can't just retire *from* something. You've got to retire *to* something," my mother says to my father at least once a day during my two-week Bonn visit. She insists, over and over, that before he retires my father has to have a plan. I bristle every time I hear my mother push her point. She sounds to me both badgering and dictatorial—and needlessly gloomy; her words are like the refrain of a dirge.

My mother rails to me about my father as we walk along the Rhine. Barges and long tour boats wend by on the gentle stream. I glance at the lovely villages of half-timbered houses and shops tumbling up forested hillsides on the opposite shore as my mother talks, looking at the ground and shaking her head.

"Here we are on his favorite continent in a country he loves and he's still not happy. Castles, history, this is his cup of tea, but nope, not happy again. It's the office, the office, and Reagan, Reagan. All the other men are getting pink-slipped. He hasn't for some reason…but he says he wants to retire early like a lot of the men are doing."

I've read back in the States that President Reagan is going all out to reduce the size of government and that pink-slipped men are getting good retirement packages.

My mother is going on. "Charlie doesn't realize he's been coddled all these years, that the office has given him a structure. A lot of men don't know what to do when they lose that. They just sit on their rumps. And if he quits, he doesn't realize that I will be giving up a lot too. All my friends, the life abroad I've cobbled together all these years. I've given up so many places. I feel like I'm one big slopping udder of places and people I've lost..."

Another day, another complaint. "Your father says I'm all speeded up since my thyroid operation. He's always wanting me to sit still. Hell if I'm speeded up. I've got things to do. I don't want to sit down. He's happy to just slump around all week and then go see cathedrals on the weekend. Well, I'm not going to slump around. I'm going to be happy, God damn it. I'm going to study my German and meet with my German ladies, and enjoy life, God damn it. I'm so tired of worrying about his happiness I could scream—or shit."

I think my mother is being very unfair to my hardworking father who has done a troubling job for the government for thirty years. He's put in his time and has a right to his freedom when he wants it. Of course, what do 27-year-olds know about careers, healthy retirement, or long marriage? And what about all the possibly sympathetic responses my mother has made to my father out of my hearing, or that I have forgotten?

My father's job in Bonn was, as usual, to keep a watch on Communists. President Reagan was obsessed with the notion that Communists were undermining him, and it was in response to a virulent spate of this that my father reached the end of his tether. Soon after the president made a showy speech accusing the Russians of fomenting anti-American sentiment in Europe, my father was tasked to look for signs of Russian backing for the sincere, homegrown, German-instigated anti-war demonstrations in Bonn. That day, outraged by yet another politically motivated use of the intelligence service, my father can swallow it no longer. He drives home to the Embassy apartment complex and announces to my mother, "Lois, I can no longer prostitute myself."

My mother's words to me, upon this news, over the phone, were: "Why does your father have to be a quitter?"

I can imagine her mind ranting as she slams the pot on the stove in the apartment kitchen and plunks in some wursts for dinner.

*I've never been a quitter... I've been telling him he's got to retire to do something, but he's just going to up and quit. He says he'll find something. That he's just got to get out. It's killing his soul, he says. Well, it's killed my soul putting up with his being-killed soul all these years. Oh, I know he's worked hard and he's been the best husband I've ever seen and I've seen a lot—he's kind and good unlike a lot of these M.C.P.s, but he's making his bed now. He's going to have to sleep in it...but so am I...*

# THE QUILT

*The mind is its own place, and in itself*
*Can make a heaven of hell, a hell of heaven.*
— John Milton
   *Paradise Lost*

"Hey Mom, why don't we make a quilt out of some of the batik," I said on the visit to Bonn, groping for something fun and neutral for us to do together.

"What a splendid idea," she said, and she went to the old Japanese tea chest and hauled out the lengths of Malaysian and Indonesian batik which both of us loved and collected back in Borneo. The piled fabrics smelled of bitter cardamom and turmeric, and sweet cloves and cinnamon. They swirled with wild colors—reds of Hornbill beaks, teals and oranges of parrot wings, pinks of orchid stamens, violets of orchid petals.

We spent an hour laying the fabrics one against the other on the bed, exclaiming. "Look at this peacock blue against that scarlet, Mom!" I said, and my mother said, "Oh, Sara, how lovely. And just look at this deep brown against that jungle green!" We were like chiming bells. We were so lightly happy—almost giddy at the prospect of a quilt pieced of festive Southeast Asian florescence spread over a bed. We were one finally again, chortling within that private, intimate, charmed sphere unique to mothers and daughters.

When I returned to the States, I bought a how-to book about quilts, and when I visited my mother again at Christmas, she said, "Here, Sara, take these three back with you and I'll keep these until you need them." She handed me three of the lengths of cloth: a multi-colored one that looked like flower petals had been crushed on it—followed by a sprinkling of tiny seeds, a brown-patterned classic in caramel, chestnut and coffee, and a third in mustard and grape. There was something a little odd in her wish to keep the other yardages with her, but I was too delighted to notice. I was off and running with my vision—which I assumed was shared.

Once back in Santa Cruz, during the few months before I headed off to my doctoral program, I set to work. I'd chosen a pattern that involved cutting out many triangles—small ones and large ones to make squares that would then be pieced together to form a cover. Evenings, after working with psychiatric emergency patients all day, I'd settle down with my pile of shapes and my needle and thread and construct fabric squares.

It was somewhat strange to be doing intense, disturbing psychiatric work in the sparkling, let's-go-to-the-beach airs of California, but such was my life in those days. It was at the hospital in San Jose that I first saw what paranoia looked like in the flesh. A grey-haired, loosely draped woman came into the clinic one day, clutching a stuffed animal so threadbare and worn it was nothing but a flattened hank of mangy fabric. She'd been picked up by the police on a street somewhere in the city, hiding behind a trash can, quaking at first and then combative, sure the police were the CIA out to get her and take her baby. She was deranged and deeply frightened, and in the examination room quick to flare if I tried to calm her by saying I didn't think the CIA was nearby. I saw terror in her, and a frightening, desperate violence. My supervisor told me to pay attention to my own instincts when with a patient. My own emotions would indicate the depth of the patient's disturbance. This woman, it was clear, would have torn out the eyes of anyone who tried to take her baby from her. Her own eyes were simultaneously vacant and too bright with conviction. I was learning a lot fast, and to come home to my pile of quilt squares was a satisfying and therapeutic evening occupation. I wrote to my mother, reporting on my progress on the quilt, and she responded that this was grand.

The quilt project dribbled along, as quilt projects often do, and it was a few years later that I discovered the pile of quilt squares tucked in a plastic bag in the bottom of a trunk. By this time I was in my doctoral program on the east coast, and I again thought it would be grounding to spend a little time working on the quilt between bouts of writing papers. I'd finished all the squares I could make with the cloth my mother had initially given me and needed to re-up my supply.

My mother was back in Washington, my father was by now retired, and my mother was going great-guns on her private physical therapy practice—a bittersweet dedication jet fueled by her resentment that my father did not have a job. I had no idea what force this resentment was building in her, how it was broiling, and, with other factors, was annealing the harsher person she'd started to become in Bonn.

I said on a visit to their Chevy Chase house, "Mom, could I have some more of that batik so I can make some more squares? I think I could make a lot of progress, and it's almost halfway done already!"

She was strangely offhand, vague in response. She nodded and then seemed to need to do something in the kitchen. For an instant, her evasion recalled to me the paranoid maneuvers I'd seen in psychiatric emergency clinic patients—the fine hairs on my arms rose—but I brushed off the sensation. When I brought the quilt up later, she said, "Sure," and promptly lost focus again. When I was about to go back to Cambridge, I asked a third time.

"I'll have to get some more batik..." she said, when she reluctantly brought out her stash of fabric. She handed me a couple more lengths of cloth, holding tight in her lap several more. "I'll keep enough for me and for Andy," she said. I had assumed the quilt was her project and mine, something we were doing together, mother and daughter. I was enjoying the making, and the making together. I hadn't given much thought to the end product or who it might go to. I assumed we might share it. I did think I might end up with the quilt in the end, though possession wasn't something I had devoted much thought to. But she had. She'd come to the conclusion that I was selfishly hogging the quilt for myself.

Perhaps there comes a time in the mother-daughter relationship when the mother gets tired of the one-way street of giving nonstop to her daughter. In any case, somehow, my mother's assumption that I assumed the quilt was for me had grown and inflated and expanded...into something I was *taking, depriving her of*, rather than something we were doing and enjoying together. And, to her eyes, I was, as usual, as the older child, trying to get something more than my brother had.

Suddenly, we needed to make three times the number of squares—in order to make three quilts. My mother went out and bought some Dutch batik in navy, and some cheap Indonesian cloth, to add to our stockpile, which had, until then, been made up solely of East Malaysian batik. The quilt project had now changed from a happy memory book of our time in Borneo into a black book, a weighing and counting affair. For my mother, it seemed, the project had transformed into a matter of protecting herself and Andy from my greediness. I had become the enemy.

There was a strain of suppressed rancor in my mother now. Joy was extinguished. She was like a squirrel hiding her nuts from a fox—me—bent on stealing her stash in order to starve her over the winter. The woman with the stuffed animal in San Jose flashed into my mind for an instant, but I didn't seize it. My mother wasn't like *that*. But things *had* changed. We were no longer aligned, no longer the mother and daughter doing a project together.

Over time, my mother's conviction about my wish to steal from her festered and grew—and became unignorable. In my magazine of my relationship with my mother, I reported that my mother had put out a new issue of her own magazine of our relationship in which I was cast as a thief and enemy, and she, as the CIA protecting the nation. My investigative reporting had yielded several indications that a switch had flipped in my mother's brain. Of course, this was *my* magazine of *my mother's* magazine, and there was a high probability that both were full of errors. One can't ever pin down what happens between two people, and it takes a family member a long time to get to even a few shards of rock bottom truth, even if she's a trained therapist.

Still, we believe our own reporting most, and as of this moment in Chevy Chase, when my mother clung to her cloth and announced that we must make three quilts, I lost heart and the quilt project came to a standstill. This was the moment, too, when the mother-daughter charm that had often sparkled between us cracked. My mother no longer trusted in my goodness, and this loss of faith in me whipped from under me the carpet I'd thought heretofore that we were flying on together. This moment, poised and shining in memory's sphericle, became one of those pivotal ones overwrought and probably overweighted amongst the thousands of others, but so pain-choked I could never again make those bright, clashing batiks cohere into a pleasing coverlet. Some views through the porthole, of their own accord, appear and appear, return and return. This almost certainly gives them too much prominence in the recollector's story of her life. On the other hand, do they inform us of us something important, even crucial, something to beware of?

Years later, when my mother died, I found a round basket

full of triangles cut from the Dutch and cheap Indonesian batiks—the squirrel's stash hidden from her conniving daughter.

# THE FURIES

Greek mythology harbors several stories of the Furies, or Erinyes. These "infernal goddesses," featuring vipers for hair and bloodshot eyes, were some of the most ancient and feared of deities. Spirits of dark fury, they were the avengers, the persecutors, the hounders and tormenters of all those judged to be transgressors. These bat-winged beings might, perhaps, be seen as the source of the strange sense of flapping that rippled through me when the more reasonable mother I mostly knew took flight at strange and disturbing moments.

Fixing on my mother: at this juncture in our lives together, the lovely Demeter—"the holy goddess... who glories in the harvest" and who guards over the "sweet young seedling" she has borne—has seemingly vanished, replaced by another. As her loyal Persephone, though, I refuse to countenance the possibility that that loving mother is gone forever. She must still linger, I feel sure, somewhere in my mother's deepest places. Once in a while, I fancy I catch a fleet softening in my mother's eye—but this softer mother, if she is still there, is now in deep shadow. It even seems that the Demeter of sorrows, the one who ceaselessly mourns and seeks her lost daughter, has also receded into the dim. Instead, that old bear of the Indiana woods seems to have seized my mother. The fears and woes seem to have mounded too high. Darker, primordial spirits hold her in sway. Flapping, flapping, they carry her away.

9

# THE RETURN

*Day and night my tears have been my bread*
— Seamus Heaney
 "Clearances"

"It was god-awful, Sara," my mother says. Whispering in the kitchen about the negotiations with the Agency over my father's retirement, my mother says to me, "It was god-awful, Sara. I thought I'd cry as he told that psychiatrist he'd have a nervous breakdown if they didn't let him retire overt. Why should your father—he's better than any of them—have to go in there and do that? And after all we've been through—all the moves, all the sacrifices, putting you kids in boarding school, his having to do awful things, working for that horrid man, and then Saigon, my god."

Chubby acorns crunched under foot and red leaves drifted as usual on the Washington lawns, but the air smelt of something new. It was 1981. The election of Ronald Reagan had ushered in a tidal shift. From an era of optimism, a strong middle class, and an emphasis on meaningful work and help for the poor, the United States had moved into an era of economic decline, decreased middle class well-being, and a new necessity for both members of a couple to work just to keep up. Gone was Kennedy's "Seek not what your country can do for you, seek what you can do for your country." Reagan esteemed the rich and placed accumulation of wealth above other values. He held a social Darwinist perspective, advocating that Americans adopt the motto, "The most terrifying words in the English language are: I'm from the government and I'm here to help." Though the president would contend differently, it was not an auspicious time in the country and not the best year for my parents—the start of a series of not-the-best years.

The household effects had arrived from Germany, my parents were back in the Chevy Chase house, and my mother was back at work. Only this time it was work with a vengeance. My father had retired and it was, as she said, *by gum, her turn.* She seemed to have come under the sway of the Reagan era, and under the new regime, the making and accumulation of money became her main goal. Joy, hobbies, relaxation were irrelevant. Within months, she was serving patients all over the Washington area, barreling back and forth to nursing homes and private patients of every age and ailment under the sun. In a few years she would receive the *Washington Home Health Care Provider of the Year* award.

My father, endlessly trying to please, was applying for jobs per my mother's orders, but his immediate project had been to gain permission from the CIA to be able to note on his resume the fact that he had given 30 years of service to the intelligence service. Though he had gained incomparable experience and earned a medal for getting the Agency's Vietnamese employees out of Vietnam under extreme duress, he was forbidden by current Agency rules to tell anyone where he'd worked. How was he to convince an employer to hire him if he couldn't say what he'd done? To gain his objective, my father was forced to humiliate himself before an Agency psychiatrist and dissemble one last time—to say he would have an emotional breakdown if he couldn't stop lying about this one fact of his life, and my mother was required to back him up. After a lifetime of exerting emotional strength and maintaining a façade of impermeability for the sake of his country, this forced testimony was an insult and violation almost beyond tolerance. The whole situation enraged my mother and would wither my father. From now on, he would keep flying the flag, his own and that of his country, but at emotional half-mast. The basic fact was, after thirty years of service, my father was so tired of lying he could burst—only, as a spy trained in self-repression, he would not. The bursting would be left to my mother.

"Damn him," my mother says, "he won't even say he's mad. He just says, 'I'm not going to lower myself to their level.' But it's not healthy to pretend all the time. That's what we've done all these years…"

This arrival home from Germany was the beginning of a cascade of losses for my mother.

First, she would lose the life structure and status she had enjoyed for thirty years—that of the diplomatic corps. Next, she would lose a working husband—a husband who brought in income, a husband to be proud of, a man who conferred prestige upon his wife through his employment. She would lose many beloved patients, including a little seven-year-old named Leah whom she adored, to cancer. She would lose friends—friends who moved to Vermont, friends who replaced her with AA, friends who drifted away after retirement, friends who were turned off by her increasingly grim outlook. Perhaps most devastating of all the losses was the death of her sister Marge, the one who cared for her like a mother.

A person might judge that my mother had, by this time, accrued a life's full allotment of loss. It seems, however, that loss is not finite, that loss is a bottomless storehouse.

In the final blow of my mother's post-retirement life, she would lose my father to a galloping form of Parkinson's Disease. She said to me, "Your father cried when he received the diagnosis. I wanted to cry too, but I couldn't cry. I can't cry anymore." I don't think my mother ever permitted herself this basic human right. No one had held that little girl poised at the edge of the woods.

Meanwhile, through all of it, she would work like a dog trying to help the world. Until her last months, despite her many ailments, she boarded a van at her retirement community and went off to a school to tutor a little boy in math. During these years, she would experience moments of pleasure but most of all she would work herself to death until she couldn't work anymore, and then she would die.

# GOODBYE TO DREAMS

"How are you, Mom?"

I am visiting my parents in the bungalow to which they've returned four times now: the modest white frame cottage at the corner of Thornapple and Ridgewood. The antique Dutch bellows and Malaysian broom are placed again beside the hearth, the watercolor of a Taipei street is over the mantle, the Japanese vase is arranged with chrysanthemums, and the German bread and jug of wine sit on the dinner table. Everything is lovely but my mother's loveliness seems to have flown and left a pitchfork.

She and I are in the kitchen where she is throwing together a dinner of fried rice. While she fetches the rice and eggs out of the refrigerator, and yanks open kitchen cabinets looking for the soy sauce, my mother says, "Oh, I've just got to make the best of it..."

"But how are you, really?"

My mother says, "Oh, I turned down all the job offers," she says, as though I would know to what she's referring.

It turns out, as she explains now, that before she and my father left Bonn, she had applied for P.T. jobs in various African countries. I hadn't known a thing about these applications. I remembered well, though, the job in Nepal she had painfully given up before they went to Germany.

"I wrote all those applications, and, well, when we got here, I got some good offers, but I couldn't make poor Charlie go to Africa. How could I?" she sighs.

"Your father's more cultured than I'll ever be," my mother is going on. "He's a Europe person—he never loved the developing world like I did. And he hates the heat...I'd have loved Africa of course, but he's been through so much. I couldn't ask him to go off with me to some village with no plumbing. What would he have done? He said he'd find all sorts of things, write a book, read...But he didn't know what he was saying. I'd have been off at the clinic all day and he'd be in all that heat..."

"Oh, Mom, that's awful. You would have loved Africa," I say. "Why couldn't you at least have tried?"

"Oh, I couldn't do that to your father." She wasn't calling him Charlie and her voice had turned hard and resolute.

She poured peanut oil into the sauté pan and dumped in the cooked rice.

"Thank God I was able to slip right back into P.T. here. I've just got to make the most of my work here and go great guns...

"But, by God," she says as she dumps frozen peas into the pan and hurls in some soy sauce, "if I gave up my cup of tea in the developing world, I'm not going to put up with any guff..."

She sounds so angry I change tacks—probably to the exactly wrong subject.

"How's Pop doing?" I ask.

"He just sits on his duff on that god-damn green chair, reading that damn paper."

My father, relieved to be out the other side of his retirement ordeal, from my point of view, is looking forward and trying hard to forge a new life. He hasn't found paid employment, which has been difficult, but he is making contributions he can feel unadulteratedly good about by volunteering at the National Archives and in Hillary Clinton's correspondence office. He's exclaimed to me about the Clinton White House, amazed and ebullient, "They're all young people!" He is taking Spanish at the local community college too, always one to keep refining his language skills.

None of my father's activities count to my mother. In her book, he should have a new high-wage job by now. She overlooks the fact that it is extremely hard in this era for any spy to find work upon retirement and most don't even look for a job as retirement in these days is viewed as a time to kick back at last.

Some sea changes in a life are slow and surreptitious and evolving but absolutely critical. My father's retirement was an enormous change in my parents' life together, its negative effects, in my mother's eyes, slowly and insidiously accruing.

# RETRIBUTION

*Fury is the high queen of strength*
— Aeschylus
*The Eumenides*

"Oh, I'd love to spend a month in the south of France," my father says, his eyes shining for a moment when I ask him what he'd like to do now that he's retired.

We're eating my mother's delicious boeuf bourguignon, and I think, *Oh, how lovely that would be for him—and for my mother too. Maybe she'd relax a little. It would be such a treat for them.* But my mother has another point of view.

"God damn it, Charles, if you think I'm going to get on a plane again, you've got another thing coming. I gave up Georgetown Dental School, a good physical therapy career at G.W., and my dream job with Tom Dooley Foundation, and spent all those years being yanked here and there by your work—and, by god, it's *my* turn now. I'll be damned if I'm going to give up *my* chance for *my* career and go off to some other damned place. And anyway, I've got to work if we're going to have a dignified old age. Your pension isn't going to get us there. You and those other men at the Agency might think you can sit back on your laurels, but I've got to work."

Trying to hang onto my father's vision and that bright look in his eyes, and wishing *I* could go to the south of France, I say, "But Mom, wouldn't it be nice for you two to have a real vacation in a beautiful place just for the pure pleasure of it? You wouldn't have to quit your job..."

My mother spits, "I'm *not* going anywhere."

Suddenly it is clear that my mother has a pile of old angers that have stacked up like books—and some new ones that she is compiling. My mother will stack up angers even more quickly from here on. She will find them everywhere and seize them like first editions—until the pile builds to toppling.

The shift in my mother is shocking to me; I had assumed some parts of my mother were hardwired. My mother's old mottoes, *"All's right with the world," "Wherever I am is best," "Don't worry. Everything will look better tomorrow,"* and *"This too shall pass,"* it becomes clear during my visit, have been replaced by their opposites: *"If it's not one damned thing it's another"* and *"No one in this world thinks of anyone but number one."* Her children are raised and educated, her husband does have a solid pension, she has a thriving physical therapy practice, and yet she feels no satisfaction. Rather, my mother considers that the world has failed her and my father stolen from her something precious. She seems to have lost any kind of faith, Presbyterian, Unitarian, humanist, or otherwise.

This is how I find her this visit: The sky sings arias, the air smells fresh blue, the apples taste crisp and hearty, but my mother's face is grim. Her eyes see nothing but the car she is heading for, her ears hear nothing but the thrumming list of the day's patients in her head, her body feels nothing but the weight of the clanking wheelchair footrests and L.L. Bean bag of weights and heat pads she's lugging to her station wagon. She is gone to all the world and whirls on her own planet of forward movement and purpose. She is a model of efficiency and accomplishment—she helps thirty people by day's end—but her eyes are dark and fixed and merciless as those of a soldier surrounded by hidden enemy. A devil's war rages inside her head.

Anger—perhaps depression's disguise—is taking hold of my mother and turning the whole world poisonous. If there are lemons on the table, she sees rotten eggs to be cleaned up. If Beethoven is playing, it clangs and grates. If the air smells of roses, she thinks it is the stink of vomit. If someone pats her on the back, she flinches and snarls, "What do you want?" Something is wrong, some malignant force has nabbed her, but neither I nor anyone else is aware of this, much less knows its identity. Her fury and tetchiness conceal the fount and repel compassion.

The time of rampage has begun.

# WEDDING

My marriage has given my mother a reprieve, a funnel for her energy, a project which permits her to translate fury's energy into beauty. Daughters' activities can provide welcome diversion for tortured mothers. For a while, as she plans the wedding, she can revel in the family she has created. Even if her husband didn't make it to the top, her two children are thriving—both getting their doctorates. Her daughter has a social work degree she can always fall back on. Her children haven't had the kinds of troubles other people's children have had—no drugs, alcohol, babies out of wedlock, nastiness...And now her daughter is marrying Peter, a dependable, kind young man who will earn a good living.

She has made a huge shortcake sprinkled with powdered sugar and violets. The circle-cut Virginia country ham has arrived, and the chicken, and salmon mousse, and salads, and curry puffs, and... and...are laid out on the colonial banquet table in the mansion's dining room under old oil paintings of pastoral scenes. All the napkins she has made out of Borneo batik are arranged into fans. The bottles of Mouton Cadet are sitting ready to be opened. The silver is sparkling, the plates stacked up, at the ready. She has placed my bouquet of daisies, black-eyed Susans, and baby's breath on the table at the bottom of the stairs, ready for me to pick up in my trembling hands on my way out to the lawn where the guests will be waiting.

Peter is off with his high school friends doing whatever men do in the moments before they tie the knot and I am upstairs in the mansion with my good friends Meg and Fiona. They are helping me slip into the white Laura Ashley dress my father

276

found for me at a Bonn flea market. I put on the lapis earrings Meg has lent me to cover both "something borrowed and something blue." We try to decide if I should fix a black-eyed Susan to the bodice of my dress, and decide not. I slip my uncomfortable, heeled sandals on my feet and tip my broad brimmed Virginia Woolf hat onto my head. It is as close to the hat the writer wore in one of the old photographs of her as I could come up with.

I am getting dressed for my big day and chattering with my friends, but I am also waiting. Waiting for what I assume will happen. Waiting for my mother to come up and flutter around me as her daughter on her wedding day, and pat my back, and give me a hug, and tell me I look beautiful and to just be calm it will be okay, and to cry a little bit with me. But I wait and she doesn't come.

At the last minute, just after my brother runs up the stairs to tell me the guests are all seated and ready, my father comes in the door in his new, trim suit. He looks handsome and freshly made, like a just-hatched diplomat. Smiling, he holds me at arm's length. "Sweetie, you look beautiful." I fall into his arms. I love my father so much. This is true. But I am still waiting. I am waiting for my mother who I love too. Who never comes.

When I descend the steps with my father, there is the bouquet my mother has made for me. I pick it up. Just outside the door is my mother—in her red dress, with the first permanent wave of her life. She's tried to look extra pretty for my wedding, for me. It broke my heart when I first saw it—to think of that extra effort she'd made; she'd always hated permanents. Ahead of me, on the lawn, all the guests are seated in folding chairs. Beyond is a pasture of sheep, and beyond that a long green hill down to the Patuxent River. It looks a little like the South Downs where Virginia Woolf used to walk with her Leonard in their dream "marriage of two minds." My mother tells me, "Hurry up, Sara. The guests have all been waiting." There is a look on her face. Her jaw is clenched.

I step into my new wedded life.

Sometime later she says about my wedding, "I wish I'd been able to go up to you when you were putting on your dress." She says this in an accusing, martyred tone, as though something is my fault. I ask her why she hadn't come; I would have liked that a lot, I say. "I kept waiting for you to send your damned father down," she says. "Someone had to look after the guests."

Why couldn't my mother have been more confident and bigger than this? More and more she seemed haunted by jealousy. Which turned into a self-fulfilling prophesy. Which begot more jealousy.

# A DAUGHTER'S RANSOM

*When those who have been close collide in conflict,*
*Their anger is incurable and terrible.*
— Euripides
   *Medea*

I am standing in the tiny galley of a graduate student apartment on Shaler Lane in Cambridge. I am thirty and in the last year of a doctoral program in human development. It is a leafy life. My days are full of ideas about human behavior and culture that nourish my brain, and I walk home from my studies every day through a beautiful neighborhood of luxuriant, overarching trees. It is a week before Thanksgiving.

"Oh, Mom, I wish I could. I just can't come down," I say to my mother over the phone. "I just have too much work." As always, I am full of longing to be with my mother. My parents have just recently moved back to Washington and the chance to see her is something precious since she and my father have been inaccessible across the world for most of my young adult life. Despite this I have decided that the upcoming Thanksgiving is a time to put aside my wish to see her, and her wish to see me, for two reasons. First, I am working frantically these days, taking classes in child and adult development, working as a research assistant on a study of adolescence across cultures, and trying to get a head of steam going on my doctoral thesis about the lives and development of Patagonian sheep ranchers. I really could use the long weekend to get ahead on my work.

The second reason for my wish to bow out of the holiday is that I don't really want to see my brother. The last time I was with him we had a stupid but steaming sibling tiff and haven't yet stopped hissing. While my brother and I both orbit our mother, pulled by a powerful gravitational force, our own planetary paths aren't crossing much anymore. He was in Alaska while I was in Argentina. Now he is in Oxford, England, while I am in Cambridge, Massachusetts, and he is headed for Paraguay soon. We are adults now, have spun in different directions, are always on different continents, and have drifted apart. Because of this and our recent contretemps, I'm sure my brother isn't that keen on seeing me either. My mother can have her son-love fest alone. My work is pressing. My mother has always understood before when I've had to postpone a holiday visit. She's said comforting things like "Oh, we can just have Christmas in January. You know the dates don't really matter, Sweetie."

How could my calculation have been so vastly and fatally wrong?

"But your brother is coming all the way from England," my mother says, her voice tightening.

"I know, Mom. I'll really miss you all…" I say, "I just can't this time."

But my mother doesn't respond with understanding or sacrifice her own preferences as she usually does.

"What about my feelings?" she says tersely. I can envision her lips pressed together, her jaw clamped. "How can you do this to me? Your brother may not be back for a couple of years."

Referring to the quarrel she knows my brother and I have had, she says, "Your brother's never done anything to you.

You've always been so jealous of him..." Her voice suddenly changes to shards and sludge hurled at me.

"How can you do this to all of us? All you've ever thought of is yourself."

"Mom!" I sputter.

I shut my eyes, trying to take a breath.

"You have ruined my life," she says, and the phone clicks dead.

Now—instantly and indelibly—my mother's feelings for me alter. As of this second, our relationship turns volatile and un-quellable. What was a mere heated sibling miscommunication has transmuted into a mother-daughter conflagration.

It is all over. This is the atom in the infinitude of time, this is the moment the fates plucked.

I am no longer my mother's daughter. I am no longer her beloved. I am her heart-churn.

Up until this point, my relationship with my mother has been merely rocky. My mother has been a *mere poule* bursting with love—a tempestuous mother hen, but still, very much a clucking chick-protector. Despite her intense and sometimes tangled-up, and crazed and streaking feelings, my mother has also been a warm and bustling body, a conveyor of heart-swelling love. Now—as though I am the sole source of a lifetime of disappointments, not just this particular one—her heart bursts.

My mother is, as of now, a bomb that instantly reloads with explosive the moment it goes off. She is angry and unsettle-able, raging and ravenous. Her pain at having an empty chair at her dinner table, at having a daughter annoyed at a son, blows into a burning hatred for the daughter whom she holds responsible for the immolation of her house. From now on, whenever she looks at me her darkened eyes flick away from my face—she doesn't want to acknowledge me unless I have done her bidding. Wordless, with jaw set, her mouth is a flat, rock line of accusation, fury, and grief. She decides now that, if I will not profess unalloyed love for my brother, she will never love me again. Moreover and much more devastating, she will never be happy again. This is to be my punishment.

A daughter can be held for ransom—for herself. In order to get herself back, she must surrender herself to her mother. Like a mugger in an alley, my mother clutches me by the collar. "If you do not deliver me absolute emotional subservience by midnight, life as you know it is dead."

My mother and I are in the hands of a great and powerful helplessness, a ferocious and overwhelming contest of wills. It is a force far beyond both of us, Olympian in scale. My mother is now firmly in the claws of those un-named spirits that have stolen her away in unexpected flashes throughout my life. I will hear the thudding of their wings as a backdrop whenever, hereafter, I am with her.

It is thus that my mother's candle winked out. From now on she waited for me, by furious self-denial, on and on, to light her again. For the next two decades, I kept striking different matches, trying and hoping to provide her what she wanted. There were times I was so desperate to make her happy I would have given her my life, but I could not find my way to yield her my self. I could not turn myself over to my mother, but, as of now, the black stone took up long-term residence in my gut—a cold sinker constantly tolling damnation: *You are bad. You are bad.* Was this perhaps actually *her* stone transferred to me? Where does a mother end and a daughter begin?

Sorrows out-weigh joys. They say it takes five or seven instances of interpersonal pleasure to un-do a single instant of wounding. Sometimes it seems like the ratio is more like 10,000 to one. Sometimes it seems like a single wound can weigh five tons and each joy a single pound, and not even a lifetime of reparation and soothing will undo the injury.

That the mother-daughter relationship is made up of innumerable moments is clear, but just as true is that it may be defined and crystallized by *a* moment. A single plucked moment, a crucial and stunning instant may alter both future and past.

If every life undergoes a breakneck travesty, a single event that plunges the knife in the heart, this was mine.

Sometimes one thing happens and everything flows from that. This single exchange when I let my mother down and failed to act my assigned part in her film, along with the volatile anger that curdled that day, seemed, until after she was gone, sufficient to explain the next 25 years. This moment seemed to rock our relationship from one spatial track to another.

As daughters will do—self-centered as some of us are when it comes to our mothers—I tended for the next 25 years to believe that this telephonic parley was the tipping point not only in my life, but in my mother's as well. Daughters are apt to assume their mothers' lives revolve around them though. (Whose life revolves around whose?) I didn't consider that my daughterly take on what went on might not be accurate. Maybe this moment wasn't the defining one for her, nor the apex of her life. Maybe it was, rather, the apex of mine, and to present it as my mother's too was making too much of it, mistakenly making it the whole story.

Perhaps, I often thought in despair, nothing could really explain my mother's change of heart; it was possible that lives made no sense. What was just was. My mother existed, ricocheting, on this earth...

Or perhaps (this was something that didn't occur to me,) something I wasn't cottoning to, something mysterious or deep or far back, something I would never think of, was the swivel, the toggle, the pivot, the on-off switch of her life...

# SPAIN

For a daughter, a mother can be a femme fatale and their relationship a tumultuous love affair.

Before I go to Spain for a stint of research among Basque villagers, I stop to see my parents. My mother will not be appeased. I know that, on some level, she is satisfied and fattened by having her daughter rightfully and dutifully there visiting her, but she is making me pay: Cooking up a storm and then resentfully plunking the plate in front of me. With a churlish face, spitting surly comments like "Oh, don't worry about us. We're fine. I'll just be here working. You just go and enjoy your Spain."

The night before I leave, I am in my old pink Chevy Chase bedroom with my duffle bag half-stuffed, typewriter, boots, and books yet to be packed scattered around.

I am sitting hunched on the bed, laden with dread. My mother has successfully infused her anger into my body and my whole corpus feels imbued with a vaporous poison. I am almost paralyzed with the feeling of failure and foul judgment. To my mother, I am a malign being.

As I sit there, lodged as cement, my mother enters the room. In two steps, she is up to me, and thrusts something into my hands. "Here, take this with you."

It is my mother's old flannel nightgown, unwashed, straight from her previous-night's body.

All the nights in Spain, huddled on a strange bed, I don the nightgown and curl up, wrapped inside the smell of my impossibly difficult, beloved mother.

Years later, as I am writing this book and still endlessly cycling between celebrating and bewailing my mother, I come across a mother poem by Sharon Olds which I suspect is my destiny. The following is a portion.

> *I think I may go on falling, like my own*
> *flesh, for the rest of my life, and maybe I'll*
> *still be falling for my mother after*
> *my death—or not falling but orbiting,*
> *with her, and maybe we'll take turns*
> *who is the moon, and who is the earth.*
> — "Still Falling For Her"

# THE BIRTH OF MY DAUGHTER

I am joy beyond joy. I dance, I twirl, I blossom, I sing. I am sky the color of bluebird wings. I am dandelion fluff spinning on breeze. I am a mango luscious and golden. I am a billowing spinnaker. I am a daffodil bobbing and sunny in spring breeze. I am a leggy and beautiful sprite bounding weightless up the sky. As I spring upward, I blend, I vanish into air. I am holding our baby daughter in my arms.

There is nothing this happy. Nothing could match this winged and clamorous, pastel delight.

*Oh, did my mother never feel this?* I suddenly wonder, my heart thumping alarm——*Never know this elation at beholding and holding a daughter?* Recalling to mind those hollow eyes, that emaciated waif on that Japanese mountain, my belly cringes. It cries. It grieves for her, my mother.

284

My mother in full pink flesh materializes at the hospital doorway, arrived to see her daughter's newborn girl.

My heart choked with pleasure and hope, I place the snug, white cocoon in her arms.

The minute she takes the bundle and looks down into it, her face blooms. My mother's face blooms.

"Oh, Sara," she says.

Her whole body is calm. For a time, all is forgiven.

The children will be the one reprieve, the one arena in which our horns unlock.

# HOW MY MOTHER SHOWS HER LOVE

When I am a baby
my mother sews for me:
a flannel blanket edged with satin

When I am five
my mother sews for me:
a pink frock smocked by hand

When I am eight
my mother sews for me:
an owl costume for Halloween

When I am eleven
my mother sews for me:
a clown suit of terry cloth with enormous colored dots

When I am fourteen
my mother sews for me:
a prom gown in dotted Swiss to match my image of Juliet's in
    the play

When I am fifteen
my mother sews for me:
a hippie dress from an Indian bedspread of large red and purple
    blooms

When I am seventeen
my mother sews for me:
a maxi skirt of black watch tartan with a swishy lining

When I am in college
my mother sews for me:
a Tibetan wraparound jumper in russet corduroy

When I am in graduate school
my mother sews for me:
a blouse to match my skirt in Liberty lawn

When I have my first baby
my mother sews for my daughter:
a flannel blanket edged with satin

# "THOU SHALT NOT REST"

Finally, I am out of graduate school. Peter and I have just moved
to a new state. I have a new, full-time academic job, a difficult
department chair, and a year-old baby. I am overwhelmed. I call
my parents from Minnesota.

At baseline, my mother disliked me now, but I forgot this
sometimes, as at this moment when I placed this call to her.

While it is difficult to forget them, I've found, it is also hard to hang onto lacerating memories. The stories that ache can so easily slip from one's mind. It is as if one is forever a child, sure that one's parent will one day see the light and brighten at the sight of one. *Hope reigns eternal*, as my mother always used to say when she was her old brighter self.

"I'm going crazy. I feel like I'm doing everything badly," I say trustingly to my mother from my phone in St. Paul.

"Yes, well, I had fifteen patients today," my mother says, her voice hard.

Gone was the woman who, in previous phone calls, had soothed me as I studied, who had urged on my academic efforts, and sympathized with my graduate school workload. My mother had graduated too, it seemed. She had graduated from the perspective that educational experiences, helping the world, learning for its own sake, and human needs and comfort were important to a good life—to the "If it doesn't kill you, it'll be good for you" school of life. With my graduation, she'd launched me into adulthood. "Thank god," I could hear her mutter under her breath, and adulthood and adult responsibilities were not to be enjoyed. I was a grown-up now; the fun was over.

At the time I made the phone call in a bid for sympathy about my work and childcare challenges, I hadn't as yet, despite the searing interaction that Thanksgiving, fully comprehended the extent and dimensions of the alteration in my mother. I didn't know she'd decided work was the be all and end all—the *only* all. She had certainly worked *like a dog*, as she said, throughout her adulthood, but work had earlier always filled her with joy. I didn't know she had cast out the joy part now and saw adulthood as a straightforward matter of nose-to-the-grindstone toil and sacrifice. She believed—and this was a *belief*—that overwork and stress were just part and parcel of it. Happiness didn't matter. Earning a good salary was what mattered. It was high time I saw what real life was.

"Just put the baby in day care. She'll be fine," my mother says. "And get on with it. Get to work."

Vanished was the tender, cherishing mother of my childhood who said, sympathetically, to me, "Oh, poor, poor. The mind won't let the body rest." Vanished was the god who embraced human beings as flawed but good-willed creatures who, of course, needed a hand along the way. In their places stood a mother and a god who cracked whips and pronounced in booming voices, "Thou shalt not rest." A tough, intractable woman in my mother's clothes had announced herself.

After the phone call, I sat alone in the kitchen of the apartment in the Victorian house we'd rented. I sat still for a long time, just letting my mother's harsh tone burn its course through my body.

Then, after a while, I rose and went to the cupboard. I opened a sack of bread, took out a piece, spread it with butter, removed the cover from the sugar bowl, took a spoon in my shaky hand, and sprinkled sugar over the slice.

As I chewed, the crashing waves of grief and defeat subsided into gentle lappings.

# WHEN IN MY KITCHEN

On a visit to Washington from Minnesota, I suggest to my mother that we wait to wash the skillets we've used to make fried chicken until after we've eaten, so we can let them soak before tackling them.

Her voice is steel. "This is my kitchen and when you're in my kitchen, you do things my way. In your own kitchen, you can do things your way."

On another visit to Washington from St. Paul, I try again to talk to my mother about my life—about the travails I am encountering at work. I've had to take several day trips to North Dakota and Kansas while my toddler daughter had strep, so that I can complete a mother-infant health needs assessment. Can't my mother see the irony of that?

"I don't want to be involved anymore in your and your brother's problems. I'm not going to have any more emotions. I've had too many," she says. "And I don't want to talk about our relationship either," she adds, as a preemptive strike. I don't hear the content of her communication, just its tone. I don't hear the part about "too many emotions." Cold water trickles through my torso.

This remark—my mother's saying she doesn't want to hear about my troubles anymore—is a punch in my heart. I've prided myself on our closeness, my ability to talk to her about anything. I've taken strength in the knowledge that she is there. Now she is slamming down the portcullis. I feel like a peasant shut out of the kingdom. It is a desolate, stony loneliness.

Looking back with the clarity of rear vision, I can see that my mother was not only angry, but deeply depressed at this point in her life. After the evacuation from Vietnam and the other moves, and my father's unhappiness, and all the other terrors and challenges she'd encountered in her life as a spy's wife, she was massively exhausted and beaten down. How could the undercover wife of an ocean-crossing spy *not* grow tired of it all?

Daughters don't want mothers to be people. They don't want them to change. They want them to be magical, like Strega Nona's ever-brimming pasta pot. But there comes a time when mothers get to be people—*or does there*?

# HOPE NEVER DIES

*...You are perhaps training me to be*
*responsive to the slightest brightening.*
— Louise Gluck
  "Vespers"

As I pack boxes of books and toys in our Minnesota house, readying for a move to Washington for Peter's new job, my belly is a hive of buzzing wasps and bees: wasps for the anticipated stings, bees for the anticipated honey. On the one hand, I know how my mother and I always seem to disappoint each other. On the other, I have always yearned for my mother—or my dream of her, or the best of her—when I've been apart from her, even when I've hated her, and despite the lingering, seemingly indelible anger she has had for me. Her love, her *involvement* with me has been the porridge of my life— sustaining even if not always comfort food. I look forward to being closer to her. She's always said, ever since I moved away at 18, "I just wish you lived close enough that you could come over and do the laundry." I've longed for that too: longed for the close, sweet mother-daughter dream come true. Perhaps a person stores a longing for a mother forever and always. Perhaps, in her longing for me, my mother was longing for *her* mother.

Maybe now that I have a child, things will be different—less fraught. I dare to think it will be fun to be near my mother, and I dare to hope it might make her happy.

This turns out to be incorrect.

# DAUGHTERS CAN
# MAKE ERRORS

I thought she would be happy. When I told my mother I was pregnant again, I thought she would be excited be able to be in on this second baby's infancy. I thought it might even bring her delight. This was a mistake.

She says to me, in my poky house five blocks from hers:

*You are ruining your daughter's life.*

*You are ruining your career.*

*You are ruining your husband's career.*

*You are ruining your financial situation.*

*You are ruining your life.*

I see now, three decades later, how my mother's thinking went. She was a believer in Zero Population Growth. She thought the planet would be healthier with fewer people on it. She was considering the planet, but she was mostly thinking of me. She knew well the consequences of having more than one child. I had one lovely child. Why risk complications? She knew, from her physical therapy work and from life, that things could go wrong with babies. Furthermore, she wanted me to have whatever career I wanted. She thought it would be easier with one child. She desperately wanted me not to experience the frustrations she had had.

But I stood before her pregnant. I'd made a decision to try for a second child, and her words, perhaps only meant as cautionary or just a flurry of maternal worry, were damning. I worried now that her predictions would come true. She was so often right. I felt like I'd been cursed by the witch in *Sleeping Beauty*.

All through the pregnancy and beyond, I worried the things in my mother's forecast would one day come to pass. Contrary to my mother's dire predictions, however, our son hurtled into the world a fount of joy.

I was taught by my mother to respect one's elders. I clasped this principle to heart and felt it my duty to imbibe whatever she told me. Certainly, all human beings are to be respected, but adults—even parents—don't always know best, despite what they may contend. It took me until my late fifties to really believe that my mother could be wrong. If I had said on occasion, "Mom, please stop!" might that have helped her as well as me?

# MCDONALD'S

My mother was giving us a little money to help pay for our first child's kindergarten. I was working on a book, teaching writing at the local adult education center, caring for two children, and holding the fort while my husband traveled all over the world for his job. We were struggling to make the payments on our tiny house in a Washington suburb as well as tuition payments, but managing to make it each month—engaging in the usual struggles of young families. My mother had seemingly freely offered to help out with our daughter's fees, and I'd accepted. What she'd offered was only a small part of the tuition, but every bit helped, and I was grateful.

One day, my mother heaves her P.T. exercise weights and barbells onto the floor, and announces, "I'm tired of supporting you."

Standing there in the doorway with her overloaded L.L. Bean bag full of case notes and heating pads, she sees me and my husband as two spoiled brats. She would never say it outright, but paying for all that education for me and my brother—college, helping out with graduate school, had worn her out. Compared to her, we *were* spoiled brats. We could never equal her in struggle, willpower, or sacrifice. We didn't get full scholarships—only partial ones—nor work our way through college as she did. Nor do we work with paraplegics. She wants us to have it easier, but she doesn't. She had a 24-hour a day job, the way she did her work—and part of her wished someone would just, God damn it, take over some of her burden. But she could never actually *let* anyone else take up her burden. Heaving heavy loads was how she paid for her existence in the world— and, seeing herself as worthless, she could never work hard enough. Hers was a strict interpretation of Eleanor Roosevelt's creed: *Usefulness, whatever form it may take, is the price we pay for the air we breathe and the food we eat and the privilege of being alive.*

Peter and I have long shared a joke that we'll only get credit from my mother if we each work a full-time job, have a night job at McDonald's, and take the Greyhound bus everywhere we go.

And now my mother actually says it. "Why don't you get a job at McDonald's? They probably have an evening shift you could do after dinner. You could work at that one nearby..."

Another day, my mother continues with her suggestions for changing my work life. "Why don't you get a teaching job with the public schools? That would be a regular paycheck..." Some of her ideas are worth considering, but, severe, humorless, she spins out so many of them, she leaves no room for any of my own ideas—much less for the notion that, just maybe, I'm doing all I can for the moment. My mother's mind is too quick for me. I've had no sleep. Baby Forrest is up all night. Somehow my mother has forgotten the exhaustion and hard work involved in child-rearing. Perhaps, it occurs to me in hindsight, she didn't really experience much of it. She had servants most of the years my brother and I were young.

My mother's sense, left over from when I was little, that she was responsible for solving my every problem, and even problems I didn't see as problems, was a heavy burden, though she would never have admitted this. Perhaps at a certain point, mothers ought to let go of the compulsion to live and relieve their daughters' lives. Can a mother ever end?

# APPLE BUTTER

"I just wanted you to come over and make apple butter."

My mother and I are on the phone: me, in my cramped, light green Sears house in Chevy Chase, standing in the cluttered kitchen full of last night's dishes, with my hungry baby beginning to whimper on the pallet I've made on the floor for him—and my mother, in her white bungalow in Chevy Chase, standing in *her* kitchen, finally free of physical therapy reports to write since it is the weekend, hoping for a peaceful moment with her 37-year-old daughter.

"Mom, I can't right now. I'm too tired. Forrest was up a lot last night and he's hungry..."

"Oh, all right. I know you don't have time for me."

After she slams down the phone without saying good-bye, I lie down beside my son on his pallet on the scraped-up wood floor, drag up my shirt front, take him up against my breast, and, as he latches on, replace his wailing with mine.

Ever since I'd moved back to Washington from Minnesota, it seemed, my mother and I were in a tug of war. It was atomically intense. A sort of shrieking fantasy- ideal clamored inside each of us, and each of us was yanking on the worn and fraying sailor's rope suspended between us for dear and desperate life.

These were the two contestants in this mortal combat:

First there was my mother, with the Indiana farm girl inside her wanting me to be her little girl self back in the log house in Henryville, amiably helping her mother cut up apples at the big wooden table in the kitchen. Those were perhaps the only sorts of moments in her childhood when she—her mother's ninth child—and her mother were in rhythm and she felt *her* mother liked *her*.

And then there was me, the cosmopolitan daughter my

mother had raised all over the world who'd just had another baby and was sensitive, with artistic inclinations—the daughter who might even be a writer instead of the money-amassing, financially secure, powerful, and self-sufficient career woman my mother had wanted to be, and now urgently wanted me to be.

The whole thing was so complicated, and so full of trapdoors through which I could suddenly pitch downward into a pit of black sludge and clamoring, biting insects and pinching crabs. I knew that I was disappointing my mother no matter what I did, and my stomach was one seasick roil of frustration and hurt and fury and yearning anytime I thought of her. And I'm sure it was the same for her.

If only we could have spit at each other, and then hugged and made up. Instead, we were each mired in our side-by-side black pits of scrambling crabs and insects, hurling fistfuls of sludge at each other, and, when we could, crabs and insects too.

I cried into my baby's sweet crown, full of guilt, frustration—and fury. I couldn't conjure the could-have-been pleasure of standing beside my mother, chopping apples, then simmering them on the stove, perhaps sprinkling in some brown sugar, then smoothing the sweet fruit butter on a piece of crispy toast, and eating it, while chatting about the day's news.

# GIFTS OF LINEN

My mother rings me up and says, "Sara, let's go get you something new at that little shop you like. You've been working so hard."

She picks me up in her Subaru after work, all pleasant and

tranquil, then patiently stands by as I try on linen blouses and skirts at our favorite clothing shop on Connecticut Avenue.

"It is lovely," she says of my new outfit as we drive back to her house for a cup of tea before the children arrive home.

Women made fragile and sturdy by each other, we sit in the living room with the brush-painted landscape on the wall that has witnessed so much. For a moment at ease side by side, we sip our Yunnan out of the moss-green, rough-beautiful Japanese cups we love.

In my relationship with my mother, a happy moment often followed a taut one. A sweet, kind mother frequently made an appearance after an angry, vindictive one. Ironically, this reappearance of benevolence made matters difficult for me as a daughter. The bear made convincing and powerful appearances, but I couldn't get that marauding beast by the girth and just hang on. It kept unexpectedly flicking into a harmless, twittering sparrow. This bear-sparrow flickery kept me on the hook and made it almost impossible for me to say, "This is who my mother is." I could never be sure of it, never settle in and stick to a course of action.

## TO COBBLE A SELF

"Hi, Mom," I say, arriving at her house finally, after another day of racing from children's schools, to work, to schools, and back again.

I try to give her a hug, but she's stiff as a plank. She refuses to soften and accept my desperate affection. She will not allow my love in—not by word, not by deed. There is a chain across the door. How can love become so dangerous?

"I wish you'd come earlier," she says, her eyes dark and

darting, her mouth a straight line. Then, the refrain to one of her songs: "But I know, you never have time."

This comment from the woman who worked every weekday from four a.m. to nine p.m., and all weekend raced from the grocery store to yard work to home repair and slammed back into the house again, as though, if she stopped, God would shoot down a special bolt of lightning aimed at her—for every moment she had wasted was a sin.

Sometimes mothers hate you for having their most glaring flaw.

It seems to me a daughter's lot to cobble a self from flashing, bright-lit recollections. These tableaux tell the daughter who she is as she watches in memory's portal how her mother receives, sees, interacts with her. This daughterly self-assembly can be a mighty task if one happens to have been assigned a complicated mother. The scenes appearing in my mind's eye show me a daughter viewed by her mother as: now beautiful, now selfish, now lovable, now lazy, now smart, now hateful. It is so confusing. Self-constellation, for me, is a mighty, wobbly, unceasing task.

After one of the rounds of disappointing my mother, I make an appointment with my internist and ask for a prescription for antidepressants. This is long, long over-due.

# A MOTHER CAN BE JEALOUS OF HER GRANDCHILDREN

"Mom, I'm sorry, I can't go to the investment club with you. I promised Maud I'd take her to the craft store." We are talking on the phone.

"Didn't you just take her there a few days ago?" my mother's voice sluiced from sweet to bitter.

Only years later do I realize my mother was jealous of my children. Most of the time, the children were a safe area for us, but sometimes resentment suddenly spewed. Maybe all creatures, out of an animal wish for survival, wish to be the sole beloved. Maybe this—and jealousy—are only natural. My mother, a grown-up, was reacting to my lack of ready availability as if she were my children's sibling, and as if I were her own unavailable mother. We human beings are so complicated—and so hungry. Our bodies are inhabited by adults and by young adults and by infants. Do we ever really grow up?

# HORNET

The anger is building and building.

We're walking through Hecht's Department store. My mother is a hornet. She is on a rampage. She despises shopping but has to get some sheets and she hasn't found them instantly, so she is buzzing all over the place, stinging every store clerk we come across. She is enjoying making others miserable. Hair wind-mussed, coat hanging off one shoulder, a shoelace untied, she marches up and asks, "Where the hell are the sheets?" of one badge-sporting woman after another.

My mother is hurtling around free, turned loose from all propriety. Her hornet self is spinning and swooping around crying out, "Great God All Mighty! Free at last!"

I am trailing behind, cringing, wishing I were anywhere but here with my mother who is so rude I want to vanish across the world. I just hope she finds the linen department soon, so we can get out of the store before I am utterly mortified. I am trying to speak in the voice I have cultivated over the years, to stay sweet and patient, so as to mollify my mother and not exacerbate her fury—and wind up with a stinger smarting in my own neck.

Finally, finally a store clerk finds the right sheets, and my mother grabs them and marches off to pay, fuming at the next innocent clerk as she slams her credit card down on the counter. By the time we leave the linens, I am sure the entire department is snarling.

As we depart the store, my marching mother—hurrying as though she is evading the Stasi—knocks against a messy-haired man, in a dirty and slouchy jacket, loping along with a companion through the cosmetics department.

"Nasty old bat," I hear him say as my mother disappears ahead.

While I agree with the man, I want to beat him up.

# GRANDDAUGHTERS ARE A DIFFERENT MATTER FROM DAUGHTERS

In the evenings or on weekends, my mother invites my daughter over to play. In her comfortable living room with objects from around the globe, she has a whole roster of activities in store for her granddaughter.

First, my mother challenges my daughter to a game. "Want to play rummy?" A pack of cards in hand, giddy as a girl herself, eyes sparking, she dares my daughter to take her on, determined, herself, to win. They are evenly matched—they share the card shark gene, both are good at math (my mother plays solitaire for hours—it is the one time I see her relax)—so on and on they play, hand after hand, laughing, each crowing and gloating when she wins, as she deals out the cards—no questions asked, they know each other's minds—for another round.

After they play themselves out, which can take an hour or even two, my mother says, "How about if we make some fudge?" and off they go, dumping chocolate chips and sugar in a pot, slopping moist chocolate on their aprons, licking chocolate off their fingers, and finally spreading chocolate glop on a sheet of wax paper to cool. My daughter eats half of the fudge as they cut it into little squares, and to my mother, this is just as it should be—just as she would have liked to have done with her mother when she was eight.

My mother offers my daughter some ginger ale, and she gets out the guinea pig my children have given her whom she's named Bill, after Bill Clinton, on whom she has a crush. They play with the tolerant, nose-twitching black and brown and white creature, sitting on the rug, holding him on their laps, letting him scamper around the room and scoot inevitably under the couch—at which point my mother urges my daughter on. "Oooh, catch him! Catch him!"

They dissolve into fits of laughter, then my mother says, "Ooh! I know what, let's have a sock war!" She retrieves one of her long, old grey knee socks—like the one she once made my daughter a sock monkey out of—and she plops back on the floor again. As my daughter runs toward her, she tries to hit her with the long and flopping sock, and my daughter swerves and twirls like the ballerina she isn't to avoid my mother's lethal weapon, and she laughs and laughs, and returns for more and more and more. And my mother is herself like a little girl, crowing and crowing as though all the world is good.

She then has my daughter stay for a special dinner with her and my father: a dinner of hot dogs or something else I discourage the children from eating, or a trip to McDonald's, something I discourage even more, or, most special of all, a dinner at Moon Lake, the Chinese restaurant where we always go with my parents to recall old China days, and order ma po tofu, mu shu pork, chicken with cashews, and maybe some Szechwan green beans. Crowned, of course, with fortune cookies—always assuring exciting, good fortunes.

And after dinner, just before they change into their similar flannel nighties and curl up to read *Charlotte's Web* or *Miss Bianca in the Salt Mines* on my parents' king size bed, my mother fixes a bubble bath for my daughter, a bubble bath so full of bubbles they bloop out onto the floor, and my daughter slides into the bath, and sometimes, even, my mother joins her there herself, and there they are, the two of them, clothed in foam, my mother and my daughter both in a state of sublime wonder and contentment.

Watching them together, for a few glowing moments, I feel as though I am both my mother and my daughter, frothed in my mother's love.

# LOVE VIA EAVESDROP

*Il faut toujours avoir deux idées: l'une pour tuer l'autre.*
— Georges Braque

My mother is talking on the phone to her friend Gloria. Her voice is merry. "Oh, the grandchildren are grand. You know how cute two-year-olds are... And Sara's doing a lot of teaching..."

My mother is bragging about me! Maybe she does love me.

Suddenly I taste the plush-melting sweetness of whipped cream.

# SHOPPING FOR BRAS

*I am so changeable, being everything by turns and nothing long—such a strange mélange of good and evil.*
— Lord Byron
  "Childe Harold's Pilgrimage"

We are both giddy. My mother is in one of her irrepressible, romping moods when everything she does and says is hilarious. She is bouncing and bopping through Woodies Department Store, like she's a six-year-old going to ride the Ferris wheel with a balloon in her hand and cotton candy in her hair.

"Let's buy bras today," she said this morning, and whisked us off to Friendship Heights in her workhorse Subaru.

My mother takes a spin around the lingerie section of the gleaming store. She is Phyllis Diller, spot-lit, traipsing through the place, knocking hangars, picking up a pair of purple panties or a see-through gown, and saying "Sara, look at this!" In her state of elation, she's a ball of light attracting grins from other shoppers and the attendants too. She splatters happiness all round, generous, bountiful.

Swinging from display to display, she grabs bras here and there, passing by the nylon ones, the plain serviceable cotton ones—the ones she usually wears—focusing on the lacy confections, the sexy ones. "Your father would like this," she says, dangling a black lace number in front of me, giggling. My parents' sex life has never been in question, but what is she telling me? I cringe for a moment, feel inadequate and undersexed, then am immediately seduced again, spirited away by my flouncing mother.

In the fitting booth, I stand by, a little girl once more, just a witness, watching what this antic mother will do next. Quickly she strips down to the buff on top, leaving on her old tan skirt and sandals. There's a roll of chub above the waistband and her breasts hang loose, like two pendulous grapefruits. I look on from above my small chest, fascinated by her endowment, as always.

Now begins the comedy. My mother's spirits seem to rise even higher, and, like a clown, everything conspires to serve her routine. She's almost tripping over her big floppy feet, or rather, floundering around her big floppy breasts.

She puts on the first bra—a white lacy one. She has me do

up the hooks at the back. Above the bra strap in back is a little bulge of skin. When she turns around, her breasts are bulging over the tops of the cups, like Marie Antoinette's.

"Oh my Lord," my mother says. "This won't do," and she flings it down.

With the next bra, her breasts squeeze out sideways. They are so soft they really don't conform to any imposed shape. They flop and smush out one direction or another, like those balls you buy to increase your hand strength. You squeeze one part of it and it pops out another side, and it happens every which way.

"Well, this is not working at all!" she says, and she laughs and laughs until she has to cross her legs.

She tries on a couple more bras, then abruptly the balloon deflates. The jaw flicks. The darkness comes into her eyes. She is sick of the whole thing. "I've got to get back to work," she says and puts her fraying plain white brassiere and blouse back on and flings on her coat. "I've got to get home."

The happiness is over. I sense the flapping of wings. Bleak now, she races out of the store. She drives back spurting anger, like angry breast milk, speeding around cars at the traffic circle as we rocket north from the District of Columbia into Maryland.

My mother's quick-change acts, over the years, lodge deep within my body a sense of imminent loss. I become wary of happiness. People's love will inevitably evaporate, relationships twist themselves away. Family members, friends, kind neighbors—harking to some signal imperceptible to me, will, in body or soul, suddenly vanish across the sea.

Years later I will have a conversation with a psychoanalyst friend. When I describe my mother, she says, "I'm pretty sure her diagnosis was bipolar-II." In this milder form of bipolar disorder people experience depression and also mania, but it's hypomania, not the full-fledged mania which turns a person certifiably mad. Still, when hypomanic they are giddy and wildly ebullient and flounce at madness's borderland.

This conversation comes as a revelation. Maybe my mother deeply couldn't help her extremities. She was made to burn bright. And crash.

# PENISES!

My mother has just served us a beautiful and gracious dinner: leg of lamb with oregano and Greek rice with cinnamon and raisins. There is lemon mousse for dessert. She has on her fawn silk shirt. She is dressed for a diplomatic do, but there is some other Mom in there inside that elegant silk. I can feel a rare giddy happiness in her, ready to burst and frolic. My mother is in her finest fettle. We are about to have a Lois Taber Show.

"You'll never guess what happened at the nursing home today!"

"What, Mom?" I ask, perfectly on cue. We're all bracing for something wild.

"One of the patients had me come and see what he'd produced in the pot. It was the biggest turd I've ever seen!" and she instantly has us all laughing, showing us with her hands.

Peter looks around guiltily, as he always does when my mother says something like this. He is from a New England family where they never mentioned that anyone had a body, much less body parts or orifices or emissions, but he can't resist. He laughs, in spite of himself.

My mother is just getting started. Now she says, "And another man beckoned to me and said, 'Look what I have!' and showed his you know what to me! He wanted to show me something special!"

My mother is fond of penises—she thinks they are fun, but she also thinks they are pretty silly things, and she pities men always being at their beck and call.

"God All Mighty, save us from the penises!" my mother says next, uproarious and antic, and cracking us all up. She now lists all the poor old penises she has seen that week: enormous ones and tiny ones, long and short, wiggly ones and hopeful ones. In short order, she has us all clutching our stomachs from too much laughing on top of too much lamb. And, for once, we all go home bubbled up and happy.

What would we do without flawed charmers?

# "I WAS JUST TRYING
# TO HELP"

"Why haven't you used those new sheets I gave you?" my mother says, her voice full of hurt, her faced streaked livid with barely suppressed annoyance. "I gave them to you last week and I saw they're still in the package by your bed. I thought you said you only had one pair of sheets."

The week before she had driven over. The hydrangeas were blooming when she arrived, and I was feeling triumphant that day that I had managed to pick up the house despite the crazy flurry of getting my daughter off for a field trip and trying to fit in three hours of editing work before picking up my son from preschool. Furthermore, I was basking in what I'd recently managed to do with our bedroom even though we had barely any money to spend.

I was at a juncture when I was craving color and desperate for a sense of possibility and control in my life. I had small children, my husband was continually overseas, and I was simultaneously bored and overbusy and understimulated. I'd splurged on a poster of Bonnard's painting *Table Set in a Garden*, which depicts a picnic table laid with a pink cloth in a pastel garden shot with sunlight. It shone with happiness and hope, and hanging it up had given me a small outlet for my urge to design, to create something—anything. To go with it, I'd managed to dig up an Indian bedspread in a pastel pink, and I was so pleased to have imposed that little bit of coordination in a house cluttered and stuffed with the primary-colored jumble of children's debris. I'd cleaned the whole room—dusted the pine bookshelf and wardrobe and bedside tables my husband had built, swept the hardwood floor, even dusted the spider-webbed window ledges during the three hours my son had been at preschool. After I'd finished, I'd lain down on the smooth, pink-clothed bed, just lay there in the pink and clean and the sense of possibility for a few minutes.

I basked in the hard-won sense of triumph crystallized in a couple of Rudyard Kipling's lines:

> *Daughter am I in my mother's house;*
> *But mistress in my own.*

It was after I'd fetched my son from school that my mother appeared with her package.

"I got these at Ikea for five dollars," she said. "Aren't they nice?"

If I'd bought a Manet poster, they'd have been perfect: they had bold black and white stripes.

My heart sank. "Oh, thanks so much, Mom," I said.

Gifts from my mother could be so loaded, so complicated. Sometimes her acts of kindness seemed made to establish her un-impeachability; they seemed a defense against possible criticism rather than a pure act of thoughtfulness. She *was* always trying to be helpful, but sometimes, as this time, gifts seemed to be wrapped with aggression.

Maybe I was completely wrong about her, but now, with the sheets, I had the acute sense of being put to a test: "I dare you to like these," my mother was secretly saying. "You *will* love whatever I give you." It was as if I was a delinquent she was testing for parole.

When she was not adored—and she tested the adoration via impossible challenges such as the sheets—she was enraged. She was so insecure about her worthiness, she required absolute authority and absolute adulation. I tried hard, day after day, to assure her of my adoration, but inevitably failed. This pattern of interaction was intensifying, and occurring with greater and greater frequency.

The question came down to: Ought I please my mother or myself?

Another gift. Another test of my love.

"Did you like the quiche from the Farmwoman's Market?" my mother says, standing at the sink, scrubbing her cast iron skillet.

"Yeah, it was great," I say, but my tone isn't quite right, not quite bright enough, not completely, unadulteratedly enthusiastic.

I liked the quiche, I loved not having to cook, but it wasn't the best quiche in the world. Certainly not as good as my mother's quiche was back in the days when she made quiche. But it was good. It was great to have it. It was a huge help and I appreciate so much my mother's having brought it.

But my mother has an uncanny ability to read people. She is too smart. It's a subliminal kind of intelligence. No philosophy or perspective or neocortex involved. Just sheer reading of the undercurrents. Never does she just accept what someone says. She reads invisible face twitches and vocal undertones not even dogs can hear. She can do this for everyone except herself.

Today she can tell that I am not saying everything I am thinking, that I am being polite, so she speeds to the conclusion that I hated the quiche, and that by extension, I hate her—

always the cleanest conclusion her mind draws, always her fallback, bottom-line truth. The truth is, she is the goddess queen, multiple in powers, controller of the universe. The world rotates around her; she is a female Atlas, responsible for everything that occurs. Most of all, all that I am and feel depends on her. There are no other determining factors in my life. In her other guise, as a vulnerable female mortal, as a mother, she wants me to be happy and this happiness is up to her, and today she has failed once again. This is a laceration. Every time I fail to have the right response of happiness—in response to what she does for me to make me happy—it is another stab in her breast. She has failed me, and now I have failed her. Around and around it goes.

Her jaw flicks. "Okay, well I'll never bring you anything from the Farmwoman's Market again. I was just trying to help."

As I look at my mother uttering these last words, I go cold. I watch the light in her eyes flash out. It is as though a switch has been flicked and instantly her eyes assume the flat black of night. I shut my eyes, trying to imagine the old, kind mother, longing for the days when I was small and my mother would take me on her lap, but I can't locate her.

As I see the darkness flood yet again into her pupils, it is the signal that there is nothing left. Sense has fled. She's been bruised and she will make up and say anything at all about me now to match whatever past experience of being wronged or ignored or deprived had been triggered. 'Don't you see all I do for you?' or 'You only think of yourself,' or 'You've never considered anyone else in your life,' she may say, jaw clenched, and keep going in this vein until I finally yell back, 'I have too!' or, helpless against her, start to well up. At that, seeing that I am aroused or upset, and sensing that the black stone in my belly is as cold and heavy as it should be, she will appear to feel satisfied and relieved and will go call a friend or start to mix up pancakes. There are times it is imperative—in this repeating cycle: She *will* be seen. She *will* be felt. Does she feel invisible otherwise?

My mother's frequent and extreme disappointment at my response to her gifts has had a profound and lasting effect on me. Gift-giving for me, too, is loaded. If I offer a book to a friend and she already has a copy, or if I bring a loaf of bread as a contribution to a dinner and the hostess says, "Oh, I already have bread," (and despite the fact that the contradictory, merciful part of my mother always said, "It's the thought that counts") I feel like a little girl tossed naked into the sea. I expect myself to present, without fail, the perfect gift. It is an internal rigor that heralds partly from growing up in a diplomatic household in which careful gift-giving to foreigners was an integral part of the job, but in largest portion this peculiar species of vulnerability may be traced to my mother. I try not to reveal the sea-lost waif and her sense of emotional shattering to my recipients, but, for me, a recipient's response to my offerings is a matter of my feeling acceptable to the world, or a bit of debris. This response, I know, is absurd. It is one I work on.

## MY MOTHER'S BEAUTY

I am sitting in my tiny porch-study, finishing up some editing when I hear a knock on the door. It is two in the afternoon, a period of grace before the children have to be fetched from their schools.

My mother is standing on the doorstep. Her gorgeous, fluffy, gardenia-white hair is a-glow around her head, her baggy canvas tote is hanging from her elbow, and she is looking plucky and bright-eyed, like this might be an appearance of her old elfin pleasant self. But there is something even more in her hazel eyes: a wistfulness, a wishing. She is tentatively daring to hope for something.

"Hi, Sweetie," she says. "I was just wondering if maybe..."

She stops, looking bashful and coquettish, like a little Indiana girl twisting her foot and hoping against hope for permission to have a cookie.

"I was wondering if maybe you'd like to come to the drug store with me to try to find an eyebrow pencil. My eyebrows are just getting so white," she says, jabbing her finger toward her face.

My heart breaks. I want to drop to the ground and bawl.

We get in the car and I take her hand.

# TURDS

*Despair is like forward children, who, when you take away one of their playthings, throw the rest into the fire for madness. It grows angry with itself, turns its own executioner, and revenges its misfortunes on its own head.*
— Lord Byron
    "Childe Harold's Pilgrimage"

"I know you hate me," my mother says. This is her opening salvo when I drop by.

Immediately my innards start to churn, and the filaments of the hairs on my arms to rise. I know what is coming but I fight it with all I've got. I will not let her do this to me, I think. I love her, God damn it. I always have. She's my mother, for heaven's sake. Doesn't she know I love her by now? I desperately try to keep my arms around the mother I can love, and around the love I have for her. But her tone is so calm. She sounds almost happy, and she says I hate her with such matter-of-fact, comfortable surety that I feel every fiber of me hackling.

I spurt out, trying to sound calm and light, "Oh, Mom, don't be dumb. I don't hate you. I love you and I always will." My voice only quavers a little bit on the last sentence.

She is quick on the uptake. Not a second goes by.

"But I *am* dumb, and of course you hate me. You know you do."

"Mo-om!"

"You know I'm right," she says, calm as Athena, the invincible, helmeted goddess of war.

My mother's utter confidence, her lance of ice, pushes me over the edge. The hairs all over my body are now standing on end. I can feel my body puffing and pawing like a riled bull. I am starting to huff and steam. Where I had a hold of the love when I entered the room, it has now evaporated and I am filled with snorting, barely contained hate. I want to bellow at her. I want to run her over with my great, heaving body and trampling hooves, then stampede from the room and away from her forever.

My mother is brilliant. Effectively and expertly, with great shine, she has brought me to my knees; turning me from a being benevolent to one malignant. I now burn with hatred, I feel hateful for hating her, and my mother is off scot-free, washed clean. Her face wears an angelic tranquility.

Via this twisting, contorting, magical thinking—and blastedly unconscious maneuver, my mother has tranquilly removed her uncomfortable ill-wishing malignancy, her intolerable self-hatred, disappointment, and fury as though they are a cloak and hung them over my shoulders. Presto! Mission accomplished! Her daughter has become her toxic, wrathful, electric-furred self.

And further vindication! See! She was right all along about my hating her.

Here is another sample of my mother's canny moves.

"I'm just a turd," my mother says.

"Oh, Mom, don't be dumb."

"But I *am* dumb. I'm a turd. You know I am."

My mother and I have this exchange, imbibe this meal, this

delicacy of pain and self-loathing—in so many words—over and over again. At her house, at my house, in shops, in cars. Each time, even though I have been through it before, it is as though a shaft of ice lances me. My mother means her words seriously, and her habit of saying she is a turd is so confounding and difficult to handle that, by the end of such an interaction, I feel, in some ways, she *is* one (so to speak). And I am left cringing and crouched, abjectly praying, scrabbling for some sprig of green growth in the dung.

It is all so painful, so *alive*, this interaction between us, indeed like a turd splatted in a dark-tangled forest, crawling with maggots.

What is the nature of loyalty? I return and return to my mother. Is loyalty obedience your mother in all things? Is it willingness to make yourself available for regular voyages between Scylla and Charybdis?

Where does a mother end and a daughter begin?

# BATHING FORREST

"Oh, Forrest, come here. Let me give you a bath!" My mother seizes my round, platinum-headed two-and-a-half-year-old, disappears with him into the kitchen and plops him on the counter. She has waiting on the dish drainer a washcloth and a bar of soap. The room already smells of Dove.

"Oh, look at your beautiful mollies," she says as she squeezes the thighs sticking out of his shorts. They're so chubby they look like they have rubber bands stretched around them at intervals.

"Hold your arms up, Forrey, so I can take off your dinosaur shirt." My son complies, miraculously. "Okay, Oma." She efficiently removes his shirt and diaper. Once he's naked, she can't resist picking him up, her hand cradling his bottom as she holds him to her bosom and squeezes his pure roundness tight.

"Oh, Forrest, you're delicious," she says.

As the water runs in the sink, she carries him to the fridge and says, "Look what I have for you!" And hands him a bottle of apple juice. He grabs it with one dimpled hand, tips it into his mouth and chugs, like a lusty drunkard.

"And look what else I got you!" she says, opening a bag of peanut butter cookies.

Once the sink is half full and my little boy's face and hands are sticky with juice and crumbs, she plops him in the sink and hands him the measuring cups and strainer, his favorite bath toys.

He pours and splashes busily as, crooning, she soaps his back and his chest and belly until they're all white suds and he's become a slopping, slippery boy. She pours water over his head. He startles and splutters a bit, but doesn't cry. He feels secure in her hands. "Oh, it's okay, Forrey," my mother says and he just retrieves the measuring cups floating in the soapy pool.

"Oh, you're so delicious," my mother says again as she lifts him up and slops a soapy washcloth around his bottom and penis, and scrubs his feet.

"What great abductors he has," she says. "He's going to be a good hiker like his Opa, aren't you Forrey?"

When she lifts him out, he squirms. He doesn't want to leave his little pool, but she wraps him tightly in a white towel and carries him around, a warm and soothing packet, holding him close, a part of her, his body her great delight.

She is deliciously round too and I am happily watching her with him. Moved, I hug her and say, "I love you, Mom."

She says, "I'm just squish."

## "I TOLD YOU SO"

My mother is standing in her clean living room on her clean carpet by her vacuum cleaner. The whole house smells of

Lemon Pledge. "If you don't clean your house, no other mother will let her child come play with your children." Her voice is dictatorial, with a spike in it.

I am too tired, too frazzled, too stretched thin to clean my house, but, nevertheless, because my daughter needs companionship, I invite to come over, a child who lives in an impeccable house approximately twenty times the size of ours, and—to up the ante—also has an impeccable mother.

The mother permits her daughter to enter our house, perhaps only because she hasn't seen its interior.

My daughter and the little girl seem to play fine. The little girls seem able to transcend the mess. The visiting girl does comment, "Gee, your whole house would fit in our dining room."

But later I hear her say to my daughter, "Wow, your mother plays with you!"

A brief unexpected vindication.

# SHE CAN STILL READ ME
# LIKE A BOOK

My mother knows what is written in the pages of my journal even before I put pen to them. She divines my moods and disgruntlements just as she did when I was small. By now, though, the knowledge seems to burden her. Her tone with me, when she's detected something off kilter in me, is sometimes emphatic, sometimes exasperated, sometimes a martyr's plaint. Two examples:

First:

I've just arrived for dinner at my mother's. I've spent the day reading manuscripts for pennies, wishing I'd never left my university job. My mother and I have only said hello. I sit down to the Trader Joe's rice and beans my mother has heated up for us in the microwave.

"You need a new job," my mother says.

Second:

I am fed up. In the last week, my mother has told me I'm ruining my career by not getting a new job teaching in a school. She's told me I'm looking frowsy. She's told me again that I'd better clean my house or no other mothers will let their children come over. (Was this true, I wonder, when I was growing up in the 50s?) I don't want to see my mother, but she wants to see the children, so I've agreed to come by for dinner. I will go but I'm gritting my teeth. I am determined to be civil, to get through another dinner with my mother, to avoid my mother's damn feelings and ideas, to not have to really talk to her, to hide my fury, to just get through it without emotional torment. I can do it. We'll eat and then we'll just go home.

"You're mad at me," my mother says when she opens the door.

# FIFTEEN WORDS FROM
# MY FATHER

"You know, I don't think your aim in life should be to please your mother."

My father's eyes are chestnut brown, quiet and serious, and looking straight into mine. His sentence comes, calm and intentional, like a tossed life ring saving me from gasping grief and desperate flabbergastion, at the end of just one more evening in my hectic life, one more dinner at which I fail my mother.

Before the dinner, I'd spent the afternoon fetching my four-year-old son from preschool; making him a hot dog for his snack; helping him find the pieces for the Lego airplane he was building; cajoling him with promises of cookies to walk with me to fetch my daughter at her bus stop; bandaging his knee after he scraped it on the walk; fixing my daughter oatmeal cookies and a ham sandwich; helping my daughter get started on a diorama of *Charlotte's Web* she was making for school; calling for prescriptions at the pharmacy—my daughter had her umpteenth strep infection; and scheduling piano lessons—all while trying to assemble an apple pie for the evening meal at my mother's.

"I'm making something special," she had said, so I wanted to contribute a pie. It took me twice as long to make the crust, though, because the crust was one of those that crumbled instead of cohering and cooperatively rolling out smoothly. At the last minute, I dashed to the neighborhood market with the kids to get my mother some flowers. Then my husband arrived home fifteen minutes late—at 6:45 instead of 6:30. We were due at 6:45 and the pie wasn't out of the oven. It was a typical day at our house: a mad scramble of juggling tasks, cock-ups, and *best laid plans*.

I don't know if I phoned to tell her that we'd be late. I might not have, and if so, this would have been inconsiderate and worthy of anger—and I might be held culpable for and might have brought on what next transpired. But what happened might also have occurred whether or not I'd informed my mother. Memory is unreliable, and not knowing, you see how one tends to cast memories in certain directions?

In any case, when we finally arrived at 7:15 at my parents' bungalow, my mother's face had the flat, stretched look of rubber bands. She didn't even come out of the kitchen to greet us. She might as well have just put me on a stool in the corner with a dunce cap on my head, for she said and asked nothing. Just slammed the serving dishes out of the oven and spat out, "Put the god-damned food on the table."

When I took the platter of chicken and walnuts, and the

bamboo bowl of fresh rice, and the cucumber and peanut salad to the table, the table was all beautifully set with a pressed white linen cloth, the silver, the best dishes, and ironed white napkins.

Guilt plummeted through me and stabbed my heart.

My father's words, quietly bestowed to me just before I left that evening, were *treasures*, gifts from some well-wishing father god of mercy. My father knew how hard my mother could be on me, and he granted me credit for effort even when my responses were less than optimal.

As he uttered those fifteen words, his eyes looked as desperate as I felt. He struggled all their lives together to understand my mother and I don't think he ever did. Her fury was now ravaging all of us.

His discreet, clandestine sentence would provide me rescue time and again when I found myself tossed into tempestuous seas with my mother. Often, I couldn't immediately locate that life-saving ring of words as I thrashed about in my mother's swamping, cold waters, but eventually, sometimes, my hand would hit upon that simple, magical circlet. I'd then grasp it tight—it was like both a float I could slip over my head to wear and keep me buoyant, and a porthole through which I could see—and I'd feel calmed and safe and able to entertain the notion that I wasn't, after all, *so* bad.

# BEAUTY LOST

We are living in France where Peter has a two-year job. I send my mother gifts from Paris: a powder blue sweater from a boutique in the 16th Arrondissement, a turquoise and teal shawl to fling around her neck like a chic Frenchwoman, and many other gifts, wanting to make her happy. Picturing that mouth of hers with the corners turned down, that narrowed look in her eyes. Wanting and wanting to make her happy. It is striking, this illogical desperation an offspring feels to make a rejecting parent happy. It is a compulsion, almost an addiction. There *must* be a way to please him or her. Again and again, it seems, we children return to the scene of the crime, trying to redo.

When I ask my mother over the telephone if she receives my packets, she ignores my question and tells me about all the things in her house that need to be thrown away. Instants after I call, she says she knows I need to go, she knows I have a lot to do, and she puts down the phone.

My mother is so angry at life, nothing can mollify her. Everything I say brings a snarl and embitters her further. I forget that this indicates depression: Social Work 101. She's so spitting furious, so surly, I forget what's underneath.

In Paris I am studying the French craft of *cartonnage*—a technique for making and decorating boxes and books with beautiful papers. Pouring into it my anguish and urgent wish to prove my love for her, I spend days making my mother a box for her physical therapy files out of beautiful Italian floral papers. When I arrive back in America, it turns out that she didn't recognize that the box was a gift. She has thrown it away. Utterly bereft of her own loveliness, my mother is no longer able to recognize beauty.

# SURRENDER

"You're always spending time with Pop," my mother says after learning I took a walk with my father one afternoon. We are back in Chevy Chase now. She has dropped by while I am chopping carrots for dinner.

I stop slicing. She is the one who is always saying my father *has* to get more exercise. I had thought I was aiding her in her mission.

"You never make time for me." She doesn't let me reply—she cuts to the chase. "I know you've always hated me. Oh, I know you like him better. You always have. I would too."

There is a sinking in my deepest precincts as I splutter, "Mo-om!"

"Of course you do."

"Mom, that's simply not true." I have loved her almost desperately all my life, and I do not always hate her now, and yet sometimes I want to throttle her. But whatever I say won't matter. She believes the stories her emotions tell her.

When my mother goes home my heart is sick. By now my stomach tightens every time I think of her. Thoughts of her intrude, in little flicking scenes, all through my days. My mother, who used to coo to dogs, who adored babies, who saved hundreds of patients, who saved her daughter ten thousand ways, seems way beyond saving. She is flailing in a vast emptiness, living now in a hollow orb. I spend hours every week obsessing, racking my brain, trying to think of something to make her happy.

When I next visit my parents, I bring a cherry pie for my father and a hunk of Brie for my mother, but it as though our last conversation hasn't stopped. "I know you've always hated me," she says.

Euripides wrote of Hecuba in *Trojan Women*:

> *If sailors have to face a storm that is not too great, they rally eagerly to the task of saving themselves from peril...But if the waves are too high, the storm too fierce, they give in to fate and submit to the mercy of the running seas.*

When I get home after dinner, I throw myself on my bed and sob.

*My mother is the most tortured and impossible person in the world,*
I think. *I cannot. I cannot. I cannot make her happy. Much as I try to
bring her pleasure, I am instead sludge under her foot. I am a thorn. I
am pricks and stabs and ice water hurled in her face. I am her despicable
torturer.*

I sob and sob. I sob and sob. I sob and sob…And slowly,
slowly I begin to believe my thoughts. The rose-yellow dawn
begins to tint the sky…*I cannot do it,* I think. *I truly cannot. I
cannot make my mother happy. Maybe no one can, or maybe someone
can, but I am the last person in the world who can.*

*It is true,* I think, my words beginning to become solid, to
take on weight: *I truly cannot make my mother happy. These six words
are true. This statement is real and firm: I cannot make my mother
happy. Nothing I do will ever, ever perform this feat.*

I sob and sob on my pink-covered bed, and eventually,
wrung out, a new thought comes: *Mom always says, "Where there's
a will, there's a way," but she is wrong. Sometimes there is no way.*

# WHAT A DAUGHTER
# IS FOR

A daughter doesn't ever really give up. Nor does a mother.
Thank goodness and alas.

I visit my mother, this time bringing a posy of wildflowers.
I find her in the kitchen yanking a frozen dinner for her and my
father from the freezer. I can see only the back of her, a frazzled
white head, a 40-year-old skirt and a worn-out blouse.

"How are you, Mom?"

"It's been an awful week. If it's not one damned thing, it's
another in this blasted world."

With the thud of her voice—so dull, so weary, so
imperious—she has me instantly in a mortis grip.

I dare look at her only for an instant. Her face is a Gorgon's
mask. She has snake tresses. She is Medusa drowning, clutching

at me. Her claws grip my hair. She pulls me toward her. My belly shrieks. She *will* own what is true——or turn me to stone.

The desperation and sorrow that must be driving this harridan are far beyond my reach, sequestered on some remote planet across the universe. I only detect the fury and I know the terms: *Only reflect. If I say the day is onerous, your job is to echo. Don't you dare contradict me. Don't be anything other than I am. You, my daughter, if you are my daughter, if you are a good person, if you are loyal to your mother, if you love me, if you don't want to massacre me, if you know what's good for you, if you don't want me to...*

I envision terrors: She lunges and lacerates me with her claws.

Even in her kitchen, as I sign myself over, I know that I am doomed. Because, though I can say what she wishes me to say, "Yes, life is dreadful. Yes, life is a horror," she's too wise to believe I believe what comes from my mouth. She can't bear it, but she can't get around it, the one ineluctable truth: a person can't demand another's thoughts or feelings. And try as I might, *wish* as I might, as her daughter, to please her, to *utter* her thoughts, to suffer her suffering as she wishes me to do, I am not her. I am not her twin. A membrane of skin separates us. Even a terrorized despot such as she is at the moment, can't get around this. She would slice the membrane off me if it would work, and meld us back together, or she would stuff me back in her womb, but she hasn't that magic. Minute by interminable minute, day upon day, this crushes her. It is utter desperation.

She clutches at me and I try, "I'm so sorry, Mom, that your week has been awful," but we're both going down.

There is no rescue. She hasn't said what she will do if I fail her——now that I *have* failed her——but I know. She will take me down. She wants company, her daughter with her, as she sinks down through the black waters. This is the final act she requires of me, the only way I will understand. In the book of this mother of my many, many mothers, a daughter's job is to accompany her mother to the bottom of the sea, into the last darkness. This is what daughters are for.

# MY WRITING

*Truth has rough flavors if we bite it through.*
– George Eliot

When my son was in preschool and I had more time for creative pursuits, I wrote a story called "Longing for America," about just that—the way I yearned for my country, to have a country of my own, during my childhood of being a foreigner overseas. In the piece I described a visit our family made to Indiana, to visit my mother's sister, one time when I was small. In that description, which spelled out my envy of my cousins' everything—their little house with the swing set out back, the pool they splashed in all summer long, the way everyone knew them everywhere they went—a piece full of praise and superlatives, I used the word "grimy," nested among many complimentary others, to describe my cousins' town.

When I showed the piece to my mother, tentatively pleased with it, she returned it to me with a grisly look. "You insulted Aunt Norma. How could you call her home 'grimy?' I could never show this to anyone in my family," she said, her voice thickening from upset.

I was crushed that my mother would pluck one word, out of the effusive many, to fix upon and to demonstrate one more time how lacking in respect I was. Out of my 10,000 words, she'd chosen one to usurp all. How woefully prone to simplification, to confirming our preconceptions we are—all of us.

And how prone some of us are to overreaction. I, in turn, interpreted my mother's response to mean she hated my writing and disapproved of my preferred occupation, and I sequestered my habit underground after that, never mentioning it—and, whenever the subject of writing arose in conversation, dismissed its importance in my life.

When my mother asked me, as she did every time I saw her,

if I'd had a productive day, I said, even if I'd spent the day writing, "Yeah, I did a lot of teaching prep," or I shifted the topic to the children. I sometimes felt, with my secret writing, like a spy conducting a chancy covert operation that I hoped would ultimately be to the good.

As I wrote, at first, my main objective was to conduct undercover surveillance on the past to catch my mother at it. My goal was to get down on the page the moments that seared. As I wrote, though, and as I got the hard stuff down, my mission shifted as contrasting, lovely moments infiltrated my mind. The past seemed to hold happy moments with my mother too. My tracking and recording expanded now to include more and more variety, more and more contrasting moments. The writing grew ampler and more complicated, and fruitfully so, as time went on. I felt I was getting closer to a whole. Something sloppier and multiple seemed more generous and loving and felt nearer to the truth—and hopefully moved toward the good. But this was taking years, and the lurching back-and-forth process brought with it moments of acute pain.

As I look back, it is clear that my choice to go into deep cover with my writing was extreme. Sometimes over the years I'd overhear my mother say to a friend, "Oh, Sara's writing something," a clear admission of, and perhaps even acceptance of or pride in my calling—but I'd overlook it. Holding fast to the idea that my mother disapproved of my writing made things simpler and cleaner. Complexity, murk, *reality* would have been so much harder to deal with.

One day, long after my mother died, my eyes settle on a small, round, white container sitting on my desk, a tiny gift my mother gave me a couple of years before she died. The container says PAPER CLIPS on it.

I suddenly remember that day when I visited my mother in

assisted living. At the end of the visit, she had put into my hands the little white pot. "This is for you," she said. She had purchased it for me at the retirement community's opportunity shop.

The sorrow and love which hit me are almost more than I can bear. I sob for a long time.

How hard our mothers try. Why can't we plow through the anger and the mess to the essence, the love?

**10**

# A MOMENT

"Can I talk to you about something that happened with my mother?" So begins my conversation with my friend Susan, my friend Cindy, my friend Elaine, my friend Nancy, my friend...

My mother was so very difficult during the last 25 years of my life with her that an enormous proportion of my conversation with my husband and my friends, and later my daughter and son, was devoted to her. The amount of emotional energy I expended on trying to understand her and manage my relationship with her is immeasurable.

If the moments when she glared at me dismayed me, the moments when my mother was sweet to me, such as when she'd spin me out for a shopping spree or suddenly appear on my doorstep with a bouquet, made her all the more confusing. They made me question my perceptions, made me feel guilty, and baffled me. They gave me the sense that I simply would never be able to get my head around her and say definitively, "This is who my mother is. This is how she feels about me." The sprinkles of sugar in the bitter tonic could mask the vitriol and make me think, "I'm making it all up. There's something wrong with me. How could I be so mean as to think my mother, who obviously loves me, is malevolent? I am just a bad person."

There seems to be something deep-lodged in human nature—I've talked to others and found I'm not alone—that resists the notion that a mother truly dislikes her offspring. A child would rather blame herself than absorb and accept the fact of a mother's hostility or derangement. Something in me insisted that my mother was good. And maybe she was. And of course she was. We all have goodness in us, and my mother, in many ways, had more goodness and was more generous than most. This made it especially challenging to encompass and account for her bouts of erratic fury and disapproval. Our battles could be so epic, so without end. What could cause this? I spent 25 years fighting self-hatred, and struggling with my mother's intermittent doses of damning and undermining, trying to fathom who my mother was and why she was so hateful toward me. Each time she did something that hurt, I spent weeks ruminating about it, trying to figure out what I'd done that had brought on the fury, endeavoring to identify its fount. I needed a clear, graspable, straightforward answer.

I racked and racked my brain:

Was it socio-cultural, historical factors that fueled my mother's fury?

Was it her era, the point in history she happened to be born into—an era when women were suffocated, regarded as responsible for the well-being of everyone in a family and blamed if anything went awry?

Was it our country—its emphasis on work, self-denial, and self-reliance which encouraged my mother to do without the support every human being needs?

Was it her childhood? The sense of having no one and nothing but her own fierce determination with which to survive a terrifying world?

Was it the countless stresses associated with being a spy's wife—most of which were and will always be completely unknown and utterly invisible to me or anyone else?

Was it something within her? The postpartum depression which established, from the very constellation of our relationship, a rivalry between her survival and mine? The thyroid operation? Menopause? Psychopathology?

Was it the dynamics of our particular family—the special challenges presented by each family member's needs? Or the marriage? Or my troubling hospitalization? Or a simple mother-daughter personality mismatch? Was it that the quarrel between my brother and me shattered my mother's picture of her perfect family? Or simply that a daughter is a natural receptacle for a mother's unhappiness?

Could it be that life's blows and losses and stresses, on top of all that moving, mounted up and simply became too much—

so that she finally blew a gasket?

The piling up of, a crescendo of all of the above?

Or: Was it possibly something I didn't know about—something that, along with all the rest, served as the match that lit the fuse that altered the balance, that led to the explosion of who my mother had been?

For years I tossed around all of these possible culprits—one month being sure hormonal changes were the key cause, another that her childhood was, another that I was a bad person, and on and on—but none of them fully satisfied.

All these factors could be true and valid, serve singly or in combination as the answer to the puzzle of Lois Taber. But then one week, when I was 63, I had two conversations—one with my husband and another with a therapist friend—and a moment sprung to me out of memory:

My mother is calling me from Taipei after her evacuation from Saigon. I am standing in my dormitory hallway, twisting the phone cord around my hand. I am expecting to hear about my father who is still in Vietnam as it's coming apart, but she is telling me about something else—an airplane full of orphans that crashed shortly before she was evacuated. I can hear in her words surging, smothered panic. Her sentences are staccato, ripe with terror. "It was awful, just awful." Three times she tells me, "Sara, the babies were shrieking."

In retrospect I can hear all of this, but at the time, my mind didn't latch on. I was much more caught up in the drama of my father's odyssey—what would happen to him, abandoned in the midst of an escalating disaster? This was my mother's emphasis as well. Quickly she shifted the conversation to her worry about him. Her orphan story was lost in the flurry of the worry about my father's safety.

It wasn't until my parents returned from Southeast Asia that I heard the full story of the orphan flight:

On April 4th, 1975, a U.S. Air Force C-5A Galaxy, serial number *68-0218*, took off from Saigon's Tan Son Nhut airport.

It was the first flight of "Operation Babylift," a massive push to get orphans scheduled for adoption out of Vietnam before the looming American departure. Many of the orphans were fathered by American servicemen. By the last American flight out of Vietnam, over 10,300 orphans would have been evacuated.

Twelve minutes after the C-5A Galaxy took off, as it was rising over the South China Sea, there was a huge explosion. With the explosion, the rear fuselage of the plane ripped apart. The locks on the plane's back loading ramp had malfunctioned, causing the door to open and separate from the aircraft's body. Decompression rapidly occurred and the cabin filled with swirling fog and debris. The cables to the rudder and elevators were cut in the blow-up, and two of the four hydraulic systems broke down. The crew frantically tried to keep control of the plane, using the plane's power, wing spoilers, and the one aileron that still functioned. They managed to lower the plane to 4,000 feet and to begin to turn the craft 180 degrees, in preparation for a return landing on Tan Son Nhut's runway 25L. About halfway into the turn, though, the plane's rate of descent rapidly increased. When they saw that they wouldn't make the airport runway, the pilots applied full power to bring the nose of the plane up just before it hit a rice paddy. The plane did not stop moving upon hitting the paddy, however. It skidded for a quarter of a mile and then became airborne again for another half a mile. It finally hit a dike, whereupon it broke into four pieces and caught fire. 138 people were killed, including defense department personnel, adult caregivers, and children.

My mother, who was intensely involved in Operation Babylift, was one of the people who gathered at Tan Son Nhut and loaded the C-5A Galaxy flight. At the airport, seeing the high ratio of children to adult caretakers gathered for the flight, she offered to hop on to help out on the journey, but, because she didn't have her passport with her, she was unable to go. Just before four p.m., my mother and others strapped into their seats 243 babies and toddlers headed for new homes across the world. She and her fellow exhausted volunteers were flooded with relief and exhilaration as they watched the plane lift off: a long struggle won. My mother's body soared at the thought that she and the other women had yanked some goodness from the maw of defeat. And then, ten minutes later, the plane's nose headed toward earth.

My mother was one of those who rushed to the U.S. military hospital to receive the victims arriving from the crash site. She hurtled as fast as her legs could carry her. I can feel, in my body, her body running: She was a winged child, winged by terror. She was a little girl racing through the forest, dodging bears. And she was Demeter, ready to blot out the sun to save the earth's children. But she was seized and carried down to the shadowy underworld.

Of the 138 people who died, over half of them were children. My mother spent the rest of her day providing assistance and weeping for the small, limp bodies, those dead and those injured, arriving by the scores into the terminal. Little Anh, the toddler my mother had chosen for our family friends, survived but was severely traumatized.

From the start, upon my parents' arrival back on U.S. terra firma from their southeast Asian evacuations, my father's story became *the* punctuating family story for my parents' Vietnam tour. Whenever people would ask about Vietnam, my father's dramatic tale—of the effort to help establish a functioning community for his Vietnamese employees and their families on Phu Quoc Island, the hailing of the freighter, the escape under gunfire, the arduous sea journey from Phu Quoc to Guam, were recounted. This continued for the next 30 years.

I know my mother deliberately tried not to let her mind dwell on the tragedy she'd experienced; she had also learned, by trial and error, that people were more interested in my father's story than her own. Once in a while, though, in the company of one or more of her women friends, with a hush in her voice, shaking her head and looking at her hands, my mother would tell the story of the orphan flight, always ending with those chilling words, "The babies were shrieking."

Only upon my husband's saying several times, "Don't you think the trauma of the orphan flight could be the story here?" and after my therapist friend's clear pronouncement, upon hearing my description of my anguished relationship with my mother, "Oh, your mother had P.T.S.D.," did the bell ring.

Blows and breakthroughs, moments of deep darkness and moments of stunning light, comprise the narrative of my mother and me. These two conversations chimed to usher in an Aristotelian moment of *recognition*, an epiphanic instant of conversion in a life or a narrative when truth becomes apparent, knowledge replaces ignorance, a sense of the eternal intrudes into the temporal realm. An answer had appeared to a question I wasn't aware I'd had, a wholeness restored to a shatter of which I hadn't known.

A second therapist friend, upon later hearing of the deaths of children that my mother witnessed, said. "How could your mother not have P.T.S.D? She was a first responder to a mass casualty."

Later, I looked up the symptoms of P.T.S.D. in the Diagnostic Statistical Manual of Mental Disorders, the DSM-5. The basic criterion for the P.T.S.D. diagnosis is *exposure to actual or threatened death, serious injury, or sexual violence*. And I look up the work of Judith Lewis Herman. She wrote this of those with P.T.S.D.:

"Survivors of atrocity of every age and every culture come to a point in their testimony where all questions are reduced to one, spoken more in bewilderment than in outrage: Why? The answer is beyond human understanding." And this: "After a traumatic experience, the human system of self-preservation seems to go onto permanent alert, as if the danger might return at any moment."

Sometime between 99 and 55 BC, Lucretius recorded the destruction wrought by trauma in his *On The Nature of Things*:

*Besides, take any creature—if a blow*
*Greater than it can withstand strike it, then this will throw*
*All senses, mind and body into disarray, and lay it low,*
*For it shakes the atoms loose from their positions…*
*For what else do we think that such a blow's able to do,*
*But strike a thing to pieces and dissolve it through and*
    *through?*

I am not aware of all that went on inside my mother. My mother concealed a lot of her feelings, and my father covered for her, often explaining her anger or impatience with quiet asides to me such as, "Your mother is a little overstressed right now," or "Your mother is a little bit rigid today." But the symptoms of P.T.S.D. glaringly describe my mother's behavior.

P.T.S.D. is recognized and diagnosed commonly now. It is freely and frequently discussed, but who thinks to consider that the diagnosis may apply to her mother?

If only I had known. Might our lives have been different?

Perhaps this is giving myself too much the benefit of the doubt, but it seems unlikely that, as her daughter, I could have figured it out on my own. After all, as close as they are, there is inevitably an unbridgeable aperture between a mother and daughter. A daughter simply cannot know a mother's experience. Even if a mother could clearly articulate her experience to her daughter, her daughter couldn't possibly fully comprehend. Each woman on this earth has a particular set of irreplicable experiences, and a daughter is a being out of a different time, but it is more than that. The truth is, she will never catch up to her mother. Age confers knowledge to a woman that cannot be had until a daughter reaches that same stage of life—and a mother would not even want her daughter to know certain things until she must. But all of this means that some things a mother knows, a daughter cannot begin to understand until her mother is gone. It is one of the heart-rending verities of life that a daughter can probably never begin to understand her mother, nor a writing daughter begin to inscribe her mother's story, until her mother is in the beyond. Even then she may merely sketch a beginning. Only far-off time can spin the threads.

But still, how could this tragic story of my mother's have been so submerged by the world? The answer is, it was deep-sixed by my father's story and by the stories of Men—and by my mother's supreme effort, as the woman of the house, to simply hold her husband, her children, our financial security, our family's life and limb together. This woman's story—the story of the woman holding the fort while the men fight highly questionable wars—is more heroic and deep-dredged in humanity and moral purity than those of the G-men she was supporting. Yet she was lost, her story was lost, and she was running as fast as she could to survive, and to keep her family alive while bearing unimaginable suffering.

I can only begin to imagine how my mother must have felt in the months and years after the orphan flight. How did she put together this impossible pair of facts: she had tried to save the children and she had been instrumental in their deaths. And what must it have been like to see the orphans' tragedy quickly forgotten in the panic to save the remaining, mostly adult male, American defense department and embassy forces?

What is notable about my mother is that, unlike many veterans with P.T.S.D. who return home and understandably withdraw from future frays, my mother went back into battle. She just continued on as a wounded warrior, seeking chances to help the most beleaguered and needy and endangered people she could find. I know my mother treasured me and my brother, as a mother does, more than any other beings on earth, but another part of her could only have seen our problems as minor relative to all she had seen.

With my two conversations I suddenly saw something new: My mother was not only Demeter in her two guises—a nurturing source of seed for the earth and a hurtling force ready

334

to block the sun and rain to save lost children. She was, simultaneously, Persephone seized by Hades and transported to the kingdom of shadows.

At last I beheld my mother.

Here is where the daughter ends and the mother finally begins.

**11**

# AT THE END

*O, to take what we love inside,*
*to carry within us an orchard*
— Li-Young Lee
  "From Blossoms"

My mother is in her last bed.

When I arrive at the hospital, the nurse tells me, "Your mother has been saying, 'I want Sara. Where is Sara?'"

My insides trill. I am a little girl twirling in her new dress.

My mother asked for Sara! She asked for *me*!

# EPILOGUE

*Life is not susceptible perhaps to the treatment we give it when we try to tell it. What is the phrase for the moon? And the phrase for love? By what name are we to call death? I do not know. I need a little language such as lovers use, words of one syllable such as children speak when they come into the room and find their mother sewing and pick up some scrap of bright wool, a feather, or a shred of chintz. I need a howl; a cry.*
— Virginia Woolf
   *The Waves*

How is one to compass a relationship as primal and essential as that of a mother and daughter?

Into these pages, I have sought to beckon every facet of my mother, every sort of moment between us, every move I could brightly recall of this wonderful and wise, terrible and troubled woman.

I have summoned and sweated and set down, and yet, still, questions remain: How much weight should I give to the dark-wracked moments, the scenes in the portal that show a girl cringing in a corner after having almost been hit by a car or a young woman told by her mother that she has ruined her mother's life? How am I to weigh those stark, wounding instants against the hundreds of more common-place harmonious, nettlesome, or simple ones enjoyed by my mother and me? Further, how ought I to weigh those, in turn, against the ten thousand tiny, nearly invisible things my mother did for me every month, every week, every day out of pure, imperishable love? Mothers and daughters are separate, yet endlessly bound. How am I to encompass the eternity that is a mother and daughter?

I summon and summon, hoping one day to hit bedrock, to with finality fathom this mother of mine who was so many mothers to me. It seems, though, and thankfully, that this is impossible—that my mother is a constant spring. It seems, perhaps, that to really embrace the full truth about our relationships, particularly complex ones, we must live without a single hard and fast definition, march on sans firm ground, and find a rocking comfort in constant, infinite, unending transition, the death of one summing-up ushering in the next, as happens perpetually in the natural world... I bow to the sense that I will go on writing and writing of my mother into all time, beyond the horizon.

For there is always more to bubble up from the infinite well of my mother. No matter how I try, so many mothers are missing from my collection, and—weightless, *surprises*—up they float: my mother eating crabs, my mother camping in the rain on a soggy English pasture, my mother as a giantess, my mother as a flea, as a cow, as a hut, as a spoon. My mother as vapor. My mother as bulk and beauty.

And not only in remembrance does my mother endlessly proliferate. I see her, too, in my daughter's deft hand as she paints a portrait of a woman, and in my son's as he stirs a delectable curry with a wooden spoon.

Oh where, oh where does she stop, this mother of mine, this human being, this world, this universe, this passing nothingness, this grass, this immortal, this night, this marvel, this miracle, this glory? Unstoppable, unquenchable, she seems...

Which shall I leave you with? Tulips or black water? The glory or the darkness? Glory-Darkness. Darkness-Glory. See how the projector is stuck endlessly shucking back and forth, and shuttling on and on and on from slide to slide to slide?

*My mother romps in the cow pasture, the corner of her frock caught in her underpants, chasing chickens. She holds up a cup of French wine, about to say something that will make her guests laugh.*

# ACKNOWLEDGEMENTS

The writing of memoir is not a solo endeavor. Though a memoirist toils away alone in her study for days on end, she does so within a nest of comrades indulgent and smart, generous and kind. To so many I owe heart-felt thanks. An abiding band of friends, colleagues, and advisors have stood by, listened to me bellow and weep and churn, and urged me onward during the many years of this book's gestation.

First, last, and foremost, I must salute Lois Louise Guernsey Taber, the strong and vital, flawed and vastly human model of womanhood I was so lucky to count as my mother. I bow to the valiant person—my mother now gone—who gave me the love and the rich, complex life that led to this contemplation on mothers and daughters.

As for others who supported me as I put pen to paper:

Chocolate and flowers go to Jana Belsky, Sharon Berlin, Deirdre Callanan, Sandra Dibble, Cynthia Eyster, Ann Harvey, Elaine Klaassen, Kerry Malawista, Catherine Mayo, Anora McGaha, Liz McKamy, Selby McPhee, Rebecca Milliken, Marianne Moloney, Hattie Myers, Susan Perkins, Lenore Pomerance, Alison Townsend, David Townsend, and Alexandra Viets, who read early and late drafts of the book and offered their support, insights, and editorial perspicacity.

I wish to thank, also, Sam Dorrance, Elizabeth Demers, and Bill Strachan, the great editors who helped this book in various ways along its passage into print.

My experiences with the editors and designers at Atmosphere Press have been wonderful. I can't thank them enough for the care they have given to *Black Water and Tulips*.

Now I must thank my friends. My friends are astonishing. Wise mothers all, they have patiently—both intentionally, and inadvertently by simply being who they are—nursed and heartened me on through the travails of both the experiencing and writing that have led to this book. They have listened, and listened, and listened, each offering me incomparable gifts. Where I'd be without this back-up crew, I can't imagine.

A special embrace goes to Mariama Bangura, who looked after my mother—and thus, also me, with patience, grace, and wisdom through my mother's last years.

My current and past students at The Writer's Center, New Directions, and The Memoir Club are also due enthusiastic and affectionate thanks. They have presented me a unique gift as I worked on this book, offering me on-going lessons about love and generosity and the curious complexities of human nature.

I wish to highlight, also, my fellow participants in the St. Johns College Year of Classics seminar. Their perspectives, lent over the past decade, have unfailingly enriched my thinking.

A series of psychotherapists have helped me to understand my mother through the years. Key among them have been Ralph Cohen, Jan Harwood, Bob Rosenthal, Suzanne Saunders, Carole Hoage, Barbara Kane, and Molly Strauss.

There aren't words in any language to thank Peter, Maud, and Forrest for the support they have given to me as I struggled with this book. Their capacities for love and delight and clarity are everything.

# ABOUT ATMOSPHERE PRESS

Atmosphere Press is an independent, full-service publisher for excellent books in all genres and for all audiences. Learn more about what we do at atmospherepress.com.

We encourage you to check out some of Atmosphere's latest releases, which are available at Amazon.com and via order from your local bookstore:

*The Swing: A Muse's Memoir About Keeping the Artist Alive,* by Susan Dennis

*Possibilities with Parkinson's: A Fresh Look,* by Dr. C

*Gaining Altitude - Retirement and Beyond,* by Rebecca Milliken

*Out and Back: Essays on a Family in Motion,* by Elizabeth Templeman

*Just Be Honest,* by Cindy Yates

*You Crazy Vegan: Coming Out as a Vegan Intuitive,* by Jessica Ang

*Detour: Lose Your Way, Find Your Path,* by S. Mariah Rose

*To B&B or Not to B&B: Deromanticizing the Dream,* by Sue Marko

*Convergence: The Interconnection of Extraordinary Experiences,* by Barbara Mango and Lynn Miller

*Sacred Fool,* by Nathan Dean Talamantez

*My Place in the Spiral,* by Rebecca Beardsall

*My Eight Dads,* by Mark Kirby

*Dinner's Ready! Recipes for Working Moms,* by Rebecca Cailor

# ABOUT THE AUTHOR

Sara Mansfield Taber is author of the award-winning memoir, *Born Under an Assumed Name: The Memoir of a Cold War Spy's Daughter*. She has also published two works of literary journalism, *Dusk on the Campo: A Journey in Patagonia* and *Bread of Three Rivers: The Story of a French* Loaf, as well as two guides for writers: *Chance Particulars: A Writer's Field Notebook* and *To Write the Past: A Memoir Writer's Companion*. A Harvard-educated psychologist and social worker, her personal essays, travel stories, and opinion pieces have been published in literary magazines and newspapers such as the *Washington Post*. She lives in the Washington D.C. area.

9 781639 882489